Post-colonial Cu
Practices in Sou

Post-colonial Curriculum Practices in South Asia gives a conceptual framework for curriculum design for English Language Teaching (ELT), taking into account context specific features in the teaching–learning settings of post-colonial South Asia. It reveals how the attitudes prevalent in post-colonial South Asian societies towards English negatively influence English language learning. The book provides a comprehensive analysis to design a course for ELT that aims at building learner confidence to speak English.

Based on original research, the study covers Bangladesh, India, Pakistan and Sri Lanka. The book focuses on the context-specific nature of learners and considers a curriculum design that binds teaching materials and teaching methods together with an aligned assessment. Chapters discuss language attitudes, learner characteristics and English in the context of native languages, and introduce a special type of anxiety that stems from existing language attitudes in a society, referred to as Language Attitude Anxiety.

The book will appeal to doctoral and post-doctoral scholars in English language education, students and researchers of sociolinguistics, psycholinguistics as well as curriculum designers of ELT and language policy makers.

Asantha U. Attanayake is Senior Lecturer in English Language at the University of Colombo, Sri Lanka.

Routledge Research in Language Education

The *Routledge Research in Language Education* series provides a platform for established and emerging scholars to present their latest research and discuss key issues in Language Education. This series welcomes books on all areas of language teaching and learning, including but not limited to language education policy and politics, multilingualism, literacy, L1, L2 or foreign language acquisition, curriculum, classroom practice, pedagogy, teaching materials, and language teacher education and development. Books in the series are *not* limited to the discussion of the teaching and learning of English only.

Books in the series include:

Further Language Learning in Linguistic and Cultural Diverse Contexts
A Mixed Methods Research in a European Border Region
Barbara Gross

Classroom-Based Research on Chinese as a second language
Fangyuan Yuan and Shuai Li

Teaching English for Tourism
Bridging Research and Praxis
Edited by Michael Ennis and Gina Petrie

Post-Colonial Curriculum Practices in South Asia
Building Confidence to Speak English
Asantha U. Attanayake

Teaching Content and Language in the Multilingual Classroom
International Research on Policy, Perspectives, Preparation and Practice
Edited by Svenja Hammer, Kara Viesca, and Nancy Commins

For more information about the series, please visit https://www.routledge.com/Routledge-Research-in-Language-Education/book-series/RRLE

Post-Colonial Curriculum Practices in South Asia

Building Confidence to Speak English

Asantha U. Attanayake

Routledge
Taylor & Francis Group
LONDON AND NEW YORK

First published 2020
by Routledge
2 Park Square, Milton Park, Abingdon, Oxon, OX14 4RN

and by Routledge
605 Third Avenue, New York, NY 10017

First issued in paperback 2021

Routledge is an imprint of the Taylor & Francis Group, an informa business

Publisher's Note
The publisher has gone to great lengths to ensure the quality of this reprint but points out that some imperfections in the original copies may be apparent.

British Library Cataloguing-in-Publication Data
A catalogue record for this book is available from the British Library

Library of Congress Cataloging-in-Publication Data
A catalog record has been requested for this book

ISBN 13: 978-1-03-209152-5 (pbk)
ISBN 13: 978-0-8153-5552-6 (hbk)

Typeset in Galliard
by codeMantra

This was a journey through divinity, humanity and jealousy: we met absolutely divine academics in Pakistan, with only one exception. Every academic we met in Bangladesh was unbelievably humane and extremely helpful, while our Indian colleagues were true neighbours in every sense. A handful of academics in Sri Lanka were also helpful.

This book is dedicated to all the academics in India, Pakistan, Bangladesh and Sri Lanka, who were there for us when we turned to them for help.

Contents

List of figures

List of tables

Foreword

Post-colonial Curriculum Practices in South Asia: Building confidence to speak English is a good addition to the study of Foreign Language Classroom Anxiety. Asantha U. Attanayake has gone round India, Pakistan, Bangladesh and Sri Lanka, collected data from selected colleges and universities, compared them and reached the conclusion that there is similarity among them.

Colonization of territory results in the colonization of mind, which is more dangerous and damaging than the former. The colonial countries are basically dominantly monolingual and monocultural. The colonized countries are multilingual and multicultural. The foundation logic of the dominantly monolingual and monocultural countries is Either Or, where as that of the multilingual, multicultural countries is Both And. The relationship among entities in the former is horizontal, big small, high low, major minor, while the relationship among the latter is vertical, complementary and converging.

The colonialist found that diversity is the greatest obstacle on the way of sustaining an empire. Therefore, they waged a battle against language, which is the foremost marker of identity as well as diversity. They declared English as the only language of knowledge and development. As a result, they not only undermined the regional communication languages, they also completely ignored the mother languages. They were eliminated from administration, education and mass communication and English was projected as the only language of elite communication.

In pre-colonial times, Both And Logic permeated the multilingual South (East) Asia including Sri Lanka. Here, the meanings of Language, Religion and Culture were different from what developed in dominant monolingual countries. In India, Hindi was a language, which constituted of 49 varieties and the boundaries between languages were so phosphorus that two or three contiguous languages operated with a single grammar, (Gumperz) Sanskrit and Pali had become national and international languages with varieties and sub varieties.

Religion is a European and Western construct. As the westerners came in contact with the Indians in the 17th and 18th centuries, they found that what existed in India was different and distinct from what they knew. The European missionaries developed Hinduism as a concept and category to project it as a dominantly mono-religious model and as an enemy of Christianity. What existed in South Asia was Dharma, the principles which held diversity together. The westerners did not understand it.

Culture in the diverse world linked the local with the global and sustained through non-violent complementarity. While civilizations like Maya, Aztec, Inca in the developed world blew up and burst like water bubbles, the Indian culture has sustained for 7,000 years. A glance at the Indian Philosophies beginning with the Vedas, Upanishads and through Advaita, Dvaita, Dvetadvaita, bisistadvaita, achintyawedabheda would go to prove the search of the relationship between One in Many and Many in One. Language is the subject, medium and foundation of this diverse cultural discourse.

The imposition of English was designed to kill the smaller languages, denigrate the larger languages and destroy the complementarity of diversity. By denying indigenous knowledge, tradition and culture, they taught British and Euro-American history and culture in a foreign language so that the products would be "Indian by birth, but English in manners and morals" (Macaulay). With the loss of commitment to mother languages and motherland, English became the aspirational language of dependence for western support for development. As the parents demand English language education from KG to PG, the vitality of mother language and other language are threatened.

The 1953 UN Declaration, signed by 200 countries, proclaimed that the mother language is the best medium of primary education for all children. Not a single country has implemented it in full. This is one example of depletion of language nationalism in all the non-English-speaking countries of the world. The English policy of UK, USA and Europe started with the slogan of cultural partnership and has ended in multibillion-dollar trade for them. In spite of multimillion dollar the support extended by the British Council, ODA, WTO, IMF for English language teaching, the English language teaching has reached a lamentable state. In India, an eighth standard child cannot read a second standard book (Asher Report). This is happening both in the mother language and in the foreign language.

The unsuccessful teaching of English, in spite of new methods, new technologies, new materials has not resulted in the change of language attitudes, "The feelings people have about their own language or language of others" (Crystal 1997, p. 215). This has immense influence in language teaching and learning.

I hope this book by Asantha will receive good readers' response. I wish her well in a prosperous academic career.

Dr. Debi Prasanna Pattanayak, Ph.D. (Cornell)
Chancellor, Centurion University, Andhra Pradesh
Chairman, Institute of Odia Studies & Research, Bhubaneswar
Honorary Consultant IGNCA
Professor Emeritus Poona University, Utkal University of Culture
Padmashree, Former Jawaharlal Nehru Fellow
Retd. Director, CIIL, Mysore
Retd, Addl. Secy, MHRD, Govt. of India.

A word from the author

'The post-colonial experience of doing research: the painful truth'

Since I have put forth a comprehensive analysis of language attitudes and Language Attitude Anxiety in the book, I do not wish to write here about the content. Instead, I intend to write a few words about our plight, doing research in post-colonial South Asia as Sri Lankans, Indians, Pakistanis and Bangladeshis. We, the post-colonial South Asian nations, are similar in many respects: we have similar histories before and after independence; we are collectively plagued by a variety of similar problems in developing and many of these problems are our own creations. Therefore, it is not surprising that we share problems in doing research as well.

This anecdote is not to be misunderstood as a complaint. It is meant to create awareness. Just as academics in the west are unaware of language attitudes and their effects on post-colonial South Asian language learners, many in the developed world may also be unaware of what being a researcher in the 'developing world' means.

Offer to publish

I received an offer to publish from Routledge on 12 September 2017. Needless to say I was very happy. My husband suggested that we started our data collection immediately as we had to cover four countries in the region. I wanted to look for grants since collecting data from four countries, including my own, was not an easy task. However, being an American who has lived in Sri Lanka for nearly five years, he wisely stated that if we waited for grants from this country, I would never write this book.

Data collection (first leg)

We set off for the first leg of our data collection on 16 October 2017. We planned our trip for three and a half months to cover Pakistan, Bangladesh and India and to return to Sri Lanka by the end of January 2018. Everything went according to plan.

Application for a small research grant

While we were mid-way through the data collection, I received notice of an advertisement for a Small Research Grant (maximum 2,700 USD) from my university in Colombo. I sent in an application on 10 November 2017, while we were still abroad, collecting data. I was awarded the grant on 1 July 2018, nine months after I applied. When I received the first instalment, which could not exceed 540 USD at a time, it was January 2019, a year and three months after the application was made. In February 2019, I received the second instalment as reimbursement for assistance with the research.

Application for a NSF grant

In June 2018, I received notice of a grant scheme (Competitive Research Grant) under the National Science Foundation (NSF), Sri Lanka. The condition for the grant was that the study had to be within Sri Lanka. So, I had to divide my study into two parts: Sri Lankan research and research in the other South Asian countries. I applied for the former on 26 June 2018. Eight months have passed and it is February 2019; the results are still pending. (Now, it is May 2019, and I am incorporating the Routledge editor's suggestions, I received a letter from the NSF stating that my application has been rejected as "research theme/objectives can't be taken as a priority area which could directly impact on socio-economic development in the country.")

Second leg of data collection

When we returned to Sri Lanka in late January 2018 from our first leg of data collection, and started to enter data, we realized that we did not have enough data representing western India. We tried to find contacts from there but failed to do so. We did not want to skip any region, as we were keen to stick to the original sample design. So, again in mid-March, we went to western India and collected data.

In addition, we realized that we needed more interview data from Pakistan, so we made another trip to Pakistan in June 2018, coinciding with my husband's teaching assignment in Lahore.

Our bills, foreign and local expenses

We kept copies of tickets and boarding passes, guest house receipts from the three countries and a record of major expenses, such as receipts of courier services that were used to get the questionnaires delivered, hoping (in vain), that someday we would be reimbursed. However, the latest information I received is that as per government regulations, nothing spent prior to the date of offer for the award (1 July 2018) can be reimbursed! By July 2018, I had already completed the second leg of foreign data collection (in Pakistan).

Moreover, we kept all of our local petrol bills, train tickets, local university guesthouse receipts, etc., thinking that they may be required to produce for grant reimbursement. However, these are also not classified as reimbursable expenses.

Easy option, not followed

Some of our colleagues in Bangladesh and Pakistan asked us why we did not use an online questionnaire, which is a common practice for a study of this magnitude and which would have been easier and more economical. However, in this research we wanted to witness the true scenario and connect the emotions of the learners after we heard from their teachers (who we met at conferences) that they suffered the same 'lack of confidence to speak English' that Sri Lankan learners face. Moreover, we did not want to collect data only from major cities like Lahore and Islamabad and say, 'Here's the Pakistani ELT Scenario!' Instead, we went to Sindh, Peshawar and even to Swat. We interacted with the students and interviewed them, both formally and informally, in all these areas. Looking back, we cannot be happier about the time, energy and money we spent on this beautiful, adventurous and rewarding academic endeavour.

The motive behind this personalized account is to create awareness among those who do not know about the difficulties faced by researchers in the developing world and to remind those who pretend not to know about it, that research suffers in our nations because of the obstacles we ourselves create.

In a nutshell

It took 11 months to complete the data collection from all four countries. It took one year and three months to receive the first instalment of the Small Research Grant. The application to the NSF grant is still pending, eight months after the application was submitted. (It took 9 months to get the rejection letter, labelling this as not having a direct impact on the country's economic and social development.)

In retrospection

I received a Fulbright Advanced Research and Lecturing Award in 2013. During the eight months I participated in the programme, I was given approximately 28,000 USD in three or four instalments, the first given in advance. Never, not even once, was I asked to produce a single receipt as to how I spent the money. (I travelled all across the USA and spent half of my time in museums and libraries.)

Developing vs. developed

We hear from all quarters in South Asia that our research is under-developed, especially in the Social Sciences, and that 'there is no serious research' being undertaken. How on earth can an academic engage in serious research when support from the system is negligible? As post-colonial South Asian neighbours, we share the same language attitudes and our students share the experience of Language Attitude Anxiety. In the same way, as academics we all experience a serious lack of support for research from our systems.

Spent vs. received

In Sri Lankan rupees, we spent about 2 million and received 0.15 million.

Given this, how can a South Asian academic do research? Why should we do research?

The other side of the story

There is another side to this story, as they say. The red tape, lack of support and lack of incentives are often caused by some of our own 'academics', abusing the few benefits available to us. Therefore, rules have to be strictly adhered to and as a result, the bureaucratic atmosphere is suffocating. At the same time, corrupt politicians in our countries steal most of the money that could go into academic advancement.

This is our story of 'the post-colonial experience in doing research: the painful truth'.

My gratitude

I wish to extend my sincere gratitude to our dear friend Pen Rendall for her interest and a preliminary edit of the manuscript. I am thankful to Professor D.P. Pattanayak, Chancellor, Centurion University, Andhra Pradesh, Chairman, Institute of Odia Studies & Research, Bhubaneswar, for writing the foreword with much enthusiasm. It is a great privilege to have a back cover comment from Professor Emeritus, James Cummins, University of Toronto, Canada, a great theorist whose work I admire and use in my own curriculum design.

I am forever grateful to my parents and my siblings for their continued support in my writing endeavours. If it was not for my husband, Col. Adam Barborich, my shadow that follows me everywhere, I would not have done this research covering all four nations. I am very fortunate to have him by my side. And he is right. If I waited for grants, I would not have written this book.

Asantha U. Attanayake
22 February 2019
Sri Lanka

1 Introduction

Introduction

More than half of the world was ruled by the British Empire. The legacy that empire left behind made many post-colonial societies more complex and confused, manifesting inferiority and superiority complexes, dependent and colonial mentalities, etc. The English language is the unmistakable carrier of this complex legacy in its various manifestations throughout former colonies. Post-colonial South Asian societies continue to form, shape and re-shape their attitudes towards those who speak English and those who do not, those who speak it better, various attitudes towards vernaculars and so on. Inevitably, such factors complicate the teaching of English and, when they are not taken fully into consideration, English language teaching (ELT) fails.

The post-colonial South Asian element in ELT

Teaching English specifically to learners in the former British colonies of South Asia is an unexplored area because of the fact that a teaching methodology has not been devised to address the issues arising from certain prevalent social attitudes and their influence on ELT. Most scholars in the field are unfamiliar with the attitude problems attached to the English language in the former British colonies in South Asia where minority elites have set themselves up as the watchdog of the masters' language. The watchdogs still exist, even decades after our countries obtained 'independence', and their role is perpetuated by the Anglophone culture of capitalism in these countries today. As a result, many, especially rural learners, the large majority, lack the confidence to speak English for fear of ridicule.

When we presented papers about the 'confidence building issue' at the University of Texas at Austin in 2014, the questions were geared, surprisingly, towards understanding *why* and *how* it was necessary to build confidence for ELT. Even in Singapore, academics were interested to know why confidence was involved with speaking English. In contrast, in the presentation we did at the North South University, Dhaka, Bangladesh in February 2015 there was great eagerness among Bangladeshi academics to know more; the problem addressed was overwhelmingly similar to their own experience in teaching English language. In March 2017, we presented on the same issue in India at a conference in Utkal

University, Odisha, and several students, as well as academics, identified the issue as one close to their experience as well. And quite surprisingly, in April 2017, when we spoke about the need for confidence to speak English at several universities in Pakistan, all of the teachers identified the problem as one they face. It was a surprise for the teachers, as well as students, in four separate universities, namely: Islamic International University in Islamabad, Fatima Jinnah Women University, Islamabad, Air University, Islamabad and the University of Lahore where we presented. Their experiences in relation to English language education were identical to those found in Sri Lanka.

In the west, scholars have discovered an anxiety related to foreign language learning which inhibits learner performance. It is called Foreign Language Anxiety (FLA)/Foreign Language Classroom Anxiety – FLCA (Horwitz, Horwitz, & Cope, 1986). However, this is quite different from the lack of confidence to speak English that is being discussed here that exists in the former British colonies in the South Asian region. How does the fear, shyness, uncertainty, etc. that makes English language learners lack confidence to speak English in South Asia differ from FLA?

The thrust of the argument in this book lies in the decisive role of attitudes present in South Asian post-colonial societies in creating psychological barriers in learners that discourage them from speaking English and how this creates a need for a context-specific teaching methodology, to arrest these attitude-related obstacles to learning in these former colonies. To this end, the book is set up to achieve some specific objectives.

The objectives

This book is set up

1 to create awareness among the experts in the field on the necessity of considering context-specific features vis-à-vis ELT in designing ELT curricula
2 to give a comprehensive analysis of curriculum design for ELT with a strong theoretical framework
3 to understand the attitudes related to and prejudices attached to languages
4 to examine new dimensions namely language attitudes and language competition (English as opposed to vernaculars) to be considered in designing curricula for ELT
5 to show how to create a 'safe zone' within the classroom for low proficiency English language learners
6 to show the importance of the context-specific nature of problems related to English language by contextualizing the materials and teaching methodologies to address the problems of teaching English in different localities
7 to show the importance of a needs analysis for ELT that is rarely carried out when undergraduates enter universities in countries like Sri Lanka, India, Bangladesh and Pakistan. (Student needs are assumed based on teachers' perceptions, which are not always accurate.)

To this end, data collected from four South Asian countries, namely India, Pakistan, Bangladesh and Sri Lanka are analysed,

- a to compare and contrast the attitudes related to speaking English among the post-colonial South Asian nations of India, Pakistan, Bangladesh and Sri Lanka
- b to examine the reasons for students not speaking English
- c to find out whether the shyness and fear of speaking in English are present in front of specific persons such as teachers, strangers, friends, etc. or whether they are present in front of everyone
- d to find out whether the lack of confidence to speak English is restricted to the English language classroom or whether it is present among the learners outside of the classroom as well
- e to carry out an in-depth analysis of the fear and shyness present among South Asian English language learners to speak English in terms of the various settings mentioned above
- f to compare and contrast the factors mentioned in objectives (b), (c), (d), and (e) among South Asian learners.

This book consists of 12 chapters. The first chapter outlines the framework of the book and the aims and specific objectives of the study. In addition, it describes the content of each chapter briefly.

Chapter 2 of the book is dedicated to a discussion on the constitutional treatment of English in Sri Lanka and other former British colonies in South Asia and the usage of it in education and higher education. The advent of the open economy in Sri Lanka made English a necessary requirement in education and higher education as employment became more 'open' to the private sector. Other post-colonial South Asian countries went through similar transformations in their economies by and large even though the pace at which the economy opened varies in each country. A survey that has been carried out from 2007 to 2018 vis-à-vis the undergraduate population of Sri Lanka discloses that the desire for English, from a student perspective, is primarily to be able to speak in English. Interestingly, the data collected over ten years has shown that this desire has remained unchanged over the entire period. At the same time, the data reveals that students' reason for not speaking in any kind of English that is understood by the linguistic community, despite having learned it over the entire course of their school careers is due to a lack of confidence. This scenario becomes complex because in spite of the student community desiring the ability to speak English most, they are not speaking it due to a lack of confidence. Upon examination, it was found out that this lack of confidence stems from shyness and a fear of being ridiculed by others in society. The chapter discusses in detail the fear, shyness and uncertainty linked to speaking English in South Asia, locating them in the attitudes of the society towards the English language and the people who speak English well and those who do not speak well.

Chapter 3 is about the study itself. It devotes its content to the sample, the tools and the approach used to collect data and the methods of data analysis and discussion. The discussion demonstrates that learners in post-colonial South Asia experience anxiety associated with speaking English both inside and outside the language classroom. While some are afraid, shy or uncertain to speak English in front of their teachers and peers, others also feel the same way in front of outsiders and strangers. Still more experience the same anxiety in front of everyone. This demonstrates another powerful area in which anxiety relates to language education in addition to the concept of FLA, the leading theory available to scholars discussing anxiety issues related to foreign and second language teaching.

The fourth chapter examines in greater detail how social attitudes towards a language and its speakers influence English language learners in post-colonial South Asia with a special focus on the learners' most sought-after language skill, speaking. The fear/shyness/uncertainty that surrounds South Asian learners is a creation of social attitudes that generate a lack of confidence in the learners when they attempt to speak English. This lack of confidence to speak in English may in turn cause the learner to develop a set of negative attitudes towards their own speaking ability, which may then be projected onto the entire English language learning process, which results in further poor performance in learning English. The effects of the societal language attitudes on the language learner can be explained in the following manner.

Language attitudes of the society –> lack of confidence to speak –> negative attitudes towards speaking –> negative attitudes toward learning.

This chapter introduces a special *type* of anxiety that is caused by the language attitudes present in society, labelled Language Attitude Anxiety (LAA). The role of LAA as a conduit between the societal attitudes towards the English language and its speakers and the lack of confidence in the learners to speak English is explained. The limitations of FLCA to capture the problems of the English language learner in post-colonial South Asia are discussed while taking the content as well as the structure of the FLCA scale into account. Two main components of LAA are identified as negative evaluation and communication apprehension. These two constituents are explained in relation to the societal language attitudes that learners come into contact with, both inside and outside the language classroom. The components are further discussed with their effects on the learners, particularly in regard to speaking English, and learning English in general. The chapter ends by establishing the centrality of building confidence to help students learn English against the backdrop of the unsuccessful practices used to teach English as a second language in Bangladesh, India, Pakistan and Sri Lanka.

Chapter 5 is dedicated to a description of the learners in terms of their existing English language abilities in their local context. The power relations between the English language and learners are seen as an affective love–hate relation. Also the social, mental and educational paradigms in which learners are immersed are analysed alongside the constructs of learner identity, possible selves and role conflict. They are further elucidated by locating the learners in terms of their language acquisition stages. Learner responses facilitate the understanding of the power relations between the English language and its learners in their local context. The battle that language learners have to fight with FLA stems from the uniqueness of the language learning process, while societal attitudes create LAA is brought out by emphasizing the need to address and re-frame language attitudes in the minds of the learners in a positive way. The chapter discusses how LAA, which creates a lack of confidence to speak English, is projected and leads to poor performance in English language learning in a general sense.

The sixth chapter details the importance of intervention to build confidence. It signifies that the identification of the stage to intervene is important as is identifying the presence of Language Attitudes Anxiety. The way to eliminate and conquer LAA involves building confidence to speak English with a psychological approach by using habituation and exposure to scenarios in which learners fear speaking English. The chapter discusses the importance of, and the need for, a special course with materials and teaching strategies specifically designed to build learners' confidence to speak English.

Chapter 7 is about the theoretical perspectives of the experimental curriculum design along the lines of the theme of confidence building. The principles include the suitability of Basic Interpersonal Communication Skills (BICS), Common Underlying Principles (CUP) and the Cognitive Academic Language Proficiency Skills (CALPS) theory of Cummins (2000) as an all-encompassing theory for the entire curriculum. This experimental curriculum has three courses given in progressive order, as sub-divided by us, and is illustrated with diagrams. The course under discussion in this book, 'Building Confidence to Speak English', is the first of the three courses, and it is discussed at length, including: the use of speech as a promoter to build confidence to speak/learn English; the use of Austin's Speech Act Theory, first discussed in his lecture series in 1955 (Austin, 1975) and as developed by Searle (1969) and further advanced by Bach and Harnish (1979) and Crystal (1994) for choosing speech functions. The use of Speech Act Theory for material design is presented with examples. The sequencing and gradation of activities is analysed by juxtaposing Dubin and Olshtain's (1987) activity potentials, namely communicative and cognitive potential development scales with Bloom's Taxonomy (Bloom, 1956). Further, how repetition of speech acts in an ascending order of difficulty to reinforce a particular speech function is examined in this chapter. An excerpt of a module (teaching material) is given highlighting these features. The chapter closes with the related logistics of the Building Confidence to Speak English course.

The eighth chapter details the Cooperative Language Learning (CLL) techniques that are incorporated into the teaching methodology of the course. The techniques of CLL are discussed at great length together with a discussion of the psycho-social features of language learners. These details are examined in relation to the 'safe zone', the classroom environment most needed to build confidence. The essential components of this safe zone are discussed along with the role of the teacher as the sole authority responsible for creating the safe zone. The discussion on the safe zone is carried out as opposed to the features found in an ordinary language classroom. For instance, error correction, the demand from individual learners for performance, homework, etc., which are found in an ordinary language classroom and create LAA in the language learners' mind. These aspects are analysed along with remedial techniques that contribute to the making of a safe zone. The teacher's transference from an 'ordinary teaching position' to that of an observer who 'overlooks' the errors and mistakes found in student speech is highlighted as one of the key characteristics of the safe zone. The necessity for teacher training is brought out with some potential challenges for teachers in deviating from their usual practice of 'mere teaching'. The process-oriented nature of the approach is stressed with an emphasis on the need for teachers to be trained to teach the confidence building course along with an emphasis on the importance of making them aware of the language attitudes and their impact on student language learning.

Chapter 9 is dedicated to discussing the assessment used in the Confidence Building Course to Speak English. The student assessment is summative and is in keeping with the course objective: to build confidence to speak English. Also, there is a clear constructive alignment with the teaching methodology in that it is a group performance in the spirit of cooperation. Learners are given the chance to perform in stage plays. Grading the plays is not mandatory, if there is a provision in the organizational logistics that allows for not grading the final assessment. However, if grading is required by the administration, certain criteria are given as guidelines. Additionally, a weekly-basis formative assessment is encouraged. However, it is emphasized that such formative evaluation must be strictly in line with assessing the students' demonstrated confidence level while engaging in group activities and performing in English.

The tenth chapter presents the course evaluation stages that are available in the discourse namely pre-evaluation, in-course evaluation (during the course) and post-evaluation. As the confidence building course is a short one, we consider post-evaluation to the most fitting to assess the effectiveness of the confidence building course. Therefore, it is discussed in detail. The main target group is students who can give feedback on the course while the teachers' views are also sought in order to complement the data from students. The areas to be evaluated include the course materials, content covered, teacher performance, the teaching methodology employed and the modes of assessment. These are identified in order to evaluate their efficacy in building learner confidence to speak in various locations with different people. A sample questionnaire is presented covering these areas. Interviews with teachers and students are recommended in order to extract more information about learner confidence levels to speak English after the course in a variety of locations with different people. It is highly recommended that teachers maintain a journal or other written records on a daily basis to record learners' exhibited confidence levels so that such records can serve as a set of data for the course evaluation. In addition, records of teacher observation can be made use of as well.

The last chapter discusses the significance of developing language attitudes as an independent academic discourse. The key concepts include examining language attitudes, analysing them in diverse contexts, assessing the effects of language attitudes on language learning and identifying rectifying measures for their negative effects in regard to language teaching. Identifying language attitudes is discussed with special reference to social variables such as class, gender, public–private education and levels of education, profession, etc. An example analysis of language attitudes in the context of vernaculars is also discussed along with the related implications. The effects of language attitudes in post-colonial South Asia are discussed along with how the consequences are manifested in the language learning domain as well as in the larger society. Remedial measures are suggested that involve teaching about these diverse aspects along with enlisting the support of political movements aiming at a mass level of attitudinal change. The envisaged outcomes are discussed in light of developing teacher awareness as the main change agent in regard to language attitudes so that building bridges between languages and cultures/knowledge can be achieved.

We consider LAA to be a very serious problem that affects the English language learning of post-colonial South Asian learners in an adverse way, contributing to the failure of English language education in South Asia in a way that has not been previously identified.

Limitations of the study

1. Due to financial restrictions, we were unable to travel to all of the locations in India we identified in our sample. Therefore, interviews could not be conducted by the native speaker of English as we did in other locations. Instead, interview questions were sent and written responses were obtained.
2. Due to security issues and the cumbersome process for obtaining NOCs (no objection certificates), we did not attempt to go to Baluchistan. The data was collected via a colleague.
3. We could not collect data from the University of Peradeniya, Sri Lanka, the only state university in the Central Province as the university administration (Dean, Faculty of Arts) refused to support us despite our having made several attempts to approach him.

References

Austin, J. L. (1975). *How to do things with words*. Cambridge, MA: Harvard University Press.

Bach, K., & Harnish, R. M. (1979). *Linguistic communication and speech acts*. Cambridge: MIT Press.

Bloom, M. (1956). *Taxonomy of educational objectives*. New York: David McKay.

Crystal, D. (1994). Words Worth. *Times Higher Education*, 11, 34.

Cummins, J. (2000). *Language, power and pedagogy: Bilingual children in the crossfire*. Clevedon, England: Multilingual Matters.

Dubin, F., & Olshtain, E. (1987). *Course design: Developing programs and materials for language learning*. Cambridge: Cambridge University Press.

Horwitz, E. K., Horwitz, M. B., & Cope, J. (1986). Foreign language classroom anxiety. *Modern Language Journal*, 70, 125–132.

Searle, J. (1969). *Speech acts*. Cambridge: Cambridge University Press.

2 Background

Introduction

This chapter discusses the place of English in Sri Lanka and other former British colonies in South Asia in terms of their constitutional treatment of the English language and its usage in education and higher education. The need for English in education and higher education arose due to the demands of the job market; this is briefly discussed against the backdrop of the advent of the open economy in Sri Lanka. Situations analogous to this are also applicable to other post-colonial South Asian countries. The survey that has been carried out over the last ten years in relation to the undergraduate population of Sri Lanka reveals that the need for English, from a student perspective, is primarily to be able to speak in English. The data collected over ten years has shown that this need has remained unchanged over the period. At the same time, the data reveals that the reason for not speaking in English[1] (despite having learned it over the course of their school careers and having the ability to speak English as their most desired skill) is their lack of confidence. This lack of confidence stems from shyness and fear of being ridiculed by others in the broader society. The fear, shyness and uncertainty attached to speaking in English are discussed in relation to the attitudes in society towards English and towards the people who speak it well and those who do not speak well.

English in Sri Lanka and other post-colonial South Asian countries

The place of English in respect to policy in the post-colonial South Asian countries, namely India, Pakistan, Bangladesh and Sri Lanka, seems to have changed from an immediate down-play of it with independence and then secured its status steadily over the course of decades along with the changes in the economic policies of these countries.

The English language has marked its unchallengeable status with its expanding and accommodating nature in the education and employment sectors, inviting policy changes at the national level. In the post-independence scenario, two decades into the 21st century, a look at the place of English in the post-colonial South Asian countries reveals that the former colonies seem to change their language policies in terms of the perceived requirements of (a) nationalism, (b) the education sector and (c) the job market throughout their shared history.

It further reveals that in the immediate post-independence era, the language policy changes in South Asian countries were influenced by one common concept: nationalism. Then in the post-post-independence period, they were subject to the needs of the education and employment sectors. Another interesting revelation is that all four countries had their initial struggles related to language issues in terms of English versus a common national language. As time went on, they have all 'meekly' accepted the global dominance of English and have come to terms with it. However, all the while they have been struggling to resolve the issues within their countries, with the exception of Bangladesh (itself founded by a minority language group in Pakistan), in regard to regional–central, minority–majority language issues that have arisen in various shapes and forms.

The discussion that follows looks at English in pre-independence South Asia briefly, and then moves on to the immediate post-independence and post-post-independence eras in South Asia in detail.

The following are a few quotes to show how language policy operated during the pre-independence era in the four South Asian nations studied here.

English in pre-independence South Asia

Sri Lanka	From 1815 until 1956, English was the official language of Sri Lanka. 'Until the vernaculars were adopted for administrative functions in Sri Lanka (as in India and other post-colonial societies), the large majority of the people had to depend on those competent in the former colonial language for the exercise even of some basic functions of citizenship' (Dharmadasa, 1996, as quoted by Attanayake, 2017, p. 77) There was no place for either of the vernaculars, Sinhala or Tamil, as a language of status in [sic] administration of the time. English was the language of administration and of business, the language of education in the good urban schools and the language of higher education (Goonatilleke, 1981, p. 63)
India	During the colonization of India by British in the 18th century, English became a lingua franca and in 1835, it was made official language at both the central and provincial or state levels. However, English was not used throughout the entire administrative system. In lower lever administration, some regional languages were used (Delican, 1998, p. 123)
Pakistan	Pakistan was part of great India, just like Bangladesh, and had similar language policies. As quoted in Javed (2017), Rahman (1995) states that before the implication of Lord Macualay 'Minute' in 1835, the Orientalist language policy had been prevalent in British India between 1780 and 1835 which favoured the teaching of the indigenous languages like 'Sanskrit, Persian and Arabic to Indians as well as the British civil servants who were supposed to rule them' (p. 7). Rahman further explains that 'in 1835, English was given the status of the language of higher administration, judiciary and education (p. 7)' (p. 47).
Bangladesh	Bangladesh was the [sic] part of the [sic] greater India and was colonized by the British rulers for about two hundred years from 1857 to 1947 and its name was East-Bengal. During the British period, English was used as the official language (Roy, 2017, p. 330)

English in the immediate post-independence era in South Asia

Nationhood, English and vernaculars

The following section briefly outlines the nation-building efforts that were made in the immediate post-independence era in South Asia, with language as an identity marker. Attitudes were mostly opposed to the English language in the quest to build a concept of 'one sovereign nation'. The English language seems to have been the most 'tangible' colonial artefact and therefore had to be downplayed to achieve this goal. The struggle to become 'truly independent' during the immediate post-independence period across the South Asian region took place in an almost identical framework with surprisingly similar situations in regard to language policy.

Sri Lanka

Nine years after independence, the Official Language Act No. 33 of 1956, commonly known as the Sinhala Only Act, was enacted, whereby the mother tongue of the majority ethnic group was made the national language of Sri Lanka. This was a result of a considerable up-tick in nationalist sentiment after independence from the British.

> With the struggle for independence, Sri Lanka, like many other South Asian countries, had an awakening of national awareness which was to be manifested mainly through language. This resulted in adopting the Swabhasha Policy, which made Sinhala, the mother tongue of the majority, the national language as opposed to English, which was the language of administration.
> (Attanayake, 2017, p. 78)

However, this policy did not work out well for Sri Lanka as language discrimination contributed to the 30-year civil war that plagued the country in later years and could be said to be a direct consequence of the Sinhala Only Act.

India

A similar move was made in India after the struggle for independence. Delican (1998) states that the leaders wanted a language that was understood by all, not only to be fair to everyone, but also to eradicate the English language. 'The imposition of a common language was nothing but a determination to eradicate all the memories of colonial rule, so that India can have its own voice' (Delican, 1998, p. 124). He further states, 'To be against English means to be against the British rulers' (p. 124). This shows that the impact of language on nation-building was found throughout post-independence British India. Gandhi himself expressed the need 'for banishing English as a cultural usurper as we successfully banished the political rule of the English usurper' (Nayar, 1969, p. 12) and developing a common Indian language for an independent country was of the utmost concern (Delican, 1998, p. 124). Gandhi 'vehemently opposed' English and wanted 'Hindustani' to be the prime language of India (Jayasundara, 2014, p. 2).

Pakistan

In Pakistan, Urdu was declared as the national language despite it being the mother tongue of just 7.5% of the entire Pakistani population. This was due to the assertion of a historical identity that linked the culture of Muslims in the sub-continent with Urdu. The cultural supremacy of Urdu aided attempts to establish a sovereign Islamic nation 'because the Muslims of the subcontinent had all along in the Pakistan movement seen Urdu language as the mark of Pakistan's identity and nationalism' (Sikandar, 2017, p. 268).

As pointed out by Haque (1983), English was still considered an official language as it was during the pre-independence period, primarily to meet the need of 'operational efficiency'. This was because, as Haque sees it, the elites were more skilled at doing their official work in English.

Bangladesh

After the partition of British India into India and Pakistan (including modern Pakistan and Bangladesh), Urdu was made the official language of Pakistan in 1952. In East Pakistan, which is modern-day Bangladesh, the results of this policy had much the same effect as Sinhala Only in Sri Lanka. The people of East Pakistan saw the Bengali language, Bangla, being marginalized and interpreted this as a suppression of their culture. This was the cause of much discontent in spite of the fact that Bengali was also given official status within Pakistan in 1956. The continued discrimination against Bengali citizens of Pakistan and the feeling that the centre of political power in West Pakistan resulted in favouritism eventually led to the Bangladesh Liberation War. As a result, Bangladesh left Pakistan and became an independent nation in 1971.

The following quote reveals how the rising nationalism in Bangladesh was manifested in its language policy:

> Being an independent nation, the spirit of nationalism, as well as a sense of decolonization, became stronger than ever which ultimately functioned in favor of Bangla as a language. Like many other post-colonial nations, Bangladesh also attempted to exclude English as it was comprehended to be a potential threat to the enrichment and domination of Bangla.
>
> (Roy, 2017, p. 332)

According to Begum (2015), there were two main objectives behind the language policies that were formulated favouring Bangla: (a) to position it at the highest level in the linguistic strata and (b) to abolish the use of the other two dominant languages, namely, Urdu and English. Thus, the 1972 Constitution of Bangladesh deemed Bangla to be the sole national language to be used in administration and the judiciary, as well as the medium of instruction in education (Chowdhury & Kabir, 2014).

English in the post-post-independence era

Policy changes

Due to the great difficulties in achieving linguistic hegemony for any single language within each of the post-colonial South Asian states, language policy changes were inevitable. The changes in language policy are found in the constitutions of these states in the post-post-independence era.

Sri Lanka

The Sri Lankan constitution recognizes English as a link language while Sinhala and Tamil are both given the status of national and official languages. As we have discussed previously, after independence, in 1956, the Official Language Act No. 33 declared Sinhala, the mother tongue of the majority population (75%), as the official language, replacing English, which had been imposed under British colonial rule. In 1958, in response to the grievances of the Tamil-speaking population (24% of the combined population divided between Hindus with 11%, Muslims with 9% and Christians with 4%) in the country, the government passed the Tamil Language (Special Provisions) Act, in which Tamil was declared an official language in the Tamil-majority North and East (Martyn, 2013). In 1987, Tamil, the mother tongue of the minority, became an official language and the medium of instruction in education for the minority throughout the country, while English was given the status of a link language.

> As a result of such debates amongst members of parliament as well as people in other fields against the Sinhala Only Act, the 13th Amendment to the Constitution eventually elevated the status of the Tamil language in 1987, at the same time establishing English as a link language.
>
> (Attanayake, 2017, p. 79)

India

In India, a tri-lingual policy has been implemented. Under this, every student is supposed to learn three languages: Hindi, their own regional language and English. According to Sridhar (1989), the Three-Language Formula is

> a compromise between the demands of the various pressure groups and has been hailed as a masterly – if imperfect – solution to a complicated problem. It seeks to accommodate the interests of group identity (mother tongues and regional languages), national pride and unity (Hindi), and administrative efficiency and technological progress (English).
>
> (p. 22)

The states of India were reorganized in 1956 on the basis of the regional languages of the majority in those states. Accordingly, India has recognized 22 languages as state languages. They are Assami, Bangla, Boda, Dogri, Gujarathi, Hindi, Kashmiri, Kannada, Konkani, Maithili, Malayalam, Manipuri, Marathi, Nepali, Oriya, Punjabi, Tamil, Telugu, Santali, Sindi, Sanskrit and Urdu (Jayasundara, 2014, p. 4), while English and Hindi serve as the official languages.

Pakistan

Pakistan is a multilingual society that is home to approximately 24 languages and a number of dialects. In Pakistan, 'Urdu is the declared national language and English is the official language making them the two dominant languages of the country, used in domains of power like offices, press, media, education, and employment' (Sikandar, 2017, p. 267). The languages that are generally spoken within Pakistan are Punjabi, Sindhi, Pashto, Urdu, Balochi and Kashmiri. The 'major ethnic groups of Pakistan include Punjabis, Pashtuns, Sindhis, Saraikis, Muhajirs, Balochis, Hindkowans, Chitralis and other smaller groups' (Seifi, 2015, p. 33).

However, as Rahman (2003) states that language policy in Pakistan has favoured two languages namely, Urdu and English at the expense of other regional languages and it has resulted in ethnic identity crisis in speakers other than Urdu. Also, it has further elevated as a symbol of the elite, sophistication and power.

Bangladesh

The Bangladesh government passed the Bangla Implementation Act in 1987 to enforce the use of Bangla (the first language of about 98% of the population) in all spheres of national life, making it the national official language of Bangladesh. English was made the lingua franca of communication with foreign countries. However, the act restricted the scope and use of English in the domestic socio-cultural domain. Nevertheless, at the tertiary level, English was allowed to continue parallel with Bangla as the language of instruction and examinations. At present, English is considered a foreign language in Bangladesh and is taught in primary, secondary, higher secondary and tertiary levels (Ali, 2013). However, English is becoming the single most important language in Bangladesh with regard to higher education and social status, a tool for social advancement and economic development. There are also more than ten other languages present in Bangladesh with small percentages of the population speaking these as their first language.

The use of English in education and higher education

During the colonial period, the medium of instruction in education was predominantly English in the South Asian colonies. Education was limited to the elite and the upper classes, and English medium education matched the social classes of the time and contributed to the maintenance of the class structures.

Sri Lanka

Today, the medium of instruction for education in Sri Lanka is predominantly mother tongue (Sinhala or Tamil) in state-run schools. However, with the tremendous changes stemming from the introduction of the open economy in 1977, the need for English became clear and prominent (Attanayake, 2017). In 2001, a bi-lingual policy in education was introduced which allowed incremental use of English as a medium of instruction with a few subjects taught in English in the secondary grades at the state schools. This policy is meant to compensate for those who are not ready for a complete switch to English medium instruction. Parallel to this policy, a separate unit for bi-lingual education has been established at the National Institute of Education in Sri Lanka to support implementation of bi-lingual education in schools. Thus, state-run schools in Sri Lanka essentially recommenced English medium instruction at the policy level, but have merely been experimenting with the policy at the ground level while trying to determine the stages at which English should be taught and the appropriate 'dosage' of English to be given. In spite of the fact that bi-lingual education has not achieved much, in the post-conflict era, under the Lessons Learned and Reconciliation Commission (LLRC), a tri-lingual policy was introduced in 2011. This involves teaching Sinhala to Tamil students and Tamil to Sinhala students while English, the link language, continues to be taught as a second language.

In response to the ineffective implementation of these policies, the number of international schools (private schools with English as the medium of instruction) is increasing and these are not limited to the urban areas of Sri Lanka. Branches of major international schools are also being established in semi-urban and semi-rural areas due to their success in urban localities while brand new international schools are also being founded in both urban and semi-urban/rural areas due to the popularity of the existing international schools. Some of these offer the London or Cambridge curricula, while others offer the local curriculum. Today, English medium international schools serve as a major player in the Sri Lankan system of general education. Also, English has become the medium of instruction in most pre-schools in Sri Lanka, especially in urban and semi-urban areas.

English is also the medium of instruction in most state universities in Sri Lanka, with the exception of a few faculties, which have mother tongue instruction. Only Sri Lankan universities that have Faculties of Arts, Social Sciences and Humanities offer mother tongue instruction in Sinhala and Tamil. However, English medium instruction is also made available for those who wish to study in English in these faculties.

India

As stated earlier, India has a tri-lingual policy named 'the Three-Language Formula', under which every student in primary and secondary education is supposed to learn three languages, with English as one of them. The Three-Language Formula was suggested by the Central Advisory Board of Education in 1956 and approved by the Conference of Chief Ministers in 1961 (Pandit, 1977, p. 28 as reported by Delican, 1998). According to the formula,

> ... three languages would be taught in schools. One language was that of the state, the others were Hindi and English. The programme suggested that students in the South [sic] states would learn their state language, Hindi and English and students in the North [sic] – Hindi spoken [sic] states – would learn Hindi, English, and one of the south [sic] states, language.
>
> (Delican, 1998, p. 123)

The scenario in Indian education seems to view the Three-Language Formula as failing in most states with English gaining prominence. Ramanujam (2011), presenting the findings of an all India survey, states that the percentage of schools teaching English as a 'first language' doubled between 1993 and 2002 from 5% to 10% in primary schools and from 7% to 13% in upper primary schools. Also, out of 35 states, 33 claim to offer English medium instruction in their schools, more than any other language. Another interesting finding is that between 1993 and 2002, there was an increase in the proportion of schools offering English as a medium of instruction with the sharpest hike from 5% to 13% being found in primary schools. In addition, in 2002, more than a quarter of all secondary schools were offering English as a medium of instruction. English is also offered as a second language in 19 states, of which 16 introduce it in Class I, one in Class III and two as late as Class V (p. 26). Although English was introduced in the Indian education system as one of the languages in the Three-Language Formula, it was 'rooted in all the lines of education' (Jayasundara, 2014, p. 2) from that time and seems to be surpassing all the other languages in education. In private sector education, English serves as the medium of instruction from the early primary grades. In Indian state universities, English serves as the main medium of instruction, although Hindi and other regional languages are available too. In private universities, a growing part of Indian higher education, the medium of instruction is predominantly English.

Pakistan

The Pakistani medium of instruction has also seen many changes in the 70 years since independence, just like the others in the region. However, Sikandar (2017) observes an inconsistency in the medium of instruction at the national level that has resulted in three distinguishable types of education systems in Pakistan:

> An ambivalence regarding the medium of instruction policy, all through the 68 years of the nation's history, has resulted in three different types of education systems in Pakistan: private, elite institutions where the medium of instruction is English; government schools where Urdu is the medium of

> instruction; and, madrassas which use Arabic and Urdu as the medium of instruction.
>
> (Sikandar, 2017, p. 270)

The private schools are where the elite send their children to follow Cambridge or London syllabi for their GCE (O/L) and GCE (A/L) Grades. These systems are completely different from government schools in regard to the curriculum, assessment system and textbooks (Sikandar, 2017).

A comparative study on state sector and private sector schools, done by Awan and Zia (2015), reveals the position English enjoys in Pakistani education:

> It is also the medium of instruction in universities that is why it is required by parents in schools. The English language was seen as the major determinant of this expansion and as a basic requirement by the parents. So, we have found a positive association between the choice of a private school and the medium of instruction as English. Medium of instruction in English along with discipline and status symbol [sic] associated with private schools is [sic] responsible for preference of private schools. On the other hand, most of the public schools are Urdu medium so parents do not prefer public schools.
>
> (p. 124)

Bangladesh

In Bangladesh, English is taught as a foreign language at the primary, secondary and tertiary levels. Even though the Bangla Implementation Act of 1987 limited the use of English in socio-cultural domain, at the tertiary level, it was allowed to continue parallel with Bangla as the language both of instruction and examination (Ali, 2013, p. 117). Despite English not being recognized as a second language in Bangladesh, but as a foreign language, it is a compulsory subject at the school and college levels (Kabir, 2017) and the growth of English medium schools is mushrooming in Bangladesh (Ali, 2013). Both public and private universities teach in English medium. During my visits to the country for the data collection and prior to that, for conferences, I was surprised at the vast number of institutes of education and higher education (public and private) advertising their curricula as taught in English medium.

Thus, in spite of their initial aversion to English, the former colonies of Bangladesh, India, Pakistan and Sri Lanka have all made English language education a top priority in their education policies for future development.

English and employment

With the opening of their economies, foreign investment increased in the post-colonial countries of South Asia. Sri Lanka opened its economy in 1977 and India in 1994. Pakistan's economy varied depending on the political climate from a 'relatively free market system at one time (mostly in democratic government periods like 1988 to 1999 and 2008 to on [sic] till now) and command [economy] at the time of 1971 to 1977 and all dictatorship eras' (Anwar & Ashfaq, 2017, p. 213) in much the same way as the economy of Bangladesh following its independence. The global advancement of science and technology helped English make its way easily and swiftly into the economic, political and social domains of these countries. While low-level, mid-level and even a few high-level professions in the South Asian public sector often do not require fluency in English as a prerequisite for employment, the private sector is constantly searching for employees with the ability to communicate in English at all levels. All countries in post-colonial South Asia seem to have an identical experience with regard to the need for English in employment.

Pakistan

In Pakistan the situation is as cited by Haidar (2017):

> English is considered a source of self-improvement and career success as it provides access to the local and global resources (Mansoor, 2003; Norton & Kamal, 2003; Rahman, 2002, 2005).
>
> (p. 1)

To quote Awan and Zia (2015):

> Proficiency in English is assumed to be required for joining and advancement in armed forces, civil services, better paying jobs in private companies and NGOs.
>
> (p. 124)

Sikandar (2017):

> White collar jobs ask for English language proficiency. English language has become one big source of economic and social stratification in Pakistani society.
>
> (p. 270)

As reported by Haidar (2017), in Pakistan, English is one of the official languages and thus a pre-requisite for most professional jobs (Rahman, 2005, p. 1).

Bangladesh

English in Bangladesh has become a prerequisite for entry into the private sector job market for professionals. Private companies, institutions, NGOs and professional employers all prefer English, because of the advance of globalization and, with job scarcity at home, people cannot but flock to employment opportunities abroad where they will have to use English (Ali, 2013, p. 129).

Sri Lanka

In Sri Lanka, graduates are measured against a fairly new set of governmental criteria measuring their employability. Therein, English is seen to be an essential component of employability, so much so that the absence of other skills is often overlooked in the presence of the ability to speak in English in the private sector. The public sector does not require English as a prerequisite for recruitment and it is not usually required for promotion to many mid- and upper-level positions, whereas the private sector requires English as a definite prerequisite at every level from recruitment to the upper layers of the employment stratum. In the face of a shrinking public sector, Sri Lanka is now struggling to equip its youth with competence in English language.

India

English is increasingly becoming dominant in the education sector in urban and semi-urban India just as it is in Sri Lanka, Bangladesh and Pakistan. It is also quickly spreading to the rural areas of India as well. Almost all the colleges and universities in India offer degrees in English medium and in order to sit for highly competitive examinations for civil service recruitment and similar positions, a sound knowledge of English is mandatory.

As we can see, the ever-growing demand for English for use in the globalized economy, coupled with the prestige and status English language enjoys in South Asian societies, has paved the way for many changes at the education policy level in post-colonial South Asia.

The failures of English teaching in post-colonial South Asia

The following section briefly outlines the outcomes of English language teaching (ELT) in the region after 70 years. All four countries are dissatisfied with their level of English language proficiency because the desired results have not been attained by way of the various policy changes and continual efforts to uplift the level of English teaching to meet the growing demand. With our extensive travels in these countries and the discussions we have had with their academic communities, we have seen that among both teachers and students, there is general dissatisfaction with the ways in which English has been taught and the poor results that have followed.

There have been numerous changes in South Asian educational policy, as discussed above, but their implementation at secondary and tertiary levels of education cannot be considered successful. As the Sri Lankan Ministry of Education has stated on its website,[2] 'When it comes to the Sri Lankan education system, English is being taught almost over 11 years as a core subject but the student performance is not at a very satisfactory level' (Ministry of Education, Sri Lanka, 2018).

At school level in Sri Lanka, the following statistics (Figure 2.1) reveal that English language education has not been effective over the seven decades spent teaching it as a second language.

After more than 70 years of teaching English as a second language in the education system, Sri Lanka was not able to attain a 50% pass rate until 2017, when it barely crossed 50%.

Most of the courses that aim at Teaching English as a Second Language (TESL) fail to produce their intended results. The number of extension courses offered by the English Language Teaching Units and the Departments of English for the general public, along with the vast numbers of students enrolled in these courses and private sector courses show that English language education in Sri Lanka at the primary and secondary school levels and in higher education is not producing successful results.

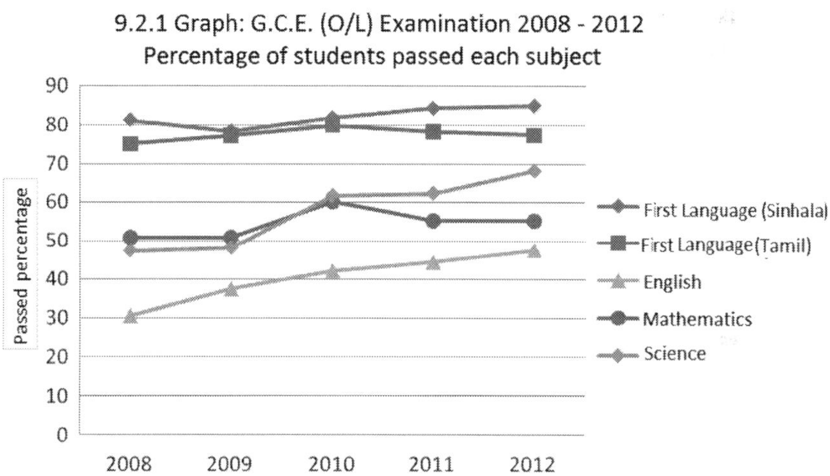

Source: Annual Performance report, Ministry of Education, Sri Lanka (above)

Year	Percentage
2014	45.08
2015	45.04
2016	47.90
2017	51.12

Figure 2.1 GCE (O/L) results from 2008/2012 to 2017, Sri Lanka.

Sources: Research and Development Branch National Evaluation and Testing Service Department of Examinations. http://www.moe.gov.lk/english/images/publications/Annual_performance_Report2013/Annual_performance_report_e.pdf.

The following excerpt from a national newspaper in Pakistan supports the contention that teaching English in Pakistan has not been a successful endeavour either.

> 92pc CSS candidates fail in English – Ikram Junaidi. Updated Dec 06, 2016 08:59 pm. ISLAMABAD: Just 2.09pc of the students who had sat the Central Superior Services (CSS) exams passed, with 92pc failing in English, the National Assembly Standing Committee on Cabinet Secretariat was told on Monday. ... The CSS exams are the most important in the country through which appointments are made in the foreign office, bureaucracy, lower judiciary, police, customs, secretariat staff and other offices and departments. ... A large number of institutions and academies offer to help students prepare for these exams and make millions of rupees in the process.
>
> *Published in* Dawn, *December 6th, 2016*
> https://www.dawn.com/news/1300724

English is taught as a foreign language in Bangladesh (Open University Publication, English Unit 1, 19 as cited by Hoque, 2008). He states that since the British invasion, English has been taught as a compulsory subject in schools, colleges and in madrasas from primary to degree level as 'a main source of up-to-date knowledge and effective means of communication' (p. 25). Yet, with regard to the results of ELT in Bangladesh, 'It is painfully observed that after long years of learning English, most of the learners cannot speak English with necessary fluency, correctness of grammar, and pronunciation' (Hoque, 2008, p. 32).

The study reports that, in spite of having studied English for nearly 12 years, a large number of students fail English in Alim (higher secondary) public examination. Monzurul (2018) states that only 18% of the total population can speak English in Bangladesh. A similar observation is made by Kabir (2017):

> ... after ten years' schooling of English, most of the students fail in English at the S.S.C. examination. Even if they pass, they get very poor marks. However, the students who pass and somehow get good marks do not seem to reflect their achievement practically. They cannot speak fluently and naturally.
>
> (p. 196)

India has produced a large number of fluent English-speaking scholars in every field, but it has also not been able to make teaching English a success at the ground level even after having taught it for nearly ten years to its youth in their school careers. Raghavachari (2013), in the article 'English for every schoolchild in India', states that

> ... English (along with mathematics) is a principal reason for failure at the Class X school-leaving examination.
>
> (p. 23)

As developing countries, India, Sri Lanka, Pakistan and Bangladesh all struggle to provide better and more equal facilities for education. Excepting Sri Lanka, all the South Asian countries are still trying to improve their literacy rates.[3] It could be argued that the failure in teaching English does not lie in the methods and approaches used to teach English specifically, but in the lack of access to education in general and a lack of resources and an environment that is not conducive to learning English. While this argument has strong points to support it, the failure of a large majority of students who have been taught English as a subject in their schools for over ten years must also be attributed to the methods used to teach English as a second language in these countries as well.

There is a conflict in these countries between the meaning of English language learning and what is actually being taught. The common and general perception in South Asia is that ELT means teaching students to learn reading and writing. A study carried out under the patronage of the British Council by Dunlea and Dunn (2013), 'English language learning outcomes at the primary school level in rural India: taking a fresh look at the data from the Annual Status of Education Report', discusses reading as the parameter to measure English education status in rural India. This raises a number of issues: everyone involved in ELT (other than the actual learners) seems to consider reading (or both reading and writing) as the primary skill/s to be taught to students who are learning English; measuring English language learning outcomes in respect to reading is believed to reflect the actual state of English language learning (as the research is examining 'reading outcomes'); and the authors, perhaps because they are native speakers of English, may take it for granted that rural Indian learners who may pass a reading assessment also acquired proficiency in speaking (and listening to) English. In fact, most of these rural learners may be unable to utter a single comprehensive sentence in English in spite of passing a written assessment. This shows a lack of understanding on the part of many English language educators of the context-specific issues related to ELT in former South Asian colonies.

In answering one of the research questions, 'Are there any trends in L2 reading performance in primary school across the different years of the survey?', the study contends:

> Yes, there is a trend. While the indication from the analysis indicates that the level of performance has been declining over the years, the difference between the initial two years (2007 and 2009) is not statistically significant. This means that any observed difference may be due to chance and should not be interpreted as reflecting a real decline. However, the decline in performance between both the 2007 and 2009 data collections and 2012 is statistically significant and can be interpreted to reflect a meaningful (if small) decline.
>
> (p. 70)

The question of whether what is taught is what the students want to learn has not been considered at all. Also, what is understood by English language *learning* seems to be learning to read in the case of the aforesaid study and/or in most other cases, learning to write. However, the preliminary studies conducted by us in Sri Lanka, starting from 2007/2008 through the past decade, continually demonstrate that the learners' most sought-after skill is learning to speak in English. This is the opposite of what students are taught in school, where reading and writing are commonly perceived to be the most sought-after skills in 'English language learning'.

Given all of this it is obvious that teaching English in the post-colonial South Asian societies has not been successful over the years. While there can be a number of reasons that may contribute to this scenario, the aforesaid discussion shows that there is a misconception of what it means to teach a language as opposed what is perceived as learnt and as a result, what is taught may not be what the learners actually need. Given such a scenario, a question can be raised as whether the content and the teaching methods that are being used to teach English to the learners in the region contextually fitting.

Having discussed the policy perspectives and the changes in English language education in the sub-continent and seeing that the results are wholly unsatisfactory, let us look at other aspects related to the English language that exist in post-colonial South Asia; intricacies that cannot be captured in a rigid policy framework as such, but are nevertheless extremely important to consider when teaching English in the region.

The colonial legacy and attitudes towards the English language

Teaching English specifically to learners in the former British colonies of South Asia is an unexplored area mainly because the prevalent attitudes in society and their influence on the South Asian English language learner have not been considered in regard to ELT. Most scholars in the field of ELT are unfamiliar with the attitude problems attached to the English language in these countries. As a result, the influence of language attitudes on the English language learner has been completely ignored, leading to a total lack of concern for their effects on the teaching and learning process.

The power that is associated with the English language is represented in the region in varying ways that indicate its high prestige: for instance, the concept of ***kaduwa*** is attached to the English language in Sri Lanka. The meaning of '***kaduwa***' in Sinhala is the 'sword' a term used for English that represents it as having power. This term was discussed by Thiru Kandiah (1984). Even today, one will often hear in local, colloquial terms, 'I need to get my ***kaduwa*** polished'. The concept of the 'sword' has varied in its meaning over the years in which it can indicate a value associated with respect or even with hatred, as stated by Braine (1998) in his anecdote 'Training College Days'; 'We were further disadvantaged as English teacher-trainees because of our tendency to speak in the detested ***kaduwa***'. In spite of its increasing utilitarian value over the years, the power-associated value of English remains unchanged in South Asia.

The English language in Pakistan has symbolic power by virtue of its British colonial history and as the language of the ruling classes after independence (Rahman, 2005). Therefore, Bourdieu's (1991) theory about the symbolic power of language is relevant for understanding access to English in Pakistan, where it is considered to be the most *prestigious* language (Haidar, 2017, p. 3). In Bangladesh, a country that was built upon a language, English is not necessarily perceived as the most prestigious language, but it is viewed as a means for upward social mobility and therefore has a high position in the language hierarchy.

> It [English] is considered in Bangladesh as a stair of prosperity, a tool of acquiring knowledge and as a sign of *sophistication*[italics added] ... The chronological history of English in Bangladesh has political as well as social background, which influence the learning of English at every level of education.
>
> (Hoque, 2008, p. 25)

Studies in the area of comparative language attitudes have shown the English language is often considered to be more prestigious, higher and/or as a competitor with the mother tongues in the post-colonial South Asian region. Sometimes, the references are obvious while some others are quite subtle: for an example, the comparative perception of Bangladeshis between English and Bangla is expressed explicitly in the quote below:

> ... new genres of knowledge, the native language has not developed much or is not doing so simultaneously. But English, being an international language is quickly adapting to the situation and enriching itself. So, English is more enriched than Bangla. A person skilled in English is highly evaluated home and abroad.
>
> (Kabir, 2012, p. 195)

A more subtle and noteworthy expression is found in discussion of the Indian tri-lingual policy, where English is included in the Three-Language Formula for its 'administrative efficiency and technological progress' (Sridhar, 1989). Interestingly, a similar observation was made by Haque (1983) with regard to the language policy in post-independence Pakistan, where English was still considered the official language as it was during pre-independence, to meet the need of 'operational efficiency' in the administration. Herein, we see two obvious connotations; either it is thought that administration will be efficient when English is the medium or that administration will be efficient when there is a common language in the administration. This leads one to question why Hindi, the other official language in the case of India, and Urdu in Pakistan are still not valued publically for their potential 'administrative efficiency'. It leads us to question whether a label like this denotes an attitude towards the English language and/or towards the people who ruled the sub-continent for decades and whose mother tongue was English.

The study we conducted in 2007, examining the language attitudes of teachers of English in Sri Lanka shows that there are contrasting views about English in relation to the vernaculars, Sinhala and Tamil, which are the mother tongues of the two main ethnic communities in the country. The teachers' perceptions were threefold: (a) some viewed English as 'threatening' and 'hostile' to mother tongues (in addition to Sinhala and Tamil being threatened by each other), thereby denoting the idea of ***competition***, (b) others perceived English as more useful and important, and therefore as a ***replacement*** for mother tongues in education, while (c) others viewed English as surpassing the local languages and empowering the individual with power and prestige which the former were unable to do, thus placing English as ***superior*** in a linguistic power hierarchy. It is important to note that none of the teachers viewed the three languages as a confluence or as complementing each other (Attanayake, 2017).

The existence of such perceptions of language positioning and the power structure associated with it is well explained by Ramanathan (2005):

> Any understanding of English and Vernacular education has to begin first by locating them side by side (as opposed to arranging them in a hierarchy). Doing so is the first step not only in addressing language-related inequalities on the postcolonial ground but in recognizing ways in which English and the vernaculars while simultaneously divided and dichotomous from some points of view are also simultaneously overlapping and conjoined.
>
> (p. 3)

Sri Lanka, India, Bangladesh and Pakistan share almost identical experiences with regard to the English language in their pre-independence, immediate post-independence and post-post-independence periods. In addition, they seem to come together on common ground in a simultaneous awakening of regional/national consciousnesses with language as an integral facet. Even though we do not intend to explore this area more deeply, it is interesting to observe regional consciousnesses expressed through language as yet another common ground that all four neighbours share in post-post-independence South Asia: India – Hindi versus regional languages like Tamil and Bengali; Sri Lanka – Sinhala versus Tamil; Pakistan – Urdu versus Sindh, Punjabi, Pashto, etc. The only exception is post-1971 Bangladesh where Bangla stands alone, but this occurred only after a bloody war of liberation. It is in this common context that English is strengthening its established position of power and prestige in the region.

The desire to speak English and the lack of confidence

Our research that has been carried out for the past 11 years (from 2007 to 2018) shows two important findings: that speaking is the most desired skill among learners of English in Sri Lanka, perhaps owing to its obvious productive quality, and they lack confidence to speak English. If someone speaks a language, it is taken as if they know the language, irrespective of whether they know how to read or write in it. The primacy that speaking English has obtained over all other language skills may be attributed to the position that the English language has secured over the years; it is considered the premiere indicator and representation of class, education, intellect, etc. Being able to speak in English means that one is presenting oneself as educated, belonging to a higher class and as a member of the intellectual community without having to prove it by writing in English (Samarakkody, 2001).

There are learners of English from all walks of life. However, for the undergraduate community, learning English does not mean learning to speak only. They also need the ability to read and write English for their immediate academic purposes and for their future occupational pursuits. They are aware of the importance of these other English language skills. Nevertheless, the primacy they give to speaking English shows the importance that is placed on the ability to speak in English over the demands of written examinations, assignments, etc. that are involved with studying in the university. Given this kind of response, one would expect, quite justifiably, that their level of proficiency in English would be higher than that of an average person[4] and that they are able to speak it appropriately with some confidence. However, the study shows otherwise. This lack of confidence results from the anxiety learners experience when trying to speak in English, an anxiety rooted in the language attitudes of the society. This lack of confidence proves to be decisively detrimental to their ability to speak in English and put what they already know into practice so that they can improve their English language proficiency. MacIntyre and Gardener (1994a, 1994b) support this view that speaking may produce more anxiety than any other skill. Therefore, anxiety may also interfere with the learner's ability to demonstrate what she or he actually knows.

Within such a scenario, we argue that the failure in English language education in post-colonial South Asia as a whole may stem from a lack of consideration and a complete disregard for the complexities attached to the learners' most sought-after skill, speaking. The lack of consideration for the (a) societal attitudes that create fear/shyness/uncertainty to speak English causes learners to (b) lack confidence to speak English, resulting in (c) poor speaking skills in English, that in turn leads to (d) poor overall performance in English.

Demand vs. supply

The changes in the language policies in post-colonial South Asia have been aimed at nation building, education and employment at different points in time in our history. The English language has secured its important place through all of the many changes that have taken place. Despite various efforts by all of the governments in the region to teach English over the past seven decades, it is unarguable that, as shown by the results, there is a definite failure in the teaching of English. With our preliminary research in teaching English in Sri Lanka and our discussions with the academic communities in the sub-continent as described in the introduction, we observe that there is a major mismatch between the demand and the supply in English language education: (a) students want to be able to speak English and consider it the prime purpose of learning the language but teachers mainly teach them reading and writing and measure their language knowledge accordingly; (b) there are power-related attitudes towards the English language and students are affected by these attitudes – in other words, learners love to speak English yet they are afraid and are shy to speak English for fear of being ridiculed by others in the society – yet we continuously ignore the deleterious effects for learning caused by these attitudes in our own ELT. It is in this context that we locate the thrust of the argument in our study: language attitudes that exist in post-colonial South Asia must be considered when teaching English. To this end, it is of extreme importance to (a) identify the existing language attitudes and related complexities in the South Asian region, (b) analyse them in terms of their effects on language learners and (c) find remedial measures in the ELT process to help learners improve their language performance. Our study, therefore, is designed to achieve these objectives by building student confidence to speak in English.

The attitude problem attached to the English language and its speakers must be considered in designing goals for English language education. Psycho-educational approaches have to be developed specifically targeting a change of attitudes in the learner. Empowering the learner to withstand the ridicule of society even if he/she speaks 'wrong English' has to be accomplished methodically by addressing the learner's psyche as part of teaching English. In such a context, 'confidence building to learn English' becomes paramount as the initial step towards eliminating the shyness and fear to speak English. The built confidence to speak in English can be used to master English in the long run if it is developed and sustained. Thus, there is sufficient evidence for the need of psycho-educational approaches in teaching English to the post-colonial South Asian learner. So far as we know, no teaching approach or method has been developed to build confidence in order to learn English and no curriculum has been designed to teach English by building confidence as a main objective. Even though there are numerous books on ELT curriculum design, none address these particular psychological aspects of the social environment, namely language attitudes, as a central theme.

Conclusion

When we consider the efforts, the money and other resources that former South Asian colonies such as Sri Lanka, India, Pakistan and Bangladesh have put into English language education, we must conclude that ELT in the region is an utter failure. While there may be a number of social, economic and political issues driving such an outcome, it could also very well be that the use of methods and approaches borrowed from the west do not suit the English language learners in these countries. Their needs, vis-à-vis English language, are different from what educators may perceive their needs to be. The context within which they operate is different from what may be generalized. This study sets out to uncover the language attitudes that exist in the sub-continent towards the English language and its speakers and to analyse their effects on the language learner in order to find remedial measures.

Notes

1 Herein, 'English' does not mean native proficiency, but a variety that is generally accepted in the community it is spoken and a variety that is comprehensible within that community.
2 Ministry of Education, Sri Lanka: 2018 advertisement on 'Insights into teaching English as a Second/Foreign Language through foreign exposure programme' http://www.moe.gov.lk/english/images/HRD/proposal.pdf.
3 Sri Lanka has the highest literacy rate, i.e., 98%, in the South Asian region.
4 In Sri Lanka, university entrance examination is considered as one of the most competitive examinations and only about 21,500 students (roughly about 5% of the total student population who sat for the examination) are able to enter the university. So, undergraduates are considered as the 'cream' of the society.

References

Ali, M. A. (2013). Language policy and planning for Bangla in the current context of Bangladesh: Possibilities and constraints. *Prime University Journal*, 7(2), 113–137.

Anwar, S. A. Q, & Ashfaq, M. (2017). Introduction to the economy of Pakistan. Retrieved from: https://www.researchgate.net/publication/321037817_Introduction_to_the_Economy_of_Pakistan. Accessed 15 December 2018.

Attanayake, A. U. (2017). *Undergraduate ELT Sri Lanka: Policy, practice and perspectives for South Asia*. New Castle upon Tyne: Cambridge Scholars Publishing.

Awan, A. G., & Zia, A. (2015). Comparative analysis of public and private educational institutions: A case study of district Vehari-Pakistan. *Journal of Education and Practice*, 6(16), 122–130.

Begum, T. (2015). The 'cultural legacy' of English in Bangladesh. *Language in India*, 15(3), 239–252.

Bourdieu, P. (1991). *Language and symbolic power*. Oxford: Polity Press.

Braine, G. (1998). *Anecdote: Training college days*. Unpublished article.

Chowdhury, R., & Kabir, A. H. (2014). Language wars: English education policy and practice in Bangladesh. *Multilingual Education*, 4, 1–16.

Dawn. (2016). Retrieved from: https://www.dawn.com/news/1300724

Delican, M. (1998). The language policy of India. *İstanbul Üniversitesi Sosyoloji Konferansları Dergisi*, 25(1), 121–130. Retrieved from http://dergipark.gov.tr/download/article-file/101067

Dharmadasa, K. N. O. (1996). *National language policy in Sri Lanka*. Colombo: ICES.

Dunlea, J., & Dunn, K. (2013). *English language learning outcomes at the primary school level in rural India: Taking a fresh look at the data from the annual status of education report. English impact report*. Ed. Vivian Berry. London: British Council.

Goonatilleke, D. C. R. A. (1981). English for university admission. *Navasilu*, 4, 63–79.

Haidar, S. (2017). Access to English in Pakistan: Inculcating prestige and leadership through instruction in elite schools. *International Journal of Bilingual Education and Bilingualism*. UK: Routledge. doi:10.1080/13670050.2017.1320352

Haque, A. R. (1983). The position and status of English in Pakistan. *World Language English*, 2(1), 6–9.

Hoque, M. E. (2008). ***English language teaching and learning at the Alim Level in the madrashas in Bangladesh: Problems and possible solutions.*** Unpublished MPhil dissertation. Retrieved from https://www.scribd.com/doc/28681752/English-Language-Teaching-and-Learning-in-Bangladesh-Dr-M-Enamul-Hoque

Javed, F. (2017). A historical perspective of Pakistan's language in education policy. ***Language in India***, 17(8), 45–55. Retrieved 15 February 2019 from: https://www.researchgate.net/publication/319276792_A_Historical_Perspective_of_Pakistan's_Language_in_Education_Policy

Jayasundara, N. S. (2014). The development of language education policy: An Indian perspective; a view from Tamil Nadu. ***International Journal of Scientific and Research Publications***, 4(11), 1–4. Retrieved from: http://www.ijsrp.org/research-paper-1114/ijsrp-p3530.pdf

Kabir, E. (2017). Is English a failed language in Bangladesh? Retrieved from: https://www.dhakatribune.com/opinion/op-ed/2017/07/07/english-failed-language-bangladesh/

Kabir, M. M. N. (2012). Causes of secondary students' failure in learning English. Retrieved from Language in India: www.languageinindia.com

Kandiah, T. (1984). Kaduwa, power and the English language weapon in Sri Lanka. In P. Colin Thomas and A. Halpe (Eds.), ***Honouring E.F.C. Ludowyk. Felicitation Essays.*** Dehiwala, Sri Lanka: Thisara Prakashakayo.

MacIntyre, P. D., & Gardner, R. C. (1994a). The effects of induced anxiety on three stages of cognitive processing in computerized vocabulary language learning. ***Studies in Second Language Acquisition***, 16, 1–17.

MacIntyre, P. D., & Gardner, R. C. (1994b). The subtle effects of language anxiety cognitive processing in the second language. ***Language Learning***, 44, 283–385.

Mansoor, S. (2003). Language Planning in Higher Education Issues of Access and Equity. ***Lahore Journal of Economics*** 8 (2), 17–42.

Martyn, S. (2013). In post-conflict Sri Lanka, language is essential for reconciliation. ***Asia Foundation***. Retrieved from: https://asiafoundation.org/2013/01/16/in-post-conflict-sri-lanka-language-is-essential-for-reconciliation/

Monzurul, M. M. (2018). The present scenario of English language teaching in Bangladesh. Daffodil International University. http://hdl.handle.net/20.500.11948/2458; Retrieved from: http://dspace.library.daffodilvarsity.edu.bd

Nayar, B. R. (1969). ***National communication and language policy in India***. New York, Washington, DC, London: Frederic A. Praeger, Publishers.

Pandit, P. B. (1977). ***Language in a plural society, the case of India***. Delhi: Delhi University Press.

Raghavachari, A. (2013). An English for every schoolchild in India. ***English Impact Report***. Ed. Vivian Berry. London: British Council.

Rahman, S. (2005). Orientations and motivation in English language learning: A study of Bangladeshi students at undergraduate level. ***Asian EFL Journal***, 7(1), Article 3. Retrieved 12 March 2008 from: http://www.asian-efl-journal.com/march_05_sr.php

Rahman, T. (1995). ***Language planning and politics in Pakistan***. Research Report Series No. 9. Islamabad: Sustainable Development Policy Institute. (PDF) A Historical Perspective of Pakistan's Language in Education Policy. Retrieved from https://www.researchgate.net/publication/319276792_A_Historical_Perspective_of_Pakistan's_Language_in_Education_Policy. Accessed 24 May 2019].

Rahman, T. (2002). ***Language, ideology and power: Language-learning among the Muslims of Pakistan and North India***. Karachi: Oxford University Press.

Rahman, T. (2003). Language policy multilingualism and language vitality in Pakistan. Retrieved 21 January 2019 from: http://apnaorg.com/book-chapters/tariq/

Ramanathan, V. (2005). *The English-vernacular divide: Postcolonial language politics and practice*. Clevedon, England: Multilingual Matters Ltd.

Ramanujam, M. (2011). Language policy in education and the role of English in India: From library language to language of empowerment. In H. Coleman (Ed.), *Dreams and realities: Developing countries and the English language* (pp. 2–30). British Council. Retrieved from: https://files.eric.ed.gov/fulltext/ED530679.pdf

Roy, S. (2017). English in Bangladesh: Resistance versus utility. *Language in India*, 17(5), 330–342.

Samarakkody, M. (2001). Motivation and acquisition of English in Sri Lanka: A linguistic and social psychological study. In D. Hayes (Ed.), *Teaching English: Possibilities and opportunities* (pp. 37–47). Colombo: British Council.

Seifi, P. (2015). Language policy in multilingual Pakistan. *Advances in Social Sciences Journal*, 2(3), 32–37. Retrieved 21 January 2019 from: https://www.researchgate.net/publication/282456093_Language_Policy_in_Multilingual_and_Multicultural_Pakistan

Sikandar, A. (2017). Language policy planning in Pakistan: A review. *Pakistan Business Review*, 19(1), 267–272. Retrieved from: http://journals.iobmresearch.com/index.php/PBR/article/view/1264/241

Sridhar, K. (1989). *English in Indian bilingualism*. Delhi: Manohar Publications.

3 The study

Introduction

This chapter discusses the sample, the tools used to collect data, the approach used for data collection and the methods of data analysis and discussion. The discussion reveals that learners in post-colonial South Asia experience anxiety related to speaking English both inside and outside the language classroom. While some are afraid, shy or uncertain to speak English in front of their teachers and peers, some others also feel the same emotions in front of outsiders and strangers. Still more experience the same anxiety in front of everyone. This shows another potent area in which anxiety relates to language education, in addition to the concept of Foreign Language Anxiety (FLA), the dominant theory available to scholars discussing anxiety issues related to foreign and second language education.

The sample

Four post-colonial South Asian countries, namely India, Pakistan, Bangladesh and Sri Lanka, were selected for the study. We selected these countries as the result of our formal and informal encounters with academics in these countries, as well as academics in non-post-colonial settings and western countries. Our discussions revealed differences in the 'confidence to speak English' among the different student communities. As discussed in the introduction, this study was triggered by one of the findings of my PhD research: Sri Lankan undergraduates lacked confidence to speak English due to their fear of being ridiculed by others in their society. I started to present these findings at conferences under the title, 'Building confidence to speak English is central to the teaching of English in Sri Lanka (rather than emphasizing the teaching of grammar and structures)'. When I presented at conferences in the USA, quite interestingly, the academics were curious to know about why confidence was needed to speak English. In Singapore, the academics were very keen to know about this seemingly novel issue of 'needing confidence to speak English'. However, at guest lectures and conference presentations in India, Pakistan and Bangladesh, almost all of the academics said their situation was identical to what we were facing in Sri Lanka and what I was presenting. The surprise, if any, was how similar our situations were. This sparked the idea that this similarity could be due to a commonality we all share: the colonial mentality. All four nations share similar characteristics as a result. Although we split hairs when discussing it, even after 70 years of being 'free', we still struggle to get out of this mentality, seem to be eternally trapped in it. This causes us to deposit all the present problems we face in our respective countries in a common 'colonial history account'.

The four countries in this study are geographically close and all four countries were under British rule and received their independence at more or less the same time (with India and Pakistan – East and West – in 1947 and Sri Lanka in 1948). All have shared colonial histories in terms of the use of English as the language both of administration and of the local elite. Therefore, it seemed that there was an intricate and complex scenario behind the English language and its representation in these countries that affected English language learning and its use that the western nations and states without a colonial history did not experience and could not readily understand. To add to that, we attribute the failures in teaching English language that we have identified in South Asian countries (discussed in the previous chapter), mainly to the failure to develop context-specific teaching methodologies to teach English as a result of our failure to identify certain context-specific problems and understand their magnitude.

The universities in which data was collected for this study were selected to represent the main geographical locations in each of the four countries to obtain a general picture of the English language teaching scenario. As Figure 3.1 shows, the main regions/divisions in each country (in terms of administration and/or cardinal directions such as north, south, east and west) were identified. In each main region, the universities located in major cities were selected. This was because students who studied in major cities generally had more contacts with the English-speaking community and were well aware of the benefits and possibilities that the ability to perform well in English language could offer them. A representative sample was used to select the major universities from each region taking into account the physical extent of the target group and the complexities, learnt through previous studies, to obtain information with regard to a topic of this nature.

All the universities considered in this study, the target group, come under the relevant administrative body regulating higher education (e.g. the University Grants Commission – UGC – or Higher Education Commission – HEC) in each country even though some universities are fee-levying while others are free. This is because in some countries university education is fee-levying while in some others it is completely free as a matter of public policy.[1] Nevertheless, the universities considered are broadly similar in their undergraduate intake.

An attempt was made to collect data from one, two or more major universities in each of the regions so that a representative sample from each identified region in each of the countries studied could be acquired. When there were many 'major' universities clustered in a particular region, the data was collected from more than two (e.g. Pakistan – Punjab; Bangladesh – Dhaka; Sri Lanka – Colombo[2]). When there was only one major university in a particular region, the data collection was limited to that one university.

Almost all of the data collection was done by going personally to each university in Pakistan, Bangladesh and Sri Lanka. There were a few exceptions

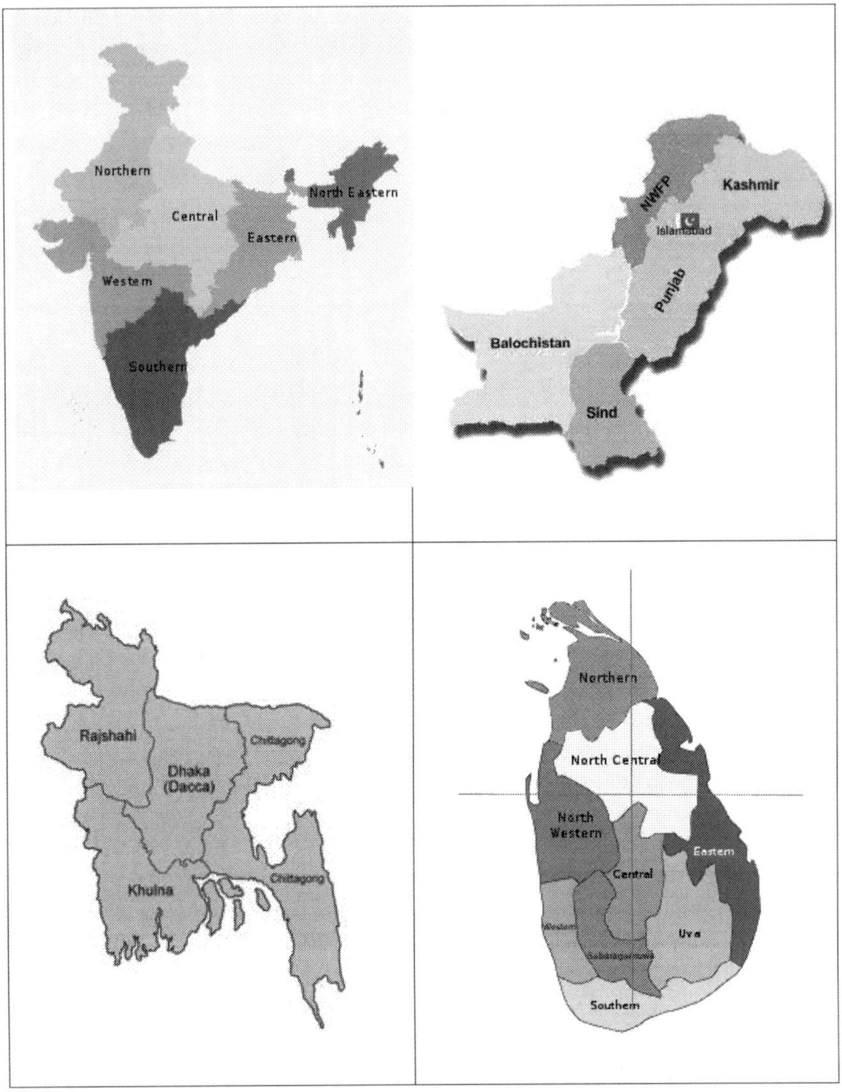

Figure 3.1 Countries and their main divisions from which data was collected.

(in Pakistan, Quetta University, Baluchistan, and Iqra University; Varendra College and Jagannagar College in Bangladesh and Ruhuna University in Sri Lanka). In India, however, except for Jawaharlal Nehru University, New Delhi, and Dempe College and Law College in Goa, all the data was collected through contact persons who were also academics in the respective universities. This was due to the vast size of India and the difficulty faced in traversing the entire country. When the help of academics was sought, they were given a detailed description of the required sample and instructions for the data collection procedure.

The criteria used to select the sample were as follows:

1 Undergraduates studying subjects other than English literature or Linguistics
2 Those who were in their first or second year of study
3 Students who have a lack of proficiency in English in spite of having studied it for years

Why were undergraduates selected for the study? The initial study upon which this work is based was related to confidence and speaking English and conducted among the undergraduates of Sri Lanka in 2007–2008. Thereafter, until 2018, as we have stated elsewhere, we have been collecting data related to the same issue from the undergraduates of Sri Lanka and the desire to develop the speaking skill in English has been observed throughout. Likewise, the lack of confidence, fear of speaking in English and shyness when speaking English were observed throughout in near-similar percentages. Even though undergraduates were selected as the sample in 2007–2008 on the basis of convenience as well as our familiarity with the Sri Lankan university system, the data collection during the years that followed and the recurrent similar findings highlighted some interesting questions to carry the current study forward with the same category of students in other South Asian countries. We chose undergraduates because they are fully adapted and socialized adults in their societies and yet they lack confidence to speak in a language they have been learning for over ten years. We want to discover why they are afraid and shy when speaking English. Undergraduates are considered as the best students in society as they qualify for their higher studies through competitive examinations, yet they say they lack confidence to speak English. We want to determine if they are reluctant to speak in English in the classroom due to the fear of being negatively evaluated by their teacher or peers and why they run away from and shun opportunities to practise speaking outside the classroom, in spite of the fact that speaking is their most sought-after skill. Undergraduates are only a few steps away from employment and are well aware of the demand for English and the higher probability of getting 'good' employment that comes with the ability to speak English. Even so, they are reluctant to speak English or to practise speaking it even when their future 'good' employment is at stake.

We want to determine who these 'others' are that the students fear being ridiculed by while speaking English. Is it their teachers, their friends and peers, or both? Are they hesitant to speak English even with outsiders and strangers? Do they feel this anxiety both inside and outside the English language classroom? Is there a single space where they feel comfortable to speak English? Do they view English language and the culture it represents through a similar fear-based lens? How do they perceive those who speak English well? All of these questions made us probe more into the English language teaching and learning scenario of South Asian undergraduates with increased vigour.

In addition, one can associate the lack of confidence to speak English with learners' low performance in English in spite of learners' overall aptitude and academic performance. Undergraduates who have passed highly competitive examinations to get into the university system in each country are considered to be the best academic performers among the student population in any given period. As such, any potential correlation between academic performance and English language proficiency can be eliminated by using undergraduates as the sample. Their high performance in other subjects while showing low performance in English clarifies the issues related to English language education and makes them more precise and specific.

With my experience teaching English in the university setting for over 18 years and prior to that studying as an English literature student at the Department of English at the University of Peradeniya, I felt that the confidence issue was either not present at all or present at a minimal level among the undergraduates who study English literature. In fact, we realized, to our great dismay, that we were part of that category of 'others' who contributed to creating the lack of confidence in students who did not study English literature. In addition, English literature students usually do not belong to the low proficiency category in English language, which was another criterion for sample selection. Therefore, we tried not to include English literature students in the sample and requested our facilitators to arrange data collection from among other students. However, there were a few exceptions, which we consider as limitations to the study: among the students in the sample in Lahore, Pakistan, and in Khulna, Bangladesh, we found out that there were some students who studied English literature. Also in Goa, India, some students who studied English literature came into the sample. This occurred when our contact persons in the those universities had difficulties finding students for the data collection: some universities had their study leave period and among those who were available, there were English literature students; also, some universities had their examinations going on and our facilitators arranged the data collection soon after the examinations were over so that we could 'catch' considerable numbers in one place easily; some English literature students slipped into the sample. However, we have entered the data under two different categories, 'English literature & Linguistics' and 'Other' so that differences, if any, can be analysed.

The target undergraduate population was predominantly from the first and second years of their degree programme in the age group 20–25. Over our years of teaching in the university system, we have observed that students who are in their initial years at the university have more inhibitions about speaking English than in their later years. Even though this is a general observation and may invite debate, the conclusion we have come to is that by the time they reach their third or fourth year, most of them have given up on speaking English and even learning English, just as they lost hope trying to learn English in the latter part of their school career.

In addition, in their final year/s they pay more attention to the core subjects of their degree programme and English language learning is usually the least prioritized subject. However, due to the same reasons mentioned above in regard to English literature students, we found some third and fourth year undergraduates in our sample. In addition, in India, a few PhD researchers volunteered to respond to the questionnaire on hearing the objective of our study and they are also included. All in all, the sample consists of a majority of undergraduates with some MA and MSc students and a few MPhil and PhD scholars.

Students with a high proficiency in English were eliminated from each university with the help of the respective department heads. Among those selected, there were students who read for degrees in their mother tongue, English or both and in other mediums. The reason for eliminating learners in the highest proficiency groups is because usually they are a small minority in all four countries at every level and need less support to improve their English than the large majority that fall under the mid- or low-proficiency level categories. Spielberger (1978) emphasizes the need for research in the area with larger samples that eliminate learners at the extreme ranges of ability. It is precisely for those students that some remedy should be found by examining major causes for the majority of students' reluctance to use English despite studying it along with those who end up at higher proficiency levels. The scenario in all four countries is such that at grade/class 10, a large majority either fail in English or pass it with a simple pass; at the university level, a large majority struggle in their programmes if the medium of instruction is English. In addition, the vast majority opt for mother tongue instruction when it is available. For instance, in Sri Lanka, mother tongue instruction is available at the Faculties of Arts in almost all the main universities. Therefore, every year, about 80% of the undergraduate population follow their BA degree programme in mother tongue due to their poor English language proficiency. In addition, about 75% of the total intake in any given year falls under the lowest proficiency category at the Faculties of Arts. As we discussed in the introduction, all four countries consider English language teaching as a failure in spite of over 70 years of teaching it as a second language since the large majority is not able to use it for communication purposes. Therefore, it was decided to examine the reasons for the situation affecting the low proficiency groups that make up the majority of English language learners in all four countries and find remedial measures to rectify this issue.

The study tried to take a minimum of 200 students from each region so that at least 1,000 respondents from each country are included in the sample. This was to obtain a fair representation of the English language teaching–learning situation in each country while also considering the diversity that may be present across regions. When we considered the general population, the undergraduate population and the geographical dispersion of universities within each country, obtaining a number based on a properly calculated ratio was deemed unachievable. For instance, Sri Lanka's undergraduate population is about 100,000 in a given year whereas India's may be 100 times larger with the other two countries falling between the two. With very limited resources (labour – only the researcher and an assistant for interviews; finance – no outside funding whatsoever for the data collection from all four countries) at our disposal, a minimum of 1,000 students seemed practical. Considering all these aspects, 1,000 students from each country, covering all regions of the country, was deemed to be a sufficiently large sample to access while also capturing the diversities in the students and teachers in relation to English language teaching–learning in each country (Tables 3.1 and 3.2).

Table 3.1 Sample of students from each country as per region/administrative division

Country	*No. of main regions (admin/direction-wise)*	*No. of regions covered*	*No. of colleges & universities*	*Total no. of students*
Pakistan	5[a]	4	10	1,318
Bangladesh	4[b]	4	8	1,013
India	6	6	20	1,297
Sri Lanka	5[c]	5	7	1,002
Total	20	19	45	4,630

a In Pakistan, data could not be collected from Kashmir.

b Old four divisions of Bangladesh were considered as convenience sampling method was used.

c In Sri Lanka, there are nine provinces of which five main provinces namely, Northern, Southern, Eastern, Western and Central were selected considering the main directions.

Table 3.2 The details on the data collected from the four post-colonial South Asian countries by city and the universities/colleges within each region

Pakistan

Administrative division	*City*	*Name of the college/university*	*No. of students*
Punjab	Lahore	National University of Modern Languages, Forman Christian College, Lahore College for Women, Lahore Government College	408
	Islamabad	Air University, Iqra University	262
Sindh	Sindh	University of Sindh	209
Khyber Pakhtunkwa (formerly NWFP)	Peshawar	University of Peshawar	197
	Malakand	University of Malakand	143
Baluchistan	Quetta	Baluchistan University of Information Technology, Engineering and Management Sciences	99
04	06	10	1,318

Bangladesh

Administrative division/district	*City*	*Name of the college/university*	*No. of students*
Barishal	Barishal	University of Barishal	169
Khulna	Khulna	University of Khulna	104
Rajashahi	Rajashahi	University of Rajashahi, Varendra University	127
Dhaka	Dhaka	University of Dhaka, Jahangirnagar University, Jagannath University	318
Chittagong	Chittagong	University of Chittagong	295
05	05	08	1,013

India			
Zone	*State*	*Name of the college/university*	*No. of students*
East	Odisha	Ravenshaw University, Stewart Science College, Rama Devi College, Utkal University	213
	Bengal	Presidency University, Calcutta University	88
	Varanasi	Banaras Hindu University	109
North East	Sikkim	Sikkim University, Tadong College, Rhenock College	137
	Assam	Assam University	95
West	Goa	Goa University (Dempe College & Salgaocar College of Law)	170
	Gujarat	Dhirubhai Ambani Institute of Information and Communication Technology	31
South	Tamil Nadu	Manomaniam Sundarnar University, University of Madras	199
	Kerala	Calicut University	53
North and Central	New Delhi	Jawaharlal Nehru University, Hans raj College, Gargi College	202
05	10	20	1297

Sri Lanka			
Province	*City*	*Name of the college/university*	*No. of students*
North	Jaffna	University of Jaffna	196
West	Colombo	University of Colombo, University of Visual and Performing Arts	329
East	Battcaloa	Eastern University	167
	Ampara	South Eastern University	100
Central	Kandy	Sri Lanka International Buddhist Academy	58
South	Matara	University of Ruhuna	152
05	06	07	1,002

Tools

A questionnaire was designed with specific questions to determine whether it was only FLA, described as 'a distinct complex of self-perceptions, beliefs, feelings, and behaviours related to classroom language learning arising from the uniqueness of the language learning process' (Horwitz, Horwitz, & Cope, 1986, p. 125) or whether it was something more than FLA arising from the society and extending into the language classroom and vice versa. The interview questions were designed to extract information along the lines of this contention: that there is more than FLA to the whole anxiety issue in relation to

English language teaching–learning in post-colonial South Asia. Since the Foreign Language Classroom Anxiety Scale (FLCAS) has 31 of its 33 questions specifically addressing the foreign language classroom context (with those who are present in it), the questionnaire and the interview questions in this study were designed to specifically distinguish between the foreign language classroom and the environment outside of the classroom so that a clear distinction between FLA and the other types of anxiety could be made. In addition, the FLA scale uses 'foreign language' as a general term encompassing both second and foreign languages but we specifically used 'English language' in our investigation of the psycho-social intricacies that stem from the power play between English language and other languages in post-colonial South Asian societies. Given the predominantly quantitative nature of language anxiety measurement in research using the FLA scale (a Likert scale with five possible responses ranging from Strongly agree to Strongly disagree), we designed our study with both quantitative and qualitative data collection and analysis methods, as our study involves identification of the contexts in which anxiety is most experienced by the learners and the attitudes that are related to English language teaching–learning in post-colonial South Asia.

The FLA scale, while exclusively testing FLA within the four walls of the classroom, uses two questions that seem to be general: 'Q 14. I would not be nervous speaking the foreign language with native speakers and Q 31. I am afraid that the other students will laugh at me when I speak the foreign language' (Horwitz et al., 1986). However, if they were used to test any anxiety outside of the language learning setting, the objective may be lost as the two questions are vague vis-à-vis context and are buried in the middle of the questions on classroom-specific situations. Also there is a very high probability that respondents may interpret the two questions as related to classroom situations amid the classroom-specific 14 questions prior to each of them. In contrast, the questionnaire and the interview questions that were designed for this study categorically asked the learners about the context in which they were reluctant to speak in English including the place and the people present.

In addition, the learners were asked to write anything that they considered relevant to their English language learning experience, English language speaking experience, what they saw as weaknesses or strengths in their English language education systems and any suggestions they had to improve the systems. From each country, the responses of 150 learners were selected randomly and analysed. They have been incorporated into the discussion as appropriate.

A randomly selected 10% of the student sample was interviewed in each location as it seemed impractical to interview all 200 who responded to the questionnaire. Gardner's (2004) Attitude/Motivation Test Battery (AMTB) was adapted for the interviews. Interviews were conducted by a native speaker of English. This was to see whether the fear/shyness/uncertainty factor when speaking English was present when learners were speaking with native speakers. However, when the data was collected via contact persons, the interview questions were sent to the respondents and written responses were collected. While admitting this as a limitation (not being able to interview students by a native speaker of English), this was the most viable strategy to collect detailed responses along the lines of the questionnaire, explaining the whys and the hows of interest to the researchers. Even though a wealth of information has come out of these semi-structured interviews, we are compelled to use only the information strictly related to the attitude-related discussion in this study. (See Appendix C for questionnaire and interview questions.)

Data analysis and methods

Both quantitative and qualitative data analysis methods were used to analyse the data. SPSS data analysis method was used for the quantitative data analysis and it was utilized to identify the basic problems related to attitudes towards speaking English. The qualitative data that was collected through interviews and the open-ended question for learners' opinions in regard to language attitudes and their English language learning experience were analysed thematically according to the development of the discussion with the aim of creating a broad picture of post-colonial South Asian English language education.

Method

To analyse quantitative data, the SPSS worksheet was used. The questionnaire was designed to capture the basic context-specific features related to anxiety issues among post-colonial South Asian learners and their attitudes towards English language, its speakers and learning English. Therefore, the typical Likert-scale-type questionnaire style was avoided, as such a tool will give us a picture of the problem in terms of numerals, which, on the one hand, we are already aware of, and on the other, does not allow us to delve deeper into the psyche of the learners. With our preliminary 'hunch' that there is more than what is immediately apparent going on in the South Asian English language classroom in regard to English language teaching–learning in our countries, we have designed the questionnaire to distinguish between Foreign Language Classroom Anxiety (FLCA) and what is not FLCA.

The depth of the problem is apparent when more than 50% of our learners fail in English at national level examinations in all four South Asian countries. We thought that even if a finding was made as to what percentage of learners experience the negative effects of language attitudes prevalent in our societies, it would not lead to a better understanding of the causes of the problem. In contrast, if our findings showed the exact colour and flavour of the language attitude problem and its effects, we believed it would lead us to understand the problem more completely at close quarters and aid us in finding context-specific remedial measures.

In addition, with our main thrust being the attitudes of learners and the broader society towards the English language and its speakers, we were determined to look at it from a qualitative angle due to (a) the difficulty in measuring attitudes quantitatively and (b) the human element involved with its psychological and emotional aspects. Thus, we did not intend to go into a heavy statistical analysis when analysing our data as we believed that a more quantitative approach would not be able adequately to capture the attitudes towards English language found in the post-colonial South Asian region. Instead, we tried to analyse the evidence in a more qualitative framework while considering the abstractness of language attitudes as the main variable in our study.

Thus, the interview questions were formulated to extract more information with open-ended questions. This proved to be both rewarding and illuminating with learners revealing their enthusiasm, frustrations and future hopes vis-à-vis speaking English.

Analysis

The comparisons are made across countries in terms of

1 The skill/s that are most desired
2 The reason for learning the most desired skill
3 The fear/shyness/uncertainty factor when speaking English
4 The domain factor in speaking English
5 The personal factor in speaking English

The section that follows shows how the analysis of the quantitative data and the qualitative data gathered in interviews are to be incorporated into the discussion.

The most desired skill among the learners in post-colonial South Asia

The data shows that the most desired language skill among the learners in India, Pakistan, Bangladesh and Sri Lanka is speaking with Pakistan at 65.1%, Bangladesh at 71.4%, India at 67.4% and Sri Lanka at 62.9% of students opting for it. At the same time, in Pakistan 10.7%, Bangladesh 4.7%, India 6.6% and Sri Lanka 11.1% learners opt for writing, reading or listening along with speaking as their most preferred skills to develop.

This is strikingly similar to the findings we have from data collected over ten years from 2007 to 2018 among the Sri Lankan undergraduate community in that the skill they want to develop the most in English is speaking.

The reason/reasons for desiring a particular skill the most

Learners gave different reasons for their preference to learn the particular skill they chose. However, most reasons indicated an instrumental slant for their preference while a few reasons could be categorized as integrated. At the same time, there was a significant percentage who preferred to learn the skill they chose in English because English is an international language.

On wanting to speak English

More than 90% of the respondents from each country answered in the positive when asked whether they would like to speak English. Among them, the highest percentage was from Sri Lanka with 99.2%; in Bangladesh it was 94.7%, in India 93.8% and in Pakistan 92.9%.

Learner self-rating on their ability to speak well in English

In Pakistan, 45.6% believed that they could speak English well, while in India it was 33.9%. In Bangladesh 30.1% believed that they could speak English well and in Sri Lanka only 4.4% rated themselves as being able to speak English well.

In Sri Lanka, 92.5% rated themselves as not being able to speak English well. In India it was 64.2% with Bangladesh at 63.4% and Pakistan at 45.4%. The highest percentage that claimed they had moderate ability in speaking English came from Pakistan at 9%, with Bangladesh at 6.5%, Sri Lanka at 3.1% and India at 1.9%.

The reason/s for students' reluctance to speak English in spite of speaking being the most desired skill

The data showed that due to fear of being ridiculed by the society, shyness or both, in Pakistan 72.1%, Bangladesh 71.2%, India 67.6% and Sri Lanka 81.5% of learners refrain from using English. Even though the 'confidence' factor was neither overtly stated in the questionnaire nor was it mentioned during the interviews, some learners themselves stated that lack of confidence was a reason for not speaking English: 3% in Pakistan, 2.6% in Bangladesh, 1.6% in India and 1% in Sri Lanka.

In addition, it is worth mentioning that some learners stated that they were reluctant to speak because they felt that their English was 'not good'. In Pakistan 6.4%, in Bangladesh 5.4%, in India 4% and in Sri Lanka 4.3% of learners voluntarily gave this as a reason.

The total percentage that stated they are 'shy or afraid, shy & afraid, no confidence, or feel English knowledge is not good enough', all of which contribute to a lack of confidence, was 81.5% in Pakistan, 79.2% in Bangladesh, 73.2% in India and 86.8% in Sri Lanka. A decade's worth of our studies on the same issue in Sri Lanka gives near identical percentages in relation to this fear/shyness/uncertainty as a factor in their avoiding speaking English.

The absence of the fear/shyness/uncertainty factor among the learners in post-colonial South Asia

The percentages of those who opted for the response that they are 'Neither shy nor fear to speak English' are as follows: Pakistan 4.1%, Bangladesh 4.2%, Sri Lanka 11.3%, with India having the highest at 20.7%.

When we examined the data in terms of cities, in India, Goa has the highest percentage of respondents who do not identify with the fear/shyness/uncertainty problem with 52.4% stating that they were neither shy nor afraid to speak English and this contributed to India having the highest percentage of students who do not report fear/shyness/uncertainty.

The context/place where post-colonial South Asian learners experience fear, shyness or both in speaking English

In Pakistan, 44.5% students stated that they felt fear, shyness or both *in* the English language classroom with 29.7% reporting the same in Bangladesh, 15.8% in India and 9.2% in Sri Lanka.

Among those who experienced fear, shyness or both in speaking English *outside* the English language classroom 23.1% were from Pakistan, 30.9% from Bangladesh, 12.9% from India and 20.8% from Sri Lanka.

In Pakistan 8.3%, in Bangladesh 20.5%, in India 45.6% and in Sri Lanka 54.4% stated that they felt fear, shyness or both in speaking English *everywhere.*

Those who stated that they had *no fear or shyness* in speaking English *anywhere* were as follows: in Pakistan 24.1%, in Bangladesh 18.9%, in India 25.8% and in Sri Lanka 15.6%.

In Goa, 57.1% stated that they were neither shy nor afraid of speaking English anywhere, which has contributed to the total figure of 25.8% in India.

The people in front of whom post-colonial South Asian learners experience fear, shyness or both when speaking in English

Table 3.3 shows the people in front of whom the learners felt fear, shyness or both when they spoke in English.

Upon looking at Indian data with the highest percentage of 22.7% stating that they were neither afraid nor shy to speak English in front of anyone, Goa is the city that had the highest percentage, with 52.9% of respondents stating the same.

Table 3.3 The people in front of whom the post-colonial South Asian learners experience fear, shyness or both when speaking in English

County	*Outsiders (%)*	*Friends (%)*	*Teachers (%)*	*Teachers & outsiders (%)*	*Teachers & friends (%)*	*Friends & outsiders (%)*	*All above (%)*	*No one (%)*
Pakistan	26.4	11.5	31.6	4.2	2.8	0.5	3.6	19.3
Bangladesh	32.2	5.5	23.8	7.5	2.4	1.7	10.7	16.3
India	18.0	5.9	17.0	2.3	0.6	0.1	33.4	22.7
Sri Lanka	23.3	2.5	6.8	6.5	0.9	0.6	44.7	14.6

The interview data

The interview questions were geared towards identifying the specific details of the contexts in which the learners felt an inhibition about speaking English. For instance, when learners stated they were reluctant to speak English in front of outsiders, who these outsiders were was probed into; whether they were foreigners, strangers or people who were outside the English language classroom. When it was outside the classroom, it was further examined so as to identify specific locations, whether it was within the university premises or outside in the larger society, including their hometowns/villages. Also, data highlights are given in terms of how learners view those who speak English *well* (as per their perception) and the detailed reasons for their reluctance to speak English as well as what they feel about their reluctance and how they perceive their future prospects in regard to their ability to speak English. The interview findings have been incorporated into the discussion.

Discussion

Speaking, the most sought-after skill

The majority of learners state that their most desired skill is speaking and almost everyone reports that they would like to speak English. This appears to show that in spite of working in an academic environment with writing in English as their primary need for academic purposes, mastery of English language, like other languages, is primarily judged by the ability to speak. However, the primacy learners give to speaking in English is not as simple as mastering spoken English for academic purposes. Their attitudes indicate that being able to speak English clearly shows a much bigger place for English in their lives and their reasons for prioritizing this skill.

Given below are example sentences/phrases the students used to express their attitudes towards *themselves if they were to become able to speak English:*

India – speaking English develops one's personality, positive attitudes and confidence and can impress and influence others; they will feel proud, independent; it is a big achievement; it leads to better careers; it will be a life-changing experience; it shows one has good manners; it 'helps me match with good English speakers' personalities'; modern (61)[3] 'English language makes me more intelligent, smart and curious'; I will be professional, talented, sophisticated; 'It sets us apart in society'; I will be empowered (54).

Pakistan – it is the main source of development (2); we can influence others by speaking in English (6); English is considered the language of the educated; it is important for success in life; it is a status symbol; society is impressed with speakers of English (21); speaking in English gives me/builds confidence/boldness (29); 'We need English to survive'.

Bangladesh – 'the ability to speak English will get us good positions'; it will give us a good personality; English will make us smart (23); 'If we good at speak in English we will get a good job undoubtedly'; 'It is the most influential language'; it is a 'weapon'; it is 'more important than the mother tongue'; 'English will give me better life'; 'it will give me confidence'; 'English is needed to increase my abilities'; 'Every educated person should know English' (43).

Sri Lanka – 'it is the best way to face challenges in life and society'; 'I will be without fear'; 'it is prestigious', 'marketable, employable', 'high class', 'important', 'good jobs', 'high society', 'get good job' (72).

The above manifests the supremacy that English language enjoys in the post-colonial societies. Those who are able to speak English, needless to say, enjoy such status by merely by virtue of being able to speak it. At the same time, those who are unable to and/or are reluctant to speak English, seem to believe that being able to speak English will give them all the status and benefits that they report perceiving in society. However, learners in these post-colonial societies are also aware of an 'other' who acts as a 'watchdog', whether present or imaginary, and judges them on the basis of their abilities in English and the quality of the English they speak. Even when the 'watchdog' is not present, the effect on the learners is not imaginary. People in South Asia who are able to speak English are well aware of the existence of a language hierarchy and are often perceived to be asserting their supremacy over those who lack the skill, resulting in English speakers in the society acting as the 'watchdog' of the former colonial master's language. The presence of this 'watchdog' serves to establish and reinforce the fear/shyness/uncertainty factor among the learners who do not speak English.

In spite of being aware of the privileges the ability to speak English can give them, the learners are often overwhelmed by the experience of fear/shyness/uncertainty and refuse to speak English however much they want to be able to. Moreover, those who are proficient in English tend to dismiss these concerns out of hand and end up reinforcing this dynamic. The findings that speaking is the most sought-after skill and that fear/shyness/uncertainty inhibit learners' ability to speak emerge throughout this study. This same dynamic is found throughout the entire post-colonial South Asian region. We must focus on what is preventing these learners who are well aware of the privileges the mere ability to speak English can bring them from speaking in English.

The inside society and the outside society

While some learners are afraid, shy or uncertain about speaking English *inside* the English language classroom, others experience the same emotions *outside* the English language classroom and some experience the same emotions *everywhere* when they try to (or want to) speak English. Also, some experience these negative emotions in front of their teachers while some feel them in front of friends and still others feel it in front of outsiders and/or in front of everyone.

This reveals that there is more to this than the presence of Foreign Language (Classroom) Anxiety (FLCA) as defined by Horwitz et al. (1986) that arises due to the uniqueness of the language learning process. While there could be traces of the impact of said 'uniqueness' in the language learning process on learner performance outside the language teaching domain, there is no evidence that the fear/shyness/uncertainty when speaking English outside the language teaching domain is due solely to the uniqueness of the language learning process. Instead, the findings in this study clearly demonstrate that some learners do have FLCA, but they also experience another type of anxiety that does not involve teachers, peers and the foreign/second language classroom but comes from the larger society outside the classroom.

We will give some examples of sentences/phrases used by the students to express *the influence of society* on speaking English below:

India – 'Our surrounding discourages us to speak English'; 'a lot of criticisms when we speak English'; 'made fun of me'; 'consider as showing off'; 'not conducive' (17).

Pakistan – 'People mock at my accent'. 'They make fun if we speak English'; 'Judge'; 'Society thinks we show off' (40).

Bangladesh – 'Our society discourages us to speak English' (67); 'People consider us mad or abnormal if we speak English'; 'My friends make fun of me when I speak English'; 'Some people look at me that I am abnormal'; 'Peers in village are uneducated'; 'Most people are uncomfortable with English'.

Sri Lanka – society discourages, various social status, intellectual levels/capacities and attitudes matter, 'people laugh', 'some friends encourage, some don't' (53).

The interview data and the voluntary expressions of the learners show that they are afraid or shy because they worry about being ridiculed by outsiders. This contributes to their lack of confidence. One may assume that the outsiders are those who speak English better, and while this is true due to the presence of the 'watchdog' in society who speaks 'better English', there is also another 'watchdog' who speaks no English at all. This is especially prevalent among learners from rural and semi-rural areas who studied in the major universities. Almost all of them lamented the lack of opportunities to speak English when they were away from the university, not only because 'no one spoke English' in their villages but also because the villagers would mock them if they spoke English by saying that they were 'showing off' or trying to be a 'gora'[4] or 'sudda'.[5] In certain cities, for example, in Chittagong, Bangladesh, students said that although their university was the main higher education institute in the region, they would refrain from speaking English outside the university walls as it would look 'odd' to speak English. Some even expressed the view that 'If we did speak English outside, people would think we are mad'. Thus, the learners are conscious of yet another group who may mock them for speaking English, a group composed of people who are completely outside the English language learning–teaching domain. In other words, they neither speak English nor belong to the English language teaching–learning environment. Those who speak English in the outside society are seen by those who do not as showing off, once again indicating that English language is considered to be higher than the native languages, even by those who do not speak English at all.

The words/phrases that students used most often to express their lack of confidence to speak English clearly bring out the power play that operates in post-colonial South Asia in regard to the English language:

India – 'nervous'; 'lack confidence'; 'hesitant'; 'shy'; 'uncomfortable to speak'; 'fear of corrected'; 'I like to speak without showing my face'; 'I speak to myself'; 'feel inferior'; 'insecure'; 'confused'; 'stutter'; 'feel humiliated' (67).

Pakistan – 'I am conscious about my pronunciation/accent'; 'No confidence to speak'; 'hesitation'; 'nervous'; 'stutter when speaking'; 'Why am I scared?'; 'What to do?' (64).

Bangladesh – 'When I try to speak in English I become afraid'; 'shy'; 'nervous'; 'hesitant'; 'glossophobia'; 'I stammer' (128); 'When I want to speak in English, my heartbeat increases tremendously'; 'I am frightened to speak English' (2).

Sri Lanka – 'Scared to speak English as I am unable to speak proper/standard/good/correct English' (90); 'afraid'; 'shy'; 'nervous'; 'hesitant'; 'fear'; 'I think my pronunciation is the problem'; 'Compared to others my English is poor'.

Given this, it was quite interesting to find that when interviews were conducted by the native speaker of English, it was clear that learners enjoyed speaking with him. In Pakistan, Bangladesh and India, with the exception of Goa, we had learners eagerly waiting to be interviewed by a native speaker of English. When asked whether they were scared or shy to speak English with a 'white man', they responded in the negative, often adding, 'He won't laugh at our mistakes'. In addition, even the interviewer's American accent did not seem to worry them much as the learners claimed they were used to watching 'Hollywood' movies.

On the other hand, quite surprisingly, Sri Lankan learners were very reluctant to speak with the native speaker of English. They were very shy and afraid to the extent that some actually got up and ran away when the native speaker started to ask questions. Those who were interviewed answered with a lot of hesitation.

Another aspect that came up in the interviews was the accent issue. In Bangladesh and Pakistan (except for the learners from Sindh), learners were conscious of the influence of their mother tongue in their spoken English. There was an overwhelming desire from the learners from Bangladesh and Pakistan to learn to 'speak "American" or "British" English'. Some learners were dismayed by their inability to speak in either of these Englishes as their mother tongue influence was very apparent in their 'Bangla English' or other indigenous Englishes and this made them less confident. In Malakand, Pakistan, learners were especially keen 'to learn' to speak with the American accent. In India (other than in Goa), there was not much desire on the part of learners to speak American or British English. However, in Goa itself, where English proficiency was high, some learners revealed during the interviews that even though they spoke English well, their main concern was with their accent. Those who came from rural backgrounds were conscious that their rural accent would betray their origins to those who spoke English with a more urbane touch, and the latter tended to look down upon those who spoke English with a Konkani (mother tongue of Goans) accent or with an accent from other regional languages. However, they did not specify which accent they would prefer to speak with, either British or

American, but were highly conscious of 'giving themselves away' with their regional language-inflected accents.

Even though there are many discussions related to global Englishes and the varieties of English found throughout the world, still the norms prevalent in these South Asian post-colonial societies are such that learners consider being able to speak either British or American English as better or indicative of higher status. This shows the unrealistic expectations (possible selves) that many learners have about English language speaking. Such expectations, we argue, may leave learners constantly frustrated over their inability to speak like a white man, giving them yet another reason to feel less confident about speaking. At the same time, even when learners are able to speak English, they are conscious of their accent and aspire to speak a 'higher variety' of English as perceived within the region.

It is noteworthy to discuss the post-colonial South Asian learners' attitude in respect to other foreign languages. In New Delhi, India, learners who studied French under the foreign languages programme said that they were conscious of the mistakes they made when speaking in English but this consciousness was not there when they spoke French, as they knew 'nobody would laugh at the mistakes they made in French' whether they were locals or native speakers of French. The response from undergraduates in Sri Lanka to the same enquiry was that they quite enjoyed practising French outside of the classroom with native speakers of French as they were sure that native speakers would not ridicule them for mistakes. Yet it is apparent that they rarely find someone to speak with in French outside the classroom in Sri Lanka. Therefore, we wanted to know whether the lack of inhibition was because there was no 'watchdog'. They reported that: 'In front of our French teachers (local) and those who know French (locals), we are afraid and conscious of our mistakes. However, when we go to functions/meetings at the Alliance Françoise, we love to talk in French and we never feel shy or scared to speak in front of native speakers of French.'

As the interviews revealed, learners from India, Pakistan and Bangladesh seemed to enjoy talking with a native speaker of English, and worries about accents were almost negligible. Bangladeshi undergraduates and undergraduates in Sindh, Pakistan, in particular, were very eager to talk with the native speaker and were following him wherever he went 'bombarding' him with questions. When asked whether they were not scared or shy to speak with the native speaker, the immediate response was 'No, because he won't laugh at our mistakes.' However, a notable difference was found among the Sri Lankan undergraduates; when the native speaker of English interviewed them, most of them shrank while a few of them ran away, without giving the chance to interview them.

This points to an interesting, mixed outcome: in both India and Sri Lanka, French is taught as a foreign language. It seems that in India, any attitude issues in relation to French are not detrimental to learners speaking it with everyone who speaks it well. In Sri Lanka however, the attitudes of local, fluent speakers of French seem to affect learners just like those of the fluent local English speakers. Is it because the attitudes of the Sri Lankan society towards the English language with its power and prestige are extended to the French language as another European language? Or is it because the local people who are exposed to western languages and cultures are operating with the same mindset and the learners are aware of that? In either case, one would expect Indian French language learners to have similar attitudes but they do not. The Sri Lankan situation may be attributed to the small size of the population and the even smaller French-speaking community, which is also associated with the English-speaking community. The Indian French-speaking community is also relatively small, but perhaps because they are not as closely associated with the educated English-speaking circles in such a heavily populated country, this problem does not arise in India. This seems possible, but we do not have enough evidence to strongly support this generalization.

The Goan experience

The much lower level of fear/shyness/uncertainty in regard to speaking English among the Goan learners contributes to the higher percentages from India in terms of (a) learners who report that they are neither shy nor afraid to speak English (b) anywhere (c) and/or in front of anyone, the three main aspects that were tested in relation to the English language related anxieties. The history of Goa and its influence on the Goans reveals something very significant to the study. Goa was a colony under the Portuguese, rather than the British, from 1510. Portugal brought not only Christianity, but European culture to its colony. In 1961, the Portuguese left, giving Goa its freedom; in 1987 Goa officially became a state of India. This means that unlike any other state/city in the four countries, Goa was more directly and strongly influenced by western culture for longer than any other place in the study, with western influence persisting until the present day. Our experience visiting two colleges in the University of Goa was quite different culturally from that in the rest of the universities. The society itself, both inside the university and in the city, was extremely westernized in nature, manifested in their attire, food, people's behaviour and their frequent use of the English language.

Even before we began to talk to students and collect data, the preliminary discussion we had with one of the deans revealed that Goan students did not have any confidence issue in regard to speaking English because their English proficiency was high and English was regularly used in the society outside of the university, including student homes. This proved to be correct as students during the interviews responded without any hesitation and the questionnaire results showed the highest percentages of students who reported no feelings of fear/shyness/uncertainty. In addition, to our immense dismay, the most arrogant respondents we met in our study were from the two colleges of the University of Goa! They showed little interest to talking to us and did not pay any heed to the instructions we, the 'foreigners', were giving, in order to complete the questionnaire. The white man (the interviewer) had to bang on the table to get their attention! One may attribute such behaviour to a weakness in the general administration in terms of discipline, but our understanding is that the Goans are most exposed to the western culture both in terms of number of years and the constant contact with foreigners, especially tourists, who speak English to communicate. Accordingly, there was nothing 'exciting' about the white man and the other Asian woman who came into their university to collect data. We can contrast this with an incident we experienced at the railway station in Dhaka, Bangladesh, during our first visit to the country in 2014: we were surrounded by a mass of people craning for a look at the white man who was waiting for the train alongside a brown woman in a different attire (Kandyan saree). The driver who took us to the station and was waiting with us until we set off acted with 'dignity' as he played the role of our guardian. The enthusiasm we saw in the learners in the universities in Bangladesh we see as an extension of this societal behaviour.

The above narratives may not appear 'academic enough' for some readers. However, we read them as a cross-section of the attitudes found in post-colonial South Asian societies towards the English language and those who speak it. The comparisons and contrasts that are discussed reveal two important facts: (a) the undeniable influence for learners of the outside, general society in learning and using a foreign/second language, and (b) the impact of the established power of English as a second/foreign language in South Asian society on both English language learners and fluent, local speakers. While the latter gain confidence by knowing and using English in the spoken form, the former lack confidence to speak, which causes difficulties in the language learning process.

Conclusion

The chapter discusses the study that has been carried out in four post-colonial South Asian countries, namely Pakistan, Bangladesh, India and Sri Lanka, with 4,630 respondents covering various regions. This data was collected over a span of one year from October 2017 to October 2018. The preliminary studies were conducted in Sri Lanka over ten years from 2007 until 2017. Responses to those studies from the international academic community, both in the west and Asia, encouraged us to extend that research to Sri Lanka's neighbours after considering the similarities and contrasting nature of the responses we received from other South Asian academics. Our findings demonstrate the unmistakable influence of the attitudes found in the larger society outside the English language domain, in addition to the influence of the attitudes found in the 'inner society' that is the English language classroom. These attitudes have an impact on learner performance in English as a foreign/second language, particularly on the speaking skill, which is the primary mode of communication.

Notes

1 In Bangladesh, India and Pakistan, higher education is fee-levying even though the fee structure may differ from university to university. Also, private sector universities may have a higher fee structure than those in the public sector. However, in Sri Lanka, higher education in the public sector universities is completely free while private sector (though not very widespread) is fee-levying.

2 From each region of India, data was collected from at least four universities.
3 The numerical value given within brackets is the number of respondents who gave the comment/a similar opinion.
4 Gora is the colloquial term in Hindi, Bengali and Urdu for a white man.
5 Sudda is the colloquial term in Sinhala for a white man.

References

Gardner, R. C. (2004). Retrieved from: http://publish.uwo.ca/~gardner/docs/englishamtb.pdf

Horwitz, E. K., Horwitz, M. B., & Cope, J. (1986). Foreign language classroom anxiety. *Modern Language Journal*, 70, 125–132.

Spielberger, C. D. (1978). Anxiety: State-trait process. In C. D. Spielberger and I. G. Sarason (Eds.), *Stress and anxiety* (pp. 115–143). Washington, DC: Hemisphere.

4 Language attitude anxiety

Introduction

The chapter investigates in more detail how the social attitude towards a language and its speakers influences English language learners in post-colonial South Asia with a special focus on the learners' most sought-after language skill, speaking. The fear/shyness/uncertainty that surrounds speaking in English is a product of social attitudes that create a lack of confidence in English language learners when they try to speak English. This lack of confidence to speak English may in turn cause the learner to develop a set of negative attitudes towards their own speaking ability, which may then be projected onto the entire English language learning process, which results in further poor performance in learning English.

Language attitudes of the society –> lack of confidence to speak –> negative attitudes towards speaking –> negative attitudes toward learning.

This chapter also discusses the *type* of anxiety that is caused by the attitudes present in society towards the English language and its speakers, labelled Language Attitude Anxiety (LAA). Next, the role of LAA as a conduit between the societal attitudes towards the English language and its speakers and the lack of confidence in the learners to speak English is discussed. The limitations of Foreign Language (Classroom) Anxiety (FLCA) as an explanation for the difficulties of the English language learner in post-colonial South Asia are then discussed. Finally, LAA is examined in terms of its main components, negative evaluation and communication apprehension, to demonstrate how the language attitudes in the society that the learners come into contact with, both inside and outside the language classroom, affect the learners, particularly in regard to speaking English, and learning English in general. The section that follows establishes the centrality of building confidence to help students learn English against the backdrop of the unsuccessful teaching practices of English as a second language in Bangladesh, India, Pakistan and Sri Lanka.

Prologue

1 In Pakistan, Urdu has been introduced by the government as the official language. There has been much debate over this policy, however, due to

the fact that indigenous languages like Punjabi and Sindhi tend to suffer as a result. For instance, in Punjab, Punjabi is often used only at home and not publicly. In other households, Punjabi is used to speak to domestic helpers only.

2 In Sri Lanka, during the civil war, one of our friends from Jaffna visited us in Colombo. While we were taking a stroll along the path in the university that borders the main road, he received a call, which he cut short, saying that he wanted to avoid speaking in his mother tongue, Tamil. (We were speaking in English.)

3 We remember two incidents in particular in the past. In Sri Lanka, Tony Greig was a popular cricket commentator during the nineties. When he started his commentaries, he would say in his Australian accent, 'Todai is a nice dai. Look at the sun! Look at the crowd at the gaite going craizi!' People simply loved him. However, in early 2000s,[1] when an Indian scholar said, 'Could you please close the doo/r/?' during a conference, no one looked at the door. Instead, they giggled.

Language attitudes

An attitude is defined as a feeling or opinion about something or someone, or a way of behaving that is caused by this. Language attitudes 'are distinguished from other attitudes by the fact that they are precisely about language' (Fasold, 1987, p. 147). Fasold further explains language attitudes:

> Some language-attitude studies are strictly limited to attitudes towards language itself … Most often, however, the definition of language attitude is broadened to include attitudes towards speakers of a particular language or dialect. An even further broadening of the definition allows all sorts of behavior concerning language to be treated, including attitudes toward language maintenance and planning efforts.
>
> (p. 147)

This broad definition of language attitudes helps one to understand the complexities attached to the English language, its speakers, how it is treated in South Asian societies and how it should be treated, etc. In Sri Lanka, India, Bangladesh and Pakistan, all former British colonies, a definite importance, bordering on reverence, is attached to English. In these countries, people who speak English are usually looked up to and those who speak it 'better' are respected more than those who do not speak well. Also, the effort exerted to maintain and upgrade English proficiency in all spheres of activity is painfully high and, in most cases, this occurs at the expense of indigenous languages. For instance in Pakistan, the current trend is to turn Urdu medium schools into English medium schools in order to attract students. As Awan and Zia (2015) state, 'Now the Punjab Government's initiative of transforming Urdu medium public sector schools into English medium may result into [sic] increase in enrolment in public sector schools' (p. 123). In Sri Lanka, the policy that, in 1956, removed English from its position as the official language has created effects that continue to the present day, such as widening the gap between rural and urban populations and creating new sets of language attitudes among Sri Lankan people. (The policy changes in the four countries with regard to the English language have been discussed in detail in the background chapter.) These types of policy changes produce effects that are embodied in Crystal's (1997) definition of language attitudes, 'The feelings people have about their own language or the languages of others' (p. 215) which are manifested in their behaviour, collectively or individually, nationally or internationally.

Language attitudes and the lack of confidence to speak English

In spite of the perceived need for spoken English and the learners' desire to speak English, our findings show that most of the learners do not speak English in their day-to-day communication, whether in academic settings or in other contexts. A recurrent set of reasons that are linked to the attitudes present in society are the central cause for this phenomenon across the post-colonial South Asian region. Even though the particular attitudes may differ in some respects, these attitudes inevitably result in lack of self-confidence to speak English among the learners in all four countries studied here.

The Merriam-Webster Dictionary defines confidence as 'a feeling or consciousness of one's powers or of reliance on one's circumstances'. A lack of confidence is a feeling or consciousness of one's lack of powers or lack of reliance on one's circumstances. By extension, the lack of confidence to speak English can be defined as a feeling or consciousness of one's lack of power or a lack of reliance on one's circumstances in regard to one's ability to speak it.

Learners are influenced by the attitudes present in their society towards any particular language and its speakers. The social attitudes related to the English language and its speakers come from two main societies: (a) the 'inner society' of the English language classroom and (b) the 'outer society' that exists outside the English language classroom. We contend that the lack of confidence that learners experience in regard to speaking English is the result of an anxiety that stems from the influence of attitudes in both the inner and outer societies. We also argue that the confidence (or lack of it) to speak a language depends on the power that language enjoys in a particular society. In addition, we view some language attitudes as temporary. Therefore, the lack of confidence to speak any particular language can also be transitory depending on the socio-politico-economic context in which the language is situated and spoken. However, in post-colonial South Asia, language attitudes in society towards the English language have not changed substantially over decades, but have been twisted and turned, only to re-establish their power.

This is apparent when analysing the learner responses about their lack of confidence to speak English; some inhibitions come from exterior origins while some others have interior origins. For instance, being shy or afraid that others may laugh at their mistakes is exterior, while 'do not know to speak in English, can't speak [sic] much fluency, do not have vocabulary', etc., are interior. It is clear that attitudes in both the inner and outer societies and learner uncertainties arising from both exterior and interior origins, all manifest themselves in a lack of confidence to speak English among South Asian English language learners.

Our study shows that learners in post-colonial South Asia are very conscious of the presence of language attitudes in society and that these attitudes affect their own relationship with the English language. Those who are unable to speak English at all or speak it 'not-so-fluently' are very conscious of their mistakes and how others look at them, while others who can speak English well are self-conscious about their accents as being different from British or American accents and are anxious about their English being judged as lower than 'posh' varieties of English. In either case, the learners end up suffering from a lack of confidence to speak English. The 'watchdogs' who create and police these societal attitudes towards English that are internalized by the learners fall into two categories, those who speak English fluently and those who do not speak English at all. At the same time, these 'watchdogs' need not be visible or present to create a lack of confidence in the English language learner. For instance, in post-colonial South Asian societies, one can easily find a pair of English language learners, outside the classroom/university environment, who will refrain from using English to speak (even to practise speaking with each other) out of a fear of being laughed at or mocked, even when no visible 'watchdog' is present. These 'imaginary others' are as influential as the 'present others' and this dynamic illustrates the power of the English language in our societies.

English language learners are part of their society, and they share our awareness of the position of the English language and of its speakers in our post-colonial societies and our common experiences. This analysis attempts to look at the processes involved in the creation and propagation of language attitudes and their effects on language teaching–learning scenario. Specifically, we will address (a) the attitudes of society towards a particular language and its speakers, (b) the attitudes present in society towards the English language learner, (c) learner attitudes towards the English language and fluent speakers of English, (d) learner attitudes towards his or her own English language speaking ability and (e) learner attitudes towards his or her own English language learning.

These five language attitudes are both cyclical and linear in terms of what they produce. At any given point in the cycle, one leads to the other and propagates the other attitude and the cycle as a whole. In a linear process, one would create the other in progression and come to a standstill.

In a totally failed or highly successful teaching–learning situations the process can be considered linear, because it produces English language learners who have either given up on their language learning completely after the going through the process in vain or learners who have succeeded in mastering the language. In a cyclical aspect, on the other hand, we find a mixture of progression that leads into the other.

This discussion is primarily concerned with the spoken form of English as the primary use of language is for communication. Also, it is the most sought-after skill of the learners. Most importantly, it is the skill that they lack confidence to use. The following diagram is an attempt to hint at what goes through the mind of the learner in the foreign/second language learning domain in terms of language attitudes (Figure 4.1).

In both, the *existing* language attitudes in society towards a language and its speakers are at the core. Depending on these attitudes, a language is *viewed* as prestigious, useful, etc., or lowly, useless, etc., and those who speak it are inevitably identified accordingly. It is at this stage that accuracy, accent, fluency, pronunciation, etc., and features that are relevant to the spoken form of the language are weighed. A language learner's use of (or attempts to use) that language is viewed in this context. The response of society to the learner's use of (or attempts to use) the language, *shapes* and *determines* the learner's attitudes (which are already partially formed by being a member of the broader society) towards the language and its speakers. This process *forms* and *shapes* learner attitudes towards speaking a language and the learning of that particular language in general.

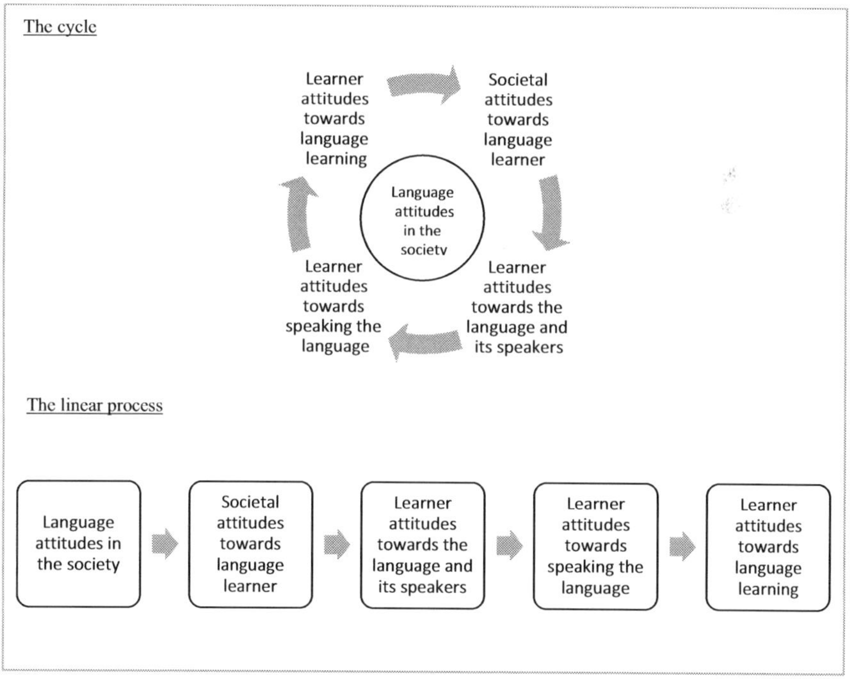

Figure 4.1 The development of language attitudes in cyclical and linear processes.

What we see in the findings of our study are the negative attitudes English language learners have towards their own English language speaking ability. These negative attitudes cripple the learner and are manifested in a lack of confidence to speak English, which is paradoxically their most-sought after skill. Their own negative attitudes towards English stem from the language attitudes present in society towards the English language and its speakers, which create a judgemental set of attitudes directed at the learners based on their speaking ability. The learners are aware of these ever-present judgements and, as a result, learners reaffirm their own negative attitudes towards the English language and its fluent speakers. These attitudes are then projected onto their own lack of speaking ability and feed into equally negative attitudes towards the entire English language learning process. From this web of interconnected negative attitudes, what manifests is a lack of confidence to speak English as learners experience anxiety in attempting to speak English. A few examples from across post-colonial South Asia are quoted below:

> I speak to myself; feel inferior; insecure; confused; stutter; feel humiliated (India). ... nervous; stutter when speaking; Why am I scared? What to do? (Pakistan) ... shy; nervous; hesitant; glossophobia; I stammer; When I want to speak in English, my heartbeat increases tremendously (Bangladesh). ... afraid; shy; nervous; hesitant; fear; I think my pronunciation is the problem; Compared to others my English is poor (Sri Lanka).

It is of paramount importance that English language curriculum designers and teachers in post-colonial South Asia come to understand this reality. Language learners come to the English language classroom not only with years of English language learning behind them, they also come with baggage from their societies. Their previous learning experiences have given them a vague understanding of grammar, vocabulary, skimming and scanning skills, etc., and a very *clear and definite* understanding of the language attitudes present in their societies. Very young learners may not be aware of societal attitudes as such, but depending on their age and experience, they will bring definite 'opinions' about the English language and those who speak it with them.

It is equally important to understand that the learners not only bring with them the language attitudes of society towards the English language and its speakers; they also bring language attitudes of their own that are directed towards their own English language learning. These attitudes are not isolated concepts operating in a vacuum, instead they are relative to their own experience in English language (speaking and) learning.

The story does not end here. In their new English language classroom, the attitudes they bring in from the societies they have encountered will be tested again and again, both outside and inside the English language classroom/s, until they are either stabilized or changed.

In our view, in the post-colonial South Asian context, where English language teaching is a failure and has not produced the desired outcomes over the past 70 years, this failure is mainly due to the fact that we have failed to identify the importance of language attitudes in English language teaching–learning. In this context, it can very well be argued that the attitudes the English language learners bring into the classroom are predominantly negative and are continually re-stabilized as negative, which results in poor performance.

The failure to recognize the importance of language attitudes vis-à-vis the English language has resulted in complete disregard of the role of these attitudes in the English language teaching–learning process. This is apparent in every aspect pertaining to English language curriculum at every level in South Asia: (a) there are no goals to achieve in terms of language attitudes, (b) there is no material to eliminate negative learner attitudes and foster positive attitudes towards English language learning, (c) there are no goals to build confidence to speak English so that learner attitudes can be made positive first towards speaking and then onto English language learning as a whole, (d) there are no teaching methodologies to eliminate negative learner attitudes and foster positive attitudes towards English language learning and (e) there are no assessments where the positive development of learner attitudes towards the English language is measured.

If the learners come into the university with positive attitudes towards their English language learning experience, they usually attain high proficiency in English in their production skill/s, (especially writing since speaking is not tested in formal examinations in South Asia at the primary and secondary levels. It is tested rarely at tertiary levels). Those who come to the university with negative attitudes towards their English language learning experience tend to remain at a low level of proficiency as their attitudes are usually reaffirmed in the university English language classroom, unless some major change to their attitudes towards English language learning occurs.

Even though what happens in attitudinal change is a complex subject, we will attempt to discuss it here. Appel and Muysken (1987) discuss two theoretical approaches that guide the studies of language attitudes.

> The first one is the *behaviourist* view, according to which attitudes must be studied by observing the responses to certain languages, i.e. their use in actual interactions. The *mentalist* view considers attitudes as an internal, mental state, which may give rise to certain forms of behaviour.
>
> (p. 16)

Fasold (1987) explains this further as 'an intervening variable between a stimulus affecting a person and that person's response' (p. 147). In such a context, what we witnessed in the respondents in this study, through their behaviour and interview responses, may help us to analyse them in both ways. However, our main interest does not lie there; we find (and some respondents are outspoken about it as well) a lack of confidence in the learners to be a result of societal language attitudes that affect them in their speech performance and this extends to the formation of negative attitudes towards English language learning in general. Within such complex attitudinal dynamics, however, a somewhat visible process in regard to the English language learner can be drawn as follows.

Language attitudes of the society –> Lack of confidence to speak –> Negative attitudes towards speaking –> Negative attitudes toward learning the language.

Language attitudes that exist in both in the small society of the language classroom and the larger society outside give rise to a lack of confidence in the learner to speak the language. As a result, the learner develops a set of negative attitudes towards speaking which may be extended to English language learning as a whole.

In this context, we argue that language attitudes that exist in society create a specific kind of anxiety resulting in the learner's lack of confidence to speak English. It is at this strategic point that we need to break this succession of negative attitudes in order to direct them towards positive attitudes by using the space for action found in the cyclic process of language attitudes development we have presented.

Learner problems that are related to learner affective domain in foreign language learning have been analysed by using FLCA, a concept developed by Horwitz, Horwitz, and Cope (1986). The scale they developed, the Foreign Language (Classroom) Anxiety Scale (FLCAS) to measure Foreign Language Anxiety (FLA) has been used extensively in many contexts, in various locales and for many different foreign languages. We would like to expand this discussion by incorporating FLA and considering (a) the relevance of two of its parallels, namely, negative evaluation and communication apprehension, to our study, (b) its wide use and (c) its relevance to classroom language teaching–learning, towards which our discussion is geared. As such, it is important to locate the FLCA in the English language teaching–learning process in varying contexts, so that what is not FLCA and effects not stemming from FLCA can be clearly established.

Foreign Language (Classroom) Anxiety and its limitations

General anxiety is defined as 'the subjective feeling of tension, nervousness, apprehension and worry associated with an arousal of the autonomic nervous system' (Spielberger 1983, as cited in Horwitz et al., 1986, p. 125). FLCA, on the other hand, is defined as 'a distinct complex of self-perceptions, beliefs, feelings, and behaviours related to classroom language learning arising from the uniqueness of the language learning process' (Horwitz et al., 1986, p. 125). Therefore, FLA is a specific subcategory of anxiety. According to Horwitz et al., FLA concerns performance evaluation within an academic and social context, and therefore, it is useful to draw attention to three related performance anxieties: (1) communication apprehension, (2) test anxiety and (3) fear of negative evaluation (p. 125).

There are many reasons behind English language learners' poor performance in English. Most of them fall under lack of motivation, lack of exposure, their environment being not conducive to learning English, a lack of facilities including a lack of qualified teachers, etc. The studies related to the reluctance to speak English have mostly been attributed, as research shows, to the presence of FLA in classroom settings.

Spielberger, in the Manual for the State-Trait Anxiety Inventory (1983), defines anxiety as the subjective feeling of tension, apprehension, nervousness and worry associated with an arousal of the autonomic nervous system. According to Horwitz et al. (1986),

> When anxiety is limited to the language learning situation, it falls into the category of specific anxiety reactions. Psychologists use the term specific anxiety reaction to differentiate people who are generally anxious in a variety of situations from those who are anxious only in specific situations. Researchers have identified several specific anxieties associated with school tasks such as test-taking and with academic subjects such as mathematics or science.
>
> (p. 125)

As described in their analysis, all three anxieties are discussed in relation to the foreign language learning process. Due to communication apprehension, a foreign language learner, who otherwise can be talkative, may become silent in the foreign language classroom. Test anxiety, as the term suggests, occurs within the classroom/examination hall. The fear of negative evaluation is described in the analysis by Horwitz et al. (1986) as something that occurs when the foreign language teacher and peers negatively evaluate learners and is discussed as mainly being confined to the classroom. Even when negative evaluation is discussed as being influential outside the language classroom setting, it does not encompass attitudes in the larger outside society in general.

> Although similar to test anxiety, fear of negative evaluation is broader in scope because it is not limited to test-taking situations; rather, it may occur in any social, evaluative situation such as interviewing for a job or speaking in foreign language class. Unique among academic subject matters, foreign languages require continual evaluation by the only fluent speaker in the class, the teacher. Students may also be acutely sensitive to the evaluations – real or imagined – of their peers.
>
> (p. 128)

Even though the researchers accept fear of negative evaluation as 'broader in scope' and something that may occur in any social, evaluative situation, they limit such situations to contexts like 'interviewing for a job or speaking in foreign language class' (ibid.). Based on the aforesaid discussion, one can ask a few questions at this point: (a) Is the negative evaluation limited to the ***uniqueness of the language learning process*** only? (b) Is negative evaluation present only in settings where the situation is formally arranged? (c) Can the fear of negative evaluation that happens outside the foreign language learning setting, in informal situations outside the classroom, also affect the language learner? (d) Can a negative evaluation occur as a result of the ***uniqueness of the language attitudes*** in society that exist outside the language classroom? (e) Can the influence of these societal attitudes come into the classroom and affect the learners in their foreign/second language learning process? Also, by the same token, can the negative evaluation that happens within the classroom also affect foreign language learners' performance outside the classroom?

The authors (1986) hint at the possibility raised in the second question:

> The effects of anxiety can extend beyond the classroom. Just as math anxiety serves as a critical job filter ... foreign language anxiety, too, may play a role in students' selections of courses, majors, and ultimately, careers. Foreign language anxiety may also be a factor in student objections to foreign language requirements.
>
> (p. 131)

However, such speculations are discussed as a result of experiencing FLA exclusively in relation to language learning situations in academic settings.

Young (1991) identifies six potential sources of language anxiety from three perspectives: those of the learner, the teacher and the instructional practice. He claims that language anxiety is caused by (a) personal and interpersonal anxiety, (b) learner beliefs about language learning, (c) instructor beliefs about language teaching, (d) instructor–learner interactions, (e) classroom procedures and (f) language testing. Young (1994) further elucidates that these sources of language anxiety are interrelated. Even though Young expands the discussion and includes many aspects related to language anxiety, one can see a complete disregard for the influence of social dynamics outside the classroom language learning setting on psychological factors that play a critical role in an individual's language learning.

According to the Linguistic Coding Deficit Hypothesis (LCDH) advanced by Sparks and Ganschow (1993), language anxiety is a reflection of a side effect caused by linguistic deficiency in processing language input. They emphasize the focus on language coding abilities, and discount anxiety and other affective variables as playing a critical role in language development. According to them, cognitive capacity is the major engine that drives second/foreign language acquisition and development.

Zheng (2008) views Sparks and Ganschow's view as closely connecting second language coding abilities with first language coding abilities, and observes that it 'in a way isolates language development from its social cultural roots' (p. 4). Zheng further observes that by exclusively emphasizing cognitive capabilities, Sparks and Ganschow's hypothesis fails to take into account the striking differences between first language development and second language development, especially the characteristics that are representative of the uniqueness of the second/foreign language learning environment (p. 4).

Even though Zheng points towards the socio-cultural roots and the significance of investigating the second/foreign language learning environment in her analysis, there is no discussion on how societal attitudes may influence second language learning, in spite of the discussion on FLA in cognitive, curriculum and cultural/policy perspectives.

In a review of Horwitz et al.'s theory of FLA, Tran (2012) challenges the theory, by bringing out arguments from other research in respect to four points: (a) the direction of the causal relationship between FLA and language learning difficulties, (b) the important role of FLA, (c) the components of FLA and (d) the validity of the FLCAS. The conclusions arrived at in these arguments are that FLA can be seen as both a consequence and a causal factor of foreign language learning; it could be that learners' cognitive abilities in respect to learning any language (including their mother tongue) also affect language learning and achievement and not FLA exclusively; the three components that Horwitz et al. have identified in relation to FLA, communication apprehension, test anxiety and negative evaluation, are not components of FLA but are related to FLA, as test anxiety could be general and is not necessarily specific to foreign language learning; and the validity of FLCAS, which tests language skills rather than the anxiety level of the foreign language learner. All such discussions focus on FLA as an entity exclusively stemming from the language learning process and creating a distinctive anxiety type.

We can see that the existing corpus of literature related to FLA discusses learners' inhibitions/reluctance to speak English (or to otherwise perform in English) as stemming from the language learning process itself and regards its effects as mostly restricted to classroom settings with very little discussion of the effects of social and cultural issues.

As South Asian undergraduates expressed themselves in this study, their shyness and a fear of ridicule contribute to their uncertainty and these are the major reasons for their *lack of confidence* to speak *English*. Other components mentioned are a dislike, or even hatred towards English. Learners do not report that these negative emotions are restricted to the language classroom or specific situations such as job interviews and public speaking. Instead, they speak about them *generally*, as relevant to all social situations in their societies. The important aspect to keep in mind in such a scenario is the need to understand the complex dynamics that surround the students in their English language learning: negative language attitudes create an anxiety that is not limited to FLA as identified by the researchers. Further, such language attitudes, which not only are present in the classroom situations, but also exist outside in the larger society, are also detrimental to speaking English inside and outside the classroom in the daily life of the learners.

Phillips (1992), in addition to her discussion on anxiety and performance, questions the impact of anxiety on *learning*. What is significant for our discussion here is her observation in regard to learner *attitudes* towards language *learning*:

> Thus, although language anxiety apparently explains a small part of a very complex picture with regard to performance, its most significant contribution to the framework may well lie in its influence on the *attitudes* of students toward language learning and on their *intentions* to continue the study of a foreign language.
>
> (p. 22)

As far as the literature related to language anxiety is concerned, the closest reference to the issues we discuss here, language attitudes and their impact on foreign language learning, is found in the above statement. It implies that the impact of anxiety on learner attitudes towards foreign language learning and some of its outcomes, i.e. learner intentions to continue to study the foreign language. It also recognizes that the fear of speaking a foreign language (and not only for formal evaluation purposes) can act as a cause for negative attitudes towards learning that language. However, the above analysis starts from a mid-way point in our analysis, in that it does not touch upon the root cause of that language anxiety in regard to language learning: the attitudes present in society that create anxiety in learners and a lack of confidence in regard to their ability to speak the foreign/second language. However, the discussion does hint at the influence of learners' attitudes as contributing to the development of negative attitudes towards language learning.

There have been some studies on the relationship between learning attitudes and anxiety. For instance, Liu and Chen (2013) discuss the influence of language anxiety on learner attitudes. Their findings show that:

> ... language anxiety appeared to have a much stronger link with learning attitude than with MI (Multiple Intelligence). A more in-depth statistical analysis revealed that the anxiety of students classified as having low- and mid-level positive attitudes (lowest 25% and middle 50%, respectively) did not differ significantly. Nevertheless, students with high-level positive attitudes (top 25%) had significantly lower language anxiety than their counterparts. (p. 932)

Research has shown that most foreign language learners suffer from FLA and that highly anxious learners perform poorly in foreign language classes and assessments. At the same time, some work has been done on the positive effects of anxiety in learning a language. Our effort is to explore the language attitudes in the society, not restricting our search to the language classroom situation only, but to the larger society as a whole, to examine their impact on English language teaching–learning. In such a scenario, FLCA poses some specific questions in regard to the situation found in post-colonial South Asia.

Issues arising from FLCA in the context of the post-colonial South Asian scenario

Negative evaluation by the teacher and peers in classroom settings

Horwitz et al. (1986) consider negative evaluation to be one of the main causes for language anxiety, but only in the context of negative evaluation from peers and teachers in the classroom setting. The negative evaluations from the larger society that the language learner brings into the classroom and the psychological barriers to learning they present have not been discussed hitherto. The effects of negative evaluation on the part of teachers and peers, as put forth in FLCA discussions, do not focus on learner performance outside the classroom and the factors of fear, shyness, etc., that create a lack of confidence in learners.

Spanish/French/other foreign languages vs. English (in post-colonial settings)

The scale was developed originally to measure classroom anxiety in Spanish language classroom settings in the United States and was then used in other foreign language teaching settings as well. However, when compared to English, Spanish, French and other foreign languages have not created comparable historic divisions among speakers and learners in South Asia and they do not play the role of representing the language of the former colonial master. Even though the scale used to examine FLCA is used in relation to English language as well, it does not capture the power dynamics that exist in the language learning context of post-colonial South Asia. Therefore, the FLCAS does not capture some of the views, emotions, beliefs, etc., that are attached to anxieties related to English language learning in South Asia. It is precisely these views that are not captured in the FLCAS that are crucial for helping to look beyond the general and umbrella terms attached to English language education to create context-specific interventions in English language teaching in post-colonial South Asian societies.

Lack of consideration of cultural and social aspects in FLCA

A personal interview with some Sri Lankan undergraduates at Sri Jayewardenepura University revealed that they did not feel any shyness or fear in speaking French with native speakers of French. However, they felt afraid and uncertain when they spoke in French with Sri Lankans who were fluent in French.[2] This aspect, although not related to English, shows that there are specific dynamics in Sri Lankan society that can create a lack of confidence among foreign language learners among their own people that is not present when speaking with foreigners. This shows the impact of specific social attitudes which go beyond mere FLA in the language learning process. It further shows that the fear and shyness to speak *English* due to the threat of being ridiculed by their own society is extended to speaking in French, but only in this local context, making this factor very society-specific. Such subtle social attitudinal nuances, which we consider as an extension of a mentality of the west-worshipping society initiated by the colonial era elites as fluent speakers of English (locally, fluent speakers of French are invariably also fluent speakers of English), are not addressed by FLCA.

FLCA as an essential component in learning a foreign language

Researchers and scholars of FLCA have discussed it as detrimental to communication, tests and evaluations, as indicated by the terms used, *communication apprehension*, *test anxiety* and *fear of negative evaluation*, respectively. However,

FLCA may also be a positive factor in motivating learners to learn and perform in a foreign language. Tran (2012) discusses this role of FLCA (p. 72). Some learners perform better and learn more effectively under pressure and this could be applied to the pressure created by FLCA. Here I recall my personal experience when I was in tenth grade and my extremely strict math teacher had everyone in the class on pins during the math period. This made everyone want to perform better and eventually everyone, with the exception of one girl, passed math with either credit or distinction! Also, the teacher held the record for bringing the highest number of distinctions in math to our school and I personally feel that it was our fear of being negatively evaluated by the teacher that forced us to go to the class regularly and perform well.

Relationship between FLCA and poor performance

Poor performance in foreign language learning is not necessarily due to FLCA, but can also stem from the poor teaching that is commonly found in South Asia in addition to the anxiety stemming from language attitudes present in society that leads to the identified lack of confidence to speak English and extends into English language learning, as is reflected in overall performance.

The structure of the FLCAS

The FLCAS is a Likert-type scale that includes responses ranging from 'strongly agree' to 'strongly disagree'. While such a structure may well capture FLA in terms of percentages, it strictly limits tapping a type of language anxiety stemming from societal attitudinal effects on anxiety. In order to examine and explore complex affective dynamics such as these, a tool that goes beyond mere mechanical measurement is required.

The social dimension of language anxiety

It is apparent that language anxiety is a social phenomenon given the primary function of language as a means of communication. Studies show that language anxiety stems primarily from the social and communicative aspects of language learning. Therefore, language anxiety can be considered as a social anxiety (MacIntyre & Gardner, 1989, 1991).

Theorists contend that anxieties that are socially based have cognitive, affective and behavioural components (Sarason, 1986; Spielberger, 1966). Schwarzer (1986) defines social anxiety as (a) feelings of tension and discomfort, (b) negative self-evaluations and (c) a tendency to withdraw from the presence of others. As a result of the arousal of anxiety in any social situation, these can become manifest along with other affective, cognitive and behavioural reactions (Clevenger, 1984; Fischer, 1988). For instance, the affective experience of anxiety includes feelings of apprehension, uneasiness and fear (Whitmore, 1987). Among the cognitive effects are an increase in distracting self-related cognitions and expectations of failure along with a decrease in cognitive processing ability (Wine,

1980). The behavioural dimension includes reactions such as increasing sympathetic nervous system arousal, inhibited actions and attempts to escape the situation (Levitt, 1980).

As cited by MacIntyre (1995), the interconnectedness among anxiety, cognition and behaviour is described as recursive or cyclical, wherein each influences the other (Leary, 1990; Levitt, 1980).

> For instance, in a situation where a demand to answer a question in a second language may cause a student to become anxious; anxiety leads to worry and rumination. Cognitive performance is diminished because of the divided attention and therefore performance suffers, leading to negative self-evaluations and more self-deprecating cognition which further impairs performance, and so on.
>
> (p. 91)

MacIntyre observes that this can be frequent and recurrent for some learners as anxiety comes to accompany any situation involving the second language. The danger is that 'once established, this association leads students to become anxious at the prospect of second language learning or communication' (MacIntyre, 1995, p. 91).

In criticizing the LCDH put forth by Sparks and Ganschow (1993), it is claimed that LCDH neglects the context in which language learning occurs (Clement, Gardner, & Smythe, 1980; Gardner & MacIntyre, 1992, 1993) and ignores the potential for social context to influence cognitive processes (Fiske & Taylor, 1991).

The social context that learners operate in is not limited to the language classroom, formally organized settings or any predictable situations. It encompasses all situations, formal and informal, predictable and unpredictable. The learners in this study report that they are not confident when speaking English in all kinds of situations. While this anxiety that creates a lack of confidence to speak English is affective in its strict disciplinary categorization, the context in which the affective entity originates and operates is essentially social, in that it includes both the classroom and the whole of society. Thus, it is imperative that we recognize the true complexity of language anxiety and the social context in which that language anxiety is created and operates, in order to analyse its effect on language teaching–learning.

Gardener's Attitude/Motivation Test Battery and its limitations

The Attitude/Motivation Test Battery (AMTB) was developed to assess the major affective components involved in the motivation of English-speaking students learning French as a second language in Canada (Gardner, 1985). Adaptations of the AMTB have paved the way for comprehensive analyses of the motivation to learn English and the attitudes of foreign language learners inside and outside classroom situations. However, in our view, a combined attitude and motivation battery does not allow for a sharp focus on language attitudes alone because much of the battery is dedicated to checking motivation as well.

As we perceive it, the motivation to learn a language, though specific, is a less complex psycho-social phenomenon than existing language attitudes, which are very complex and have various dimensions that are hard to measure. Also, the language attitudes of learners may be similar to the attitudes prevalent in their society towards a particular language and its speakers as the learners are integrated into their society. Furthermore, learner attitudes towards a particular language and its speakers may be coloured by their experience of learning the language and what their future prospects are in relation to that particular language.

In addition, the definition of language attitudes suggests an 'even further broadening' of it that 'allows all sorts of behavior concerning language to be treated, including attitudes toward language maintenance and planning efforts' (Fasold, 1987, p. 147). This, as we perceive it, has both national as well as individual dimensions. The national dimension has been discussed widely at the level of policy changes in post-colonial South Asian societies in the background chapter and elsewhere (Attanayake, 2017). The individual dimension forces us to examine the language attitudes that drive a learner either to make an effort to develop and maintain language proficiency for future use or to drop out completely. While the AMTB helps identify the language attitudes, it limits learner attitudes to attitude specificities at the individual level. In addition, due to the structure of the AMTB, which is also a Likert scale, it further limits to the ability to recognize the specific attitudinal recognition that is given to a particular language in relation to geographical and other variations. For instance, the call words that have been used for the English language by learners in the various locations we visited in our study reveal more than merely positive or negative attitudes towards the English language among the learners and their anxieties. Also, where negative language attitudes are concerned, the details show more of 'the why and the how', as well as the nervousness, lack of confidence, anger and even hatred towards the language that is creating anxiety in the learners, all of which the AMTB is unable to capture.

It must be noted that even though many studies find a positive correlation between motivation and performance in the English language, the learners who lacked confidence to speak English were some of the most highly motivated English language learners we have ever met. Especially, learners in Bangladesh and Sindh, Pakistan, who demonstrated a significantly higher motivation than others to learn and speak English and were nevertheless inhibited by their fear, shyness or a combination of both. This clearly merits thorough investigation.

To this point, the discussion of the social dimensions of language anxiety and the limited paradigms within which the FLCA is situated indicate that the attitudinal complexities that surround the English language learner in post-colonial South Asia cannot be analysed by using concepts that limit the scope of analysis in many respects. The AMTB, while helpful for us to identify the attitudes related to foreign/second language as negative or positive and the various intermediate shades between, does not allow us to delve deeper into the learner emotive domains to understand the shifts in language attitudes. Nevertheless, the strong presence of social attitudes in relation to foreign/second languages and their negative influence on language learners compel us to add another dimension to the discussion of FLA in relation to language attitudes.

Language Attitude Anxiety

In this study, we have identified another type of anxiety related to language learning, which is different from FLCA. We refer to this as LAA, and it stems from the societal attitudes towards a language and its speakers. Unlike FLCA, it is not caused by the uniqueness of the language learning process. Instead, LAA is caused by the existing specific societal attitudes towards a language and its speakers, which affect learners in their language performance, which in turn affects the entire language learning process; also, the attitudes that exist and are created in the language classroom also extend into the society outside the classroom and affect learners in their speaking of the target language. Thus, LAA can be defined as a complex of self-perceptions, beliefs, feelings and behaviours that affect language performance, which arise from the uniqueness of the language attitudes existing in both the larger society as well as in classroom situations.

LAA includes some aspects of FLCA (communication apprehension and negative evaluation, but not test anxiety) and expands them to encompass the anxiety created by societal attitudes towards a language and its speakers.

LAA is a specific kind of anxiety that inhibits a person from speaking in a language due to shyness and fear of being negatively evaluated in society or due to a dislike or hatred of the target language. It is common to second/foreign language learners in contexts where the second/foreign language has more power than the mother tongue of the learner. Further, it can be created (a) by the actual presence of a more powerful second/foreign language other, or 'watchdog' or (b) by an imaginary, more powerful second/foreign language other and/or (c) in contexts where the second/foreign language other is completely absent, but the power of the latter is well established and (d) in the presence of one's own first language group who do not understand the second/foreign language. In addition, LAA can cause the learner to move from a mere reluctance to *speak* the target language to an actual dislike for *learning* the target language, as is often the case with English language in post-colonial South Asian societies.

Moreover, LAA can originate with regard to one's mother tongue as well and is not restricted to a second language use. Where there is a complex power play between ethnic groups with different languages, the more powerful group may be deemed to be a threat to the less powerful, which creates an anxiety in members of the latter group when speaking in their mother tongue in certain situations. This may be present where there are prolonged tensions between communities. The less powerful may refrain from using their own mother tongue when the two groups are mixed in the larger society for fear of being negatively evaluated by the more powerful.

A similar study we carried out in 2013/2014[3] with the international student community in the United States shows that foreign students often avoid the company of native speakers of English and that they do not have native speakers in their circle of friends. This may indicate less of a power play between languages and more of a power play between cultures/nations which is manifested in their language use when extended to ordinary social activities such as moving in university circles.

We have identified three LAA types based on their longevity: (a) temporary, (b) transitional and (c) permanent. If and when circumstances/contexts change, language attitudes may also change. These three types of LAA are explained by locating them within the contexts narrated in the prologue to the chapter. Some of these circumstances have changed since we experienced them whereas some remained unchanged over centuries.

LAA as a temporary entity

The circumstances producing the incident reported in Prologue (2) above have changed completely in the nine years since the end of the civil war in Sri Lanka. This change took place almost immediately after the cessation of hostilities. Now it is commonplace among Sri Lankans who belong to the Tamil ethnic group to speak their mother tongue in formal and/or informal settings. Therefore, we see that when the context in which the power relations between groups speaking different languages changes, the power play between languages also changes, paving the way for attitudinal changes towards the respective languages. This in turn changes/eliminates LAA. Consequently, this type of LAA is considered to be temporary.

The second part of Prologue (3) too has changed now as we have hundreds of conferences taking place in Sri Lanka annually and most of them are graced by Indian scholars, not only as presenters but also as prestigious key-note speakers. This has made Sri Lankans more familiar with one of the strongest elements of 'Indianness' in Indian English, the pronounced /r/ at the end of words. This, however, does not account for any LAA as such on the part of the Indians who speak English in Sri Lanka. We simply feel it is worth mentioning to show how the language attitudes in a society can change as circumstances change and hence can be deemed to be temporary.

LAA as a transitional entity

In the case of the language learning contexts, the presence and duration of LAA depends on the mechanisms the learners adopt to learn and/or the strategies the teachers use to teach the language and/or the societal response one receives. For instance, one quote in Chapter 8, Teaching Methodology (see Teacher's role under *no error correction*) is from an Indian student who stated that his or her lack of confidence to speak English diminished with the encouragement he or she received from the audience in the form of applause at a debate session in his or her class. The learner revealed that this incident gave him or her 'a lot of confidence' and that it made 'English language learning much easier' (Student code I-261). This not only reveals the influence of social attitudes on the language learner, but also the transitional nature of LAA.

In addition, it is important to realize that almost all language learners experience LAA at some point in their language learning career. In fact, LAA can be considered as a characteristic of language learners who are trying to use the language in a useful manner in a real-life situation. While advancing in their learning careers, some learners will overcome LAA and become proficient language users. In such a context, LAA is transitional, a fleeting stage and it characterizes active language learning. At the same time, just as with FLCA, LAA may even prove to be a positive factor in motivating learners to learn and perform in a foreign language. Therefore, LAA can be considered as constructive in its transitional state, as some learners will be motivated to learn the language by overcoming LAA.

LAA as a permanent entity

However, it must be noted that certain language attitudes are deeply embedded in societies and their effects can be pervasive and difficult to root out. In the Prologue point (1), Urdu remains more powerful than Punjabi and the latter is not used among themselves by many in the upper or upper-middle classes but may be spoken to domestic help at home to reinforce the status hierarchy. Therefore, it is unsurprising that native speakers of Punjabi, even those who are also fluent in Urdu, may experience some level of LAA in certain contexts. In the episode (3) from the first section, where Tony Greig plays a role, the prestige of the English language remains unchanged and unchallenged in post-colonial South Asia when it is spoken by a native speaker of English with a white skin, in spite of any linguistic idiosyncrasies. On the one hand, local learners who want to speak English are affected by LAA created in settings where attitudes related to the English language and 'white standards' are set by local elites who act as 'watchdogs' for the 'white master's' language. On the other hand, local learners who are able to speak some English experience LAA due to the perception that their efforts to speak like a native (white) speaker of English are futile. Both types of learners end up lacking confidence to speak English, although we find in our study that the former group greatly outnumbers the latter because the majority struggle to speak any English.

In Bangladesh, one pressing question we were constantly asked by the learners was which English they should speak: British or American. Some almost pleaded with us to teach some American or British English as they were worried about using their English with a heavy Bangla accent. In Pakistan, in remote areas like Swat Valley, learners are eager to learn American English. It is important to understand that these learners who manage to learn some English still experience some form of LAA stemming from the sense that their spoken English is inferior.

We find it ironic that all of the post-colonial South Asian countries in the study, 70 years after their 'independence' from the British, are still 'trapped' within a colonial mindset in regard to English language attitude issues. It is also noteworthy that this status quo resembles in most ways the pre-independence scenario as it has been reported by many, as far as language attitudes and their manifestations are concerned. The locals who spoke English then and were able to communicate with the British rulers in their respective countries looked down upon their fellow countrymen who could not. And some of the locals developed a dislike and hatred towards the British and their language just as today some learners express dislike and hatred towards the English language and its speakers.

Another twist in regard to language attitudes (not necessarily LAA) in the modern 21st-century context is that all these countries have high tolerance for native speakers of English and it has remained this way as long as it is restricted to certain domains such as teaching, cricket (commentaries), helping South Asians to meet requirements to migrate to western countries, etc., just as we have seen in regard to the Tony Greig narrative. However, attitudes towards native speakers of English take a complete turn, in all four countries, in matters relating to politics where native speakers English become 'outsiders' with no value and are often seen as part of a 'foreign conspiracy' thus shifting language attitudes towards native speakers of English to a completely different paradigm.

Where English language learning is concerned, it can be argued that a large majority of learners in South Asian countries experience LAA throughout their student life as well as afterwards. An overwhelming majority of the undergraduates in this study state that they are afraid/shy/uncertain about speaking English due to a fear of ridicule by others in society; and the vast majority (almost all from rural and semi-rural backgrounds) cannot speak English in a coherent manner for two minutes continuously. National level English language performance indicators in each country also reflect our failures in teaching English (notwithstanding the fact that these failures can be attributed to other factors as well). When we move away from the study of undergraduates, we find that LAA has caused the vast majority of South Asians who have attempted to learn English to simply give up. All of this indicates that LAA in relation to English language learning in post-colonial South Asia has been a more or less permanent phenomenon since the pre-independence era, with occasional twists and turns that do little to undermine the continual perpetuation and reinforcement of the established linguistic power hierarchies.

As the discussion reveals, LAA can act as a type of 'permanent' hindrance that reinforces English language attitudes that were established and determined in the past. They have been affecting the local rural and semi-rural language learners in the decades since independence and continue to bind post-colonial English language learning to remnants of the colonial past.

LAA as a bridge between causes and consequences

The same arguments that have been made in regard to FLA about whether it is a cause or a consequence are valid for LAA as well. For instance, Tran (2012) discusses the opposing views that have been found in terms of the direction of the causal relationship between FLA and language learning difficulties. While Horwitz et al. focused on the detrimental effects of FLA on language learning, some other researchers considered it a consequence rather than a cause of poor outcomes in the language learning process (Argaman & Abu-Rabia, 2002; Ganschow et al., 1994; Sparks and Ganschow, 1991, 1995). According to Sparks and Ganschow (1995), 'one cannot discuss anxiety without inferring a cause' (p. 236) and although they agreed that anxiety could hinder learning and students might experience anxiety while learning a foreign language, it was their view that anxiety is more likely to be a consequence rather than a cause of poor achievement in foreign language learning. In supporting Sparks and Ganschow's hypothesis, Argaman and Abu-Rabia (2002) examined the influence of language anxiety on achievement in English writing and reading comprehension tasks and found a significant relationship between language anxiety and both reading and writing skills. However, they argued that language anxiety might not be a cause of failure in learning a foreign language, but a consequence.

Therefore, it cannot be denied that anxiety, whether it is FLA, LAA or both, is likely to be both a cause and an effect of language learning difficulty. However, an issue raised by Horwitz (2001) is that what is more challenging is not conceptualizing FLA as a result of poor language learning ability (as opposed to her view of it as a cause) but to determine 'the extent to which anxiety is a cause rather than a result of poor language learning' (p. 118). However, the extent to which anxiety, both as a cause and as a result of poor language learning, is manifested throughout the post-colonial South Asian region in regard to English language performance is readily apparent.

Despite many arguments on this aspect, we argue that LAA acts as bridge between the learners' negative attitudes towards speaking in English and their lack of confidence to speak English. Also, just as a bridge supports journeys to and fro, it acts both ways: when the learners are overwhelmed by negative attitudes towards speaking in English, they become anxious, which leads to a lack of confidence. On the other hand, the lack of confidence to speak English can create a higher level of anxiety that will cause the learner to develop negative attitudes towards speaking English.

Therefore, it is at this juncture that an intervention must take place (a) to prevent learners from experiencing anxiety and (b) to build learner confidence to speak English.

Components of Language Attitude Anxiety

As this study reveals, learners experience LAA and this leads to lack of confidence to speak English with the root causes found in language attitudes that exist in the larger society. MacIntyre's (1999) remark sheds light on the complexities involved with foreign or second language learning, which 'has more potential for students to embarrass themselves, to frustrate their self-expression, and to challenge their self-esteem and sense of identity than almost any other learning activities' (p. 33). The findings of our study and our extensive interviews with learners from across South Asia also support this view; learners go through very difficult phases in their second/foreign language performance (speaking) in front of an attitude-loaded audience, which leads to them developing LAA. In such a scenario, when students manifest a lack of confidence to speak in their own classroom, it is hardly surprising that the idea of speaking in front of outsiders becomes paralysing, as 'the single most important source of language anxiety seems to be the fear of speaking in front of other people using a language with which one has limited proficiency' (MacIntyre, 1999, p. 33). As such, we can identify two main components of LAA: (a) negative evaluation and (b) communication apprehension. Both of these contribute to the creation of LAA in second/foreign language learners.

Negative evaluation

Why negative evaluation contributes to creating LAA in second language learners is as complex as language attitudes themselves. Watson and Friend (1969) define fear of negative evaluation as 'apprehension about others' evaluations, avoidance of evaluative situations, and the expectation that others would evaluate oneself negatively' (p. 449). We have identified a number of negative evaluation types based on their origin: (a) from the teacher and peers, (b) from the outside society, and (c) from the learner's personal perceptions (self-directed).

By the teacher and peers

Second language learners are affected by the fear of negative evaluation in classroom situations where the language teacher and peers are their audience. Learners are shy and/or are afraid of direct, implied or suppressed mockery from their audience. In addition, overcorrection by teachers is a definite cause of the fear of negative evaluation as most learners are convinced that their performance, especially with regard to speaking, is not acceptable because of being overcorrected. Not only that, learners fear that the teacher's negative evaluation will affect their grades even in settings in which they are not being assessed. Learners may even be affected by assumed or actual negative evaluation from their teachers outside the second/foreign language classroom walls, within the broader academic setting. Negative evaluation in foreign language classroom settings has been much discussed under FLA (Horwitz et al., 1986).

By the outside society

The fear of being ridiculed by others outside in the larger society is the main thrust of our study. As our findings show, the large majority of learners throughout South Asia experience anxiety that stems from the attitudes of the larger society outside the language classroom towards English, in addition to the presence of FLCA. As stated before, direct, implied or suppressed mockery 'frightens' the learner to the extent that some report 'increased heart-beat', sudden 'loss of words', etc. It is important to identify negative evaluation of this type since it is not a product of learners feeling that they would disappoint their teacher or 'fail' a course due to their lack of competence to speak the foreign/second language. If that were the case, the anxiety created by the presence of the specific audience (teacher and/or peers) should diminish in their absence. Instead, the reported lack of confidence to speak English *everywhere* and in front of *everyone* due to their fear of negative evaluation (e.g. being ridiculed) demonstrates the broad scope of the problem. At the same time, the learners' tongue-loosening in front of native speakers of English has to be taken into account as it shows that the cause is not found in the English language or its teaching–learning method *per se*, but in the society and the people in front of whom they are afraid to speak. This clearly brings out the local attitudinal dimension of the problem. Also, that the highest percentage of learners who lack LAA in regard to speaking English come from Goa supports this point, by bringing into focus the impact of the societal attitudes in which English language learning takes place.

Learners' fear of negative evaluation at the hands of people who speak English 'well' (as per learner perception) is easy to understand when we consider that learners' speech production may belong to a substandard variety of English or include a great deal of mispronunciation. However, another complexity arises when learners report their fear of negative evaluation from an audience which is completely illiterate in the English language. The negative evaluation comes from an attitude that the speaker of another language is trying to 'show off', and the learners are afraid of this judgement. This brings out one type stereotype which is applied to people who speak English in these societies: they either act or are perceived to be acting as if they are superior by virtue of speaking English. In turn, this stereotype contributes to (i) discouraging the learners to practise speaking English for the fear of being stereotyped and (ii) the re-establishment of the 'watchdog' role in South Asian society. A fear of negative evaluation from real and/or imaginary English speakers and non-English speakers both serve to bring about the same results in learners. The effects of such a scenario on language learning are two-fold: learners do not get the chance to practise speaking English anywhere else other than inside the language classroom; and the fear factor manifests in a complete lack of confidence to speak English that is then projected to other skills and cripples learners in their language production.

In addition, learners' aspiration to develop the ability to speak English because of the perceived benefits it will give them are continually frustrated by their non-action vis-à-vis speaking English in front of others. This causes learners to associate those who speak English 'well' with extremely positive traits, describing them as 'smart', 'confident', 'stylish', 'intelligent', 'can handle any situation', etc., which further complicates the scenario and decreases learner confidence. In spite of learners having such strong positive ideas about being able to speak English, negative evaluation from the outside society can override all of them very quickly, producing sheer terror in learners as anxiety begins to take over.

By learner's personal perceptions (self-directed)

Self-directed negative evaluation was identified as coming from learners' personal perceptions (i) of their own speaking aptitude and of their learning, (ii) of the second language itself as opposed to one's mother tongue and (iii) of their mother tongue as superior to other languages (manifested in linguistic nationalism or even jingoism).

The fear of self-directed negative evaluation is even more damaging than the fear of negative evaluation from external sources. Of the three types of self-directed negative evaluation we have identified, the first is of his or her own speaking aptitude and of the learning of it. The expressions learners used reveal that they evaluate themselves as not capable of speaking like 'others' who speak 'better' English. Once they speak, they judge their own English as 'not good' or 'not up to the standard' and that leads them to feel anxious, producing a sense of inadequacy. Learners' negative self-evaluations have a bearing on their apprehension for communication as well (Manninen, 1984). This is further compounded by their aspiration to speak like native speakers of English as they continually stated during the interviews: 'I want to speak like an American'; 'Which English do you think we should speak, American or British?' etc. These unrealistic expectations only serve to frustrate them continuously, thereby contributing to the tendency to evaluate themselves negatively. This sense of inadequacy or lack of confidence may eventually lead to the learner developing a negative evaluation of the English language as a whole and/or their learning abilities in general.

The second type of self-directed negative evaluation is the negative evaluation of the second language itself in the context of one's mother tongue. Learner expressions, such as 'more comfortable in speaking in the mother tongue', indicate that the learners are less comfortable in speaking in English than in mother tongue. This is hardly surprising, but there is yet another self-directed negative evaluation that is generated from this preference for one's mother tongue (expressed in a nationalistic or even jingoistic tone) which may manifest itself in dislike or hatred for the target language. Learner expressions of 'not liking to speak English' because they 'do not like English' are usually accompanied by hatred towards English language and/or by being passionate about the mother tongue. It is noteworthy that this is most noticed in Sindh, Pakistan, and in Bangladesh.

The discussion brings into focus how the fear of negative evaluation begins in response to language attitudes in society, extends into the classroom and then into the mind of the learner as well. Learners, as a result of being negatively evaluated by the society (both inside and outside the language classroom) or imagining negative evaluations from others, start to evaluate themselves negatively. This self-directed negative evaluation, in our view, is more harmful than the negative evaluation that comes from society in creating a debilitating lack of confidence in learners. Negative evaluation turned inwards can leave a learner with a deep sense of inadequacy, which is more harmful because the negative evaluation is internalized and therefore, more difficult to eliminate.

Communication apprehension

According to McCroskey (1977), communication apprehension is the broad term that refers to an individual's 'fear or anxiety associated with either real or anticipated communication with another person or persons' (p. 78). The learner's fears are not always real, but may be imaginary, and they are based on anticipatory circumstances. McCroskey and Richmond (1995) divide communication apprehension into four different subcategories: trait-like, context-based, audience-based and situational communication apprehension. One can see an array of communication apprehension types between the two extremes, the trait-like and the state-like.

Trait-like communication apprehension is akin to a personality type or synonymous with personality (Booth-Butterfield & Booth-Butterfield, 1992) and can be highly resistant to change. In contrast, context-based communication apprehension is 'a relatively enduring, personality-type orientation toward communication in a given type of context' (McCroskey and Richmond, 1995, p. 45). They also found a correlation between trait-like and context-based communication apprehension in that the higher an individual's trait-like communication apprehension, the more contexts he will find apprehensive (Lahtinen, 2013). Context-based communication apprehension can be seen with people at job interviews, meeting strangers, etc., and should not be mixed with the apprehension most people experience in contexts such as public speaking, which is quite normal and experienced by many (ibid.).

Learners experience audience-based communication apprehension due to the presence of a particular person or certain people in a communication situation. McCroskey and Richmond (1995) define this type as 'a relatively enduring orientation toward communication with a given person or group of people' (p. 46). For instance, an employee may experience audience-based communication apprehension when communicating with his or her boss. Learners may go through the same inside (and outside) the classroom when talking to their teacher and/or to peers. Most importantly, McCroskey and Richmond (ibid.) emphasize that audience-based communication apprehension is not personality-based, but a response to situational constraints created by another person or group.

McCroskey and Richmond (ibid.) state that situational communicative apprehension is 'a transitory orientation toward communication with a given person or group of people' (p. 48). It is similar to context- and audience-based communicative apprehension in that it is a reactive, passing state and should not be considered to be a personality-based condition.

From our study findings, it is clear that the learners in the post-colonial South Asia experience context-based, audience-based and situational communication apprehension types. However, what percentage of the sample experience trait-like communication apprehension is not known as we did not attempt to examine personality traits in our study. In a given population, there is always a combination of personality types and we may assume that some learners belong to the category with trait-like communication apprehension as well.

Learners reported increased heart-beat, loss of words, nervousness, etc., either at the thought of having to speak in English or when they speak English in front of audiences who are known as well as unknown to them, inside the language classroom as well as outside. It is noteworthy that the communication apprehension types that are discussed above are reactive and created by contexts, situations and audiences. All three, even though they are divided into different categories, involve an audience, that is, people. For instance, a context does not exist without people; a situation does not arise without people and an audience necessarily involves people. Learners state that they are afraid/shy/uncertain to speak English in front of 'others' who exist in the aforesaid contexts, situations and audiences. Since all three types of communication apprehension are considered to be reactions, we argue that all three types of communication apprehension are reactions created by the learner's society, which is loaded with language attitudes. Korpela (2010) observes that the presence of other people monitoring one's speech is a potential cause for communication apprehension. While agreeing to this, we elaborate it so that it is understood that it is not only the 'presence' of other people's 'monitoring' that has the potential to cause communication apprehension in the learners but even the 'imaginary presence' of other people monitoring their speech. Furthermore, the presence of other people's 'imaginary monitoring' also causes learners to experience communication apprehension. Thus, learners are more susceptible to communication apprehension as a result of various external or internal causes, such as counterproductive fears and negative self-beliefs (Korpela, 2010).

There is yet another context-specific feature that may contribute to creating communication apprehension in the English language learner in South Asian teaching–learning contexts: the traditional power structure in the classroom. That is to say that the teacher–student relationship in the South Asian countries predominantly expresses the utmost respect for the teacher. This is sometimes characterized by the presence of almost no arguments, little discussion and few questions, all of which reinforces communication apprehension. It is unarguable that without actual communication, a language cannot be learnt. With learners who are habituated in such teaching–learning environments, it can be expected that they will experience communication apprehension more often than students in looser environments. Also, those who already suffer from the said communication apprehension types will have them reinforced in a South Asian classroom and this communication apprehension in the language classroom will contribute to further anxiety. Amid the power dynamics in the South Asian classroom where teachers of English may pose to be even 'more respectable' than teachers who teach in mother tongues, there is a possibility that learner tongues are even more tied, reinforcing their communication apprehensiveness.

LAA, with fear of negative evaluation and communication apprehension as its main components, seems therefore to be the main problem in regard to English language teaching in South Asia, manifest as a lack of confidence in learners.

Throughout this chapter, we have discussed the importance of the social context in language learning with reference to our study on speaking in English in post-colonial South Asia. We have found that language attitudes exist in South

Asian societies that create LAA in learners, which hinders them from performing well in their most-desired language skill, speaking. In discussing the importance of social context, MacIntyre (1995) criticizes the LCDH put forth by Sparks and Ganschow (1993) on the grounds that it neglects the context in which language learning occurs (Clement et al., 1980; Gardner & MacIntyre, 1992, 1993) and ignores the potential for social context to influence cognitive processes (Fiske & Taylor, 1991). Further, anxiety about speaking English may project its damaging effects onto English language learning in general. As MacIntyre (1995) states:

> ... anxious students are in a double bind; they have learned less and may not be able to demonstrate the information that they have learned.
>
> (p. 97)

Further, the cyclical relationship between anxiety and task performance suggests that as students experience more failures, their anxiety level may increase even more (ibid.), making them more hesitant to speak, which then leads to anxieties that are projected onto the English language learning process and feeds into a cyclical process of interlocking and self-reinforcing anxiety. Therefore, it is crucial for teachers to intervene at a point in the cycle where LAA can be eliminated and confidence to speak can be built so that the improved confidence to speak English can be projected into the entire English language learning process.

Conclusion

This chapter identifies some language attitudes that exist in South Asian societies and discusses their effects on the English language learner in post-colonial South Asia in terms of the learners' most sought-after skill, speaking. As a result of the existing language attitudes that create norms and set standards, and the prejudice against learners who do not meet these expectations, the vast majority of South Asian learners, especially rural and semi-rural learners, develop LAA. This is experienced in their speech performance and manifests in a lack of confidence to speak English.

FLCA and the associated scale that is widely used throughout the world to discuss language anxiety related to foreign/second language learning does not capture the entirety of social attitudes and their influence on foreign/second language learning. AMTB is discussed in regard to its limitations in capturing the context-specific attitudes in the foreign/second language learning scenario that are prevalent in South Asia, thus establishing the need for and validity of a different type of anxiety, that we call LAA, that is experienced by most foreign/second language learners in post-colonial South Asian societies. LAA stems from language attitudes in the larger society that the foreign/second language learners come into contact with, both inside and outside the language classroom, and manifests itself in the learner's lack of confidence to speak in English. The next section discusses the two main components of LAA, the fear of negative evaluation and communication apprehension as identified in learner responses.

The chapter ends by noting that as a result of learners developing negative attitudes towards their own speaking of English there may be a projection of this negativity onto their own language learning in general. The discussion leads to the identification of a point at which an intervention is made to help learners develop positive attitudes towards their own English-speaking ability through building confidence to speak English and eliminating LAA.

Notes

1 During the civil war in Sri Lanka until it ended in 2008, there were hardly any conferences. The only one on English language teaching was organized by the SLELTA (Sri Lanka English Language Teachers Association) which was held once in two years. So, the contacts with foreigners within Sri Lanka were sparse.

2 A personal interview with the final year English Special undergraduates at the University of Sri Jayewardenepura, Sri Lanka in December 2016. They have offered French as their minor.

3 The researcher was a Fellow of the prestigious Fulbright Advanced Research and Lecturing Award at the Pennsylvania State University, USA.

References

Appel, R., & Muysken, P. (1987). *Language contact and bilingualism*. London: Edward Arnold.

Argaman, O., & Abu-Rabia, S. (2002). The influence of language anxiety on English reading and writing task among native Hebrew speakers. *Language, Culture and Curriculum*, 15, 143–160. doi:10.1080/07908310208666640

Attanayake, A. U. (2017). *Undergraduate ELT in Sri Lanka: Policy, practice and perspectives for South Asia*. New Castle upon Tyne: Cambridge Scholars Publishing.

Awan, A. G., & Zia, A. (2015). Comparative analysis of public and private educational institutions: A case study of district Vehari-Pakistan. *Journal of Education and Practice*, 6(16), 122–130.

Booth-Butterfield, M., & Booth-Butterfield, S. (1992). Communication apprehension and avoidance in the classroom. In J. C. McCroskey and V. P. Richmond (Eds.), *The Burgess series on communication in instruction*. Edina, MN: Burgess Publishing.

Clement, R., Gardner, R. C., & Smythe, P. C. (1980). Social and individual factors in second language acquisition. *Canadian Journal of Behavioural Science*, 12, 293–302.

Clevenger, T. (1984). An analysis of research on the social anxieties. In J. A. Daly and J. C. McCroskey (Eds.), *Avoiding communication: Shyness, reticence, and communication apprehension* (pp. 219–236). Beverly Hills, CA: Sage.

Crystal, D. (1997). *A dictionary of linguistics and phonetics* (4th ed.). Oxford, UK: Blackwell.

Fasold, R. (1987). *The sociolinguistics of society*. Oxford, UK: Blackwell.

Fischer, W. F. (1988). *Theories of anxiety* (2nd ed.). Lanham, MD: University Press of America.

Fiske, S. T., & Taylor, S. E. (1991). *Social cognition*. New York: McGraw Hill.

Ganschow, L., Sparks, R., Anderson, R., Javorsky, J., Skinner, S., & Patton, J. (1994). Differences in anxiety and language performance among high and low anxious college foreign language learners. *Modern Language Journal*, 78, 41–55.

Gardner, R. C. (1985). Attitude/Motivation Test Battery. International AMTB Research Project. Retrieved from: http://publish.uwo.ca/~gardner/docs/englishamtb.pdf

Gardner, R. C., & MacIntyre, P. D. (1992). A student's contribution to second language learning. Part I: Cognitive variables. *Language Teaching*, 25, 211–220.

Gardner, R. C., & MacIntyre, P. D. (1993). A student's contribution to second language learning. Part II: Affective variables. *Language Teaching*, 26. 1–11.

Horwitz, E. K. (2001). Language anxiety and achievement. *Annual Review of Applied Linguistics*, 21, 112–126.

Horwitz, E. K., Horwitz, M. B., & Cope, J. (1986). Foreign language classroom anxiety. *Modern Language Journal*, 70, 125–132.

Korpela, L. (2010). *Why don't students talk? Causes of foreign language communication apprehension in English classes: A comparison of high apprehensive and low apprehensive upper secondary students.* Helsinki: University of Helsinki, Department of Teacher Education.

Lahtinen, L. (2013). *Communication apprehension in the EFL classroom: A study of Finnish and Finnish-Swedish upper secondary school students and teachers.* Unpublished MA thesis. Department of Languages English University of Jyväskylä, Finland. Retrieved from: https://www.merriam-webster.com/dictionary/confidence

Leary, M. R. (1990). Anxiety, cognition and behavior: In search of a broader perspective. In M. Booth- Butterfield (Ed.), Communication, cognition, and anxiety (pp. 39–44). Newbury Park, CA: Sage.

Levitt, E. E. (1980). *The psychology of anxiety.* Hillsdale, NJ: Erlbaum.

Liu, H., & Chen, T. (2013). Foreign language anxiety in young learners: How it relates to multiple intelligences, learner attitudes, and perceived competence. *Journal of Language Teaching and Research*, 4(5), 932–938. Academy Publisher Manufactured in Finland. doi:10.4304/jltr.4.5.932-938. Retrieved from: http://www.academypublication.com/issues/past/jltr/vol04/05/05.pdf

MacIntyre, P. D. (1995). How does anxiety affect second language learning? A reply to Sparks and Ganschow. *The Modern Language Journal*, 79(1), 90–99.

MacIntyre, P. D. (1999). Language anxiety: A review of the research for language teachers. In D. J. Young (Ed.), *Affect in foreign language and second language learning: A practical guide to creating a low-anxiety classroom atmosphere* (pp. 24–45). New York: McGraw-Hill College.

MacIntyre, P. D., & Gardner, R. C. (1989). Anxiety and second language learning: Toward a theoretical clarification. *Language Learning*, 32, 251–275.

MacIntyre, P. D., & Gardner, R. C. (1991). Language anxiety: Its relation to other anxieties and to processing in native and second languages. *Language Learning*, 41, 513–534.

McCroskey, J. C. (1977). Oral communication apprehension: A summary of recent theory and research. *Human Communication Research*, 4, 78–96.

McCroskey, J. C., & Richmond, V. P. (1995). *Communication: Apprehension, avoidance and effectiveness* (4th ed.). Scottsdale, AZ: Gorsuch Scarisbrick.

Manninen, S. (1984). *Communication apprehension. A study of the factors contributing to anxiety experienced by Finnish speakers of English.* Unpublished M.A. thesis. Finland: University of Jyväskylä, Department of Languages.

Phillips, E. M. (1992). The effects of language anxiety on students' oral test performance and attitudes. *Modern Language Journal*, 76(1), 14–26.

Sarason, I. G. (1986). Test anxiety, worry, and cognitive interference. In R. Schwarzer (Ed.), *Self-related cognition in anxiety and motivation* (pp. 19–34). Hillsdale, NJ: Erlbaum.

Schwarzer, R. (1986). Self-related cognition in anxiety and motivation: An introduction. In R. Schwarzer (Ed.), *Self-related cognition in anxiety and motivation* (pp. 1–17). Hillsdale, NJ: Erlbaum.

Sparks, R. L., & Ganschow, L. (1991). Foreign language learning differences: Affective or native language aptitude differences? *Modern Language Journal*, 75, 3–16.

Sparks, R. L., & Ganschow, L. (1993). The impact of native language learning problems on foreign language learning: Case study illustrations of the linguistic coding deficit hypothesis. *Modern Language Journal*, 77, 58–74.

Sparks, R., & Ganschow, L. (1995). A strong inference approach to causal factors in foreign language learning: A response to Maclntyre. *Modern Language Journal*, 79, 235–244.

Spielberger, C. D. (1966). Complex learning and academic achievement. In C. D. Spielberger (Ed.), *Anxiety and behavior* (pp. 361–398). New York: Academic Press.

Spielberger, C. D. (1983). *Manual for state-trait anxiety inventory* (form Y). Palo Alto, CA: Consulting Psychologists Press.

Tran, T. T. T. (2012). A review of Horwitz, Horwitz and Cope's theory of foreign language anxiety and the challenges to the theory. Retrieved from: http://files.eric.ed.gov/fulltext/EJ1078777.pdf. Accessed 30 October 2018.

Watson, D., & Friend, R. (1969). Measurement of social-evaluative anxiety. *Journal of Consulting and Clinical Psychology*, 33(4), 448–457.

Whitmore, R. (1987). *Living with stress and anxiety.* Manchester, England: Manchester University Press.

Wine, J. D. (1980). "Cognitive-attentional anxiety of test anxiety." In I. G. Sarason (Ed.), *Test anxiety: Theory, research and applications* (pp. 349–385). Hillsdale, NJ: Erlbaum.

Young, D. J. (1991). Creating a low-anxiety classroom environment: What does the language anxiety research suggest? *Modern Language*, 75, 426–437.

Young, D. J. (1994). New directions in language anxiety research. In C. A. Klee (Ed.), *Faces in a crowd: The individual learner in multisection courses* (pp. 3–46). Boston, MA: Heinle and Heinle.

Zheng, Y. (2008). Anxiety and second/foreign language learning revisited. *Canadian Journal for New Scholars in Education*, 1(1), 1–12.

5 Understanding the English language learner

Introduction

This chapter discusses the power relations between the English language and learners in terms of affective love–hate relations. Also the social, mental and educational paradigms in which the learners are immersed are analysed alongside the constructs of learner identity, possible selves and role conflict. The positioning of the learners in question is explained in relation to the language acquisition stages. Understanding the power relations between the English language and learners in their local context is facilitated by way of learner responses. On the one hand, the Foreign Language Anxiety (FLA) that stems from the uniqueness of the language learning process has to be fought. On the other hand, the societal attitudes that create Language Attitude Anxiety (LAA) need to be addressed and train the learners to face them in a positive way. The chapter ends by discussing how LAA, which creates a lack of confidence to speak English, is projected and leads to poor performance in English in a general sense.

A 'love–hate' relationship

As already discussed, Sri Lankan undergraduates have been stating for over a decade that the skill they most desire to develop in regards to English language education is the speaking skill. The reason why they do not speak English when opportunities are presented, in spite of having studied it for over ten years (from grade 3 until college/university), is that they lack confidence as a result of the language attitudes prevalent in their society. The findings of this study, which also includes undergraduates in Pakistan, Bangladesh and India, show that the majority of students in all four countries would most like to develop the speaking skill. The same lack of confidence to speak English is found among these learners, also a product of the language attitudes prevalent in society, leading to LAA caused by a fear of being ridiculed by others in the society. However, the reasons behind the societal attitudes that cause LAA vary slightly in the different countries are as follows: in Sri Lanka learners mainly fear locals who speak better English and look down upon those who speak 'not-so-better' or 'bad' English, while in Bangladesh and some parts of Pakistan, learners fear locals who do not speak English at all and mock people who do speak English.

As a consequence of these language attitudes towards the English language and its speakers, LAA inhibits learners and discourages them from speaking English. This retards their ability to learn the language and become familiar with its usage while impeding their efforts to expand their vocabulary and express themselves in English. This produces a lack of confidence that creates and reinforces LAA to the detriment of the learner's ability to benefit from the English language learning process. Some examples of how this lack of confidence is created are given below:

1 A learner might have had a teacher/friend or someone else who spoke English 'well'[1] and who laughed at/ridiculed/mocked that learner's mistake in pronunciation when he or she was in their primary schooling.
2 A learner might have witnessed a friend being subjected to such mockery by a teacher/friend or someone else.
3 A learner might have been made to feel (not through overt actions like those described in 1 and 2, but in a more covert manner) that he or she or a friend who mispronounces a word in speaking was 'wrong' to have spoken English in the first place.
4 A learner might have been continually overcorrected by a teacher in regard to pronunciation and/or grammar.
5 A learner might have been made to feel that they were not understood when they spoke in English in spite of many attempts.
6 A learner might have faced/heard of cases like these many times in his or her learning career.
7 A learner might be mocked for speaking English by friends or strangers who do not speak English at all.
8 A learner might be negatively evaluated for his or her writing by teachers in the classroom in spite of being unable to express concepts in English due to a lack of practice in regard to speech.

In such cases, it is quite natural for learners to try and avoid the recurrence of these scenarios and avoid situations that create anxiety-related feelings in them. In psychology this is known as avoidance and it hinders the nervous system from becoming habituated to stressful circumstances like those found in the language classroom. Insofar as these anxiety-producing scenarios remain novel, they will continue to arouse the nervous system and create anxiety.

Given the attitude problems that are prevalent in post-colonial South Asian countries vis-à-vis the English language and its speakers, a learner will likely experience the situation/s described both inside and outside the classroom. As a result, what tends to happen initially is that the learner will avoid speaking in English with, or in the presence of, the person who made the learner feel anxious.[2] Then, as psychology suggests, avoidance will tend to become more general over time. Learners will gradually avoid people who speak to them in English, then people who speak English, then instances/situations in which English may be spoken, etc. Thus, the fear/shyness/uncertainty felt when speaking English always remains novel and continues to arouse their nervous system while preventing the learner from becoming habituated to speaking in English.

It is noteworthy to state here an observation made by us in our own university in Sri Lanka: among the Sri Lankan undergraduates in this study and all throughout time during which data was collected for our previous study, the vast majority of undergraduates showed extremely high levels of confidence in all other areas of their academic life. There were students who were very forward and took part in student union activities, dances, dramas, singing, announcing, etc. However, they were very fearful, meek and silent in the English language classroom. When given a chance to speak in English, both inside and outside the classroom, they simply shrank. Among these students were great dancers, actors, musicians, announcers, student union leaders, etc., who were all outstanding in their academic and social performance in their mother tongues, but were reduced to nervous wrecks when asked to speak English. This was also found to be true among the students of Pakistan, Bangladesh and India. An informal discussion with a student who was in the remedial English class at a university in New Delhi, India, revealed that he was an active member of a protest against the university administration, a union action that crippled the functioning of the university for a week or so, yet he was afraid to speak English.

This duality between a high level of confidence in their academic and social lives accompanied by very low confidence in English language learning is supported by Norton's (1995) emphasis on the importance of considering the reciprocal effect of the social context on the learner during the language acquisition process:

> ... many have assumed that learners can be defined unproblematically as motivated or unmotivated, introverted or extroverted, inhibited or uninhibited, without considering that such affective factors are frequently socially constructed in inequitable relations of power, changing over time and space, and possibly coexisting in contradictory ways in a single individual.
>
> (p. 12)

In our view, some of the elements that are linked to the insecurity and a lack of confidence in the English language classroom are best explained by locating them in three concepts: learner identity, possible selves and role conflict.

Social and mental constructs

Learner identity

Identity refers to 'how a person understands his or her relationship to the world, how that relationship is constructed across time and space and how the person understands possibilities for the future' (Norton, 2000). Identity is dynamic, contextual and evolves over time. A poor learner identity is often the result of many negative learning experiences in the classroom and discouraging language experiences outside the classroom (Koay, 2018).

Foote (1951), as cited by Marcus and Nurius (1986), that all motivation was a consequence of an individual's set of identities. The individual acts so as to express his or her identity: 'Its products are ever-evolving self-conceptions' (p. 17), and 'When doubt believed of identity creeps in, action is paralyzed' (p. 18).

Going beyond the concept of learner identity in general, learner social identity is also an important factor in L2 acquisition as discussed by McDonald and Mitsutomi (2005). Learners must acquire a social identity in order to have social opportunities to develop their L2. Of the 13 acculturation areas researched, eight of them involved social interaction (hobbies/activities, insider/outsider dynamics, peers, culture, friendships and dating). Psychological distance between two cultures is also a consistent predictor of a learner's success in L2 acquisition (McDonald & Mitsutomi, 2005). By the same token, when the learner's social identity is associated more with L1 speakers, the opportunities for L2 exposure are minimal. However, if the learner is willing to acquire another social identity which is less distant from his or her L2 culture, the chances of learning L2 are high. This is supported by McDonald and Mitsutomi (2005), in that students who experienced long exposure to communication with native speakers also acquired stronger speaking skills.

Ellis (1985) states that age, sex, social class and ethnic identity are some of the specific factors that have to be considered as crucial in second language acquisition due to their influence on the attitudes of learners and the development of L2 proficiency. As Preston (1989, cited in Ellis, 2008) has pointed out, there is a clear parallel between sociolinguistic phenomena associated with social class and interlanguage development. Moreover, clear evidence points to a relationship between social class and overall L2 achievement that is actually more conspicuous for learners studying in an L2 setting (p. 104). It is inevitable that the social groups to which learners belong give them a social identity that affects not only their L2 achievement but their overall learner identity as well.

Coll and Falsafi (2010) suggest that educational situations in which learning is taking place foster a specific type of identity that is constructed alongside other identities, but that this identity is context specific according to the characteristics of the activity. Learner identity is defined by the specific situation and the diverse aspects of the learning activity and its particular characteristics, in terms of, tasks, objectives, learned subjects or abilities, etc. (Coll & Falsafi, 2010, p. 220).

As Johnson (2011) puts it, this 'reciprocal and variable relationship between learner and context underscores the idea that learners identify themselves and others around them as changeable' (p. 2). This is complemented by Osguthorpe's (2006) conceptualization (as cited by Coll and Falsafi, 2010) of the relationship between learning and identity construction. According to him, there are at least five different kinds of identity that are influenced by learning, namely, professional, personal, talent, character and learner identity. For instance, those who are skillful dancers, announcers, etc., may develop a strong talent identity while being timid and backward in the English language classroom, resulting in a poor learner identity. This partially explains why the student union leaders who manifested strong character identities cut such a poor figure in the English language classroom and in contexts where English is used.

We would argue that these identities in a learning environment are influenced not only by learning, but by other learners as well. Even though learners seem to accept their 'changeable' identities, the manifestation of these multiple identities in one person when they are contradictory in nature, may not work out well in settings where both learning and totality of education are concerned, and this is not necessarily restricted to academic settings only (see role conflict).

Granger's (2004) psychoanalytic approach to language and identity describes language as a tool for individuals to express their inner self to the world. As for children, the gradual emergence of the first language (L1) itself constitutes an identity which is combined with self-awareness and the beginning of language use. By contrast, second language acquisition limits the learner in presenting their inner self, even for a child. This incompatibility between the fully developed L1 psyche and the emerging second language self can be extremely frustrating for adult learners. Even though Granger argues that this mismatch makes learners silent, 'as they mourn the loss of their L1 communicativeness and negotiate a functional L2 self' (Johnson, 2011, p. 4), learners may actually build a wall, a barrier between themselves and English language use (in settings both formal and informal) to feel safe in their insecure L2 self. This insecure L2 self, therefore, is an identity learners are compelled to create as a result of the varied social forces in their lives including language attitudes.

Quite interestingly, Coll and Falsafi (2010) suggest that this identity is present and active in formal as well as informal learning situations, though the latter is rarely described at length. However, they do not specify what these 'informal learning situations' are, implying that it is the learner's first socializing agents, parents, with the researchers' immediate reference to 'parents who might be aware of the class, ethnic and gender identities that they want to foster, but do not really have a concept that facilitates the recognition of their children as learners' (p. 220).

Following this, in regard to 'informal situations', we consider them to be more expansive, including the society in which learners move outside the English language classroom, encompassing friends, relatives, guests, strangers and the society at large. Furthermore, we would argue that the learner identities that are created and fostered in formal learning settings are projected into the informal settings, creating a similar and an extended identity even outside the language classroom situations where English language is used. At the same time, a learner identity that is created and fostered in informal settings may be projected into the English language classroom to be nurtured as an extended learner identity. When informal settings create poor, negative learner identities, learners carry these identities with them into the English language classroom. By the same token, when pathetic learner identities are created within the four walls of the English language classroom, learners carry them with them outside the classroom and act on and live these identities in settings where the English language is used.

As cited in Coll's and Falsafi's (2010) work, Burke's (2006) definition of identities as an individual's understanding about what it means to be who they are and Bernstein's (Bernstein & Solomon, 1999) description of identities as a way of achieving a sense of belonging and recognition of self and others to manage specific situations, learner identity consists of generalized meanings about how one is recognized as a learner both by oneself and others. This then mediates the sense making of participation and the perceived sense of recognition as a learner in specific situations and activities of learning. If this were to be taken seriously alongside the observation made by Coll and Falsafi (2010) that 'learner identity is defined by the specific situation and the diverse aspects of the learning activity with particular characteristics, in terms of, for example, tasks, objectives, learned subjects or abilities etc.' (p. 220), then there are ample opportunities for the teachers to make use of by creating specific situations whereby tasks, objectives, etc., are designed so that the negative identities of learners are changed into positive ones. This may bring a sense of belonging to a group that emerges from a poor language learning identity and allows for a better learner identity to be developed.

Possible selves

Another concept that is related to this discussion is possible selves, as discussed by Marcus and Nurius (1986). Possible selves represent individuals' ideas of what they might become, what they would like to become and what they are afraid of becoming, and thus provide a conceptual link between cognition and motivation (p. 954).

These possible selves are individualized or personalized, but they are also distinctly social. Many of these possible selves are the direct result of previous social comparisons in which the individual's own thoughts, feelings, characteristics and behaviours have been contrasted with those of salient others. What others are now, I could become (Marcus & Nurius, 1986). This is where friends' and peers' negative experiences in the English language classroom can cause dread in other learners, which can encourage them to completely shut themselves off in the English language classroom. Also, the perceived notion that their English is lower than British or American English in status, which causes them to aspire to speak with a British or American accent may make learners increase their efforts to speak like a native speaker of English and contribute to generating a possible self. However, it may also make them frustrated about their inability to speak like a white man and constitute another reason for them to feel less confident in speaking English. The latter was expressed quite often in learner responses in this study. When we consider the varieties that exist within the spoken forms of American and British Englishes themselves, the efforts of learners in relation to their aspirations to be English-speaking selves may cause confusion as locally available resources may be limited for practising a native-like accent. This in turn may make the learners lose confidence in their spoken English. Horwitz (1988) discuss the positive relationship between high anxiety and negative concepts among students as language learners that lead to negative expectations for language learning. Also, it encourages learners to imitate others and learners may end up with an artificial type of English which may be considered eccentric in their society. Lastly, in terms of values, there is a propensity for learners to pay more attention to 'how' a person speaks English rather than to the substance of 'what' is said, reinforcing the already existing false values prevalent in the society in regard to language attitudes.

Needless to say, the role models for learners' vis-à-vis speaking English can be made use of to help learners develop possible selves so that their realistic aspirations can be realized. However, here again, what the learners are afraid of is becoming a (yet again) humiliated self and this fear must be eliminated systematically.

Role conflict

Another concept that emerges from contradictory learner identity is role conflict. In order to conceal poor learner identities and a sense of inferiority owing to these poor learner identities in the English language classroom, learners who have strong character or talent identities may resort to learner-unfriendly measures as a result of their conflicting role performances. For instance, students who are seniors (in their third or fourth year) and who are influential union leaders, dancers, singers, etc., performing in media other than English, may face role conflict when they fail to perform in the same manner in English, both inside and outside the classroom. This creates a role conflict within themselves.

Considering the power that English language enjoys in the post-colonial South Asian societies, this conflict can often create a sense of inadequacy, which is manifested in either hatred or envy (in addition to a complete withdrawal from anything to do with the English language). This is a psychological complex and it is expressed by many undergraduates in the Faculties of Arts/Humanities/Social Sciences in Sri Lankan universities that have mother tongue instruction. It is manifested in a number of anti-social ways: senior students banning junior students from speaking in English outside the English language classroom; severely ragging/hazing students who come from English-speaking backgrounds (or who are perceived as coming from such backgrounds including those from the best schools. Ironically, some of these students may not come from affluent classes but get into the best schools on merit while being from remote areas and/or belonging to the same social class as the raggers/hazers themselves); isolating the freshers who come from English-speaking backgrounds for the rest of their undergraduate life is another reaction to this role conflict. These facts are well known to incoming students who speak English well and they will often behave as elitists and may end up acting as the 'watchdog' of the colonial master's language when spoken by their perceived 'inferiors'.

Our experience as an academic in the Faculty of Arts, University of Colombo, with over five years of experience as a student counsellor, indicates that the 'big figures', especially union leaders in student social circles, create fear among their juniors so that the 'tradition' of not speaking in English in the university premises is carried on. As a result, the efforts of English language teachers to make students practise speaking English outside the classroom fail miserably. This situation is less prevalent in the Medical, Science, Engineering, Management and other faculties where the medium of instruction is English.

There is another dimension in this scenario: the class distinction. Those who come from rural and semi-urban areas usually end up in the Faculties of Arts/Humanities/Social Sciences in the universities of post-colonial South Asia owing to the limited subject stream options and poor facilities in non-urban schools. Almost all rural schools and most semi-rural schools in countries like Sri Lanka and her South Asian neighbours lack facilities to offer natural science or pure mathematics at the university entrance examinations. In cases where these options are available, non-urban schools are plagued with poor facilities, a lack of qualified teachers, non-existent laboratory facilities, etc. Therefore, students are compelled to follow the subjects in the Humanities and Social Sciences stream. Just as these schools have poor facilities for certain subject streams, the resources for learning English are also lacking. Sometimes it is reported that students in these schools do not have an English teacher and must learn English from the teacher of another subject for a number of years, which causes major difficulties in their English language education. In addition, the quality of English language teachers in these schools, when they are available, is also questionable due to the lack of pre-service and in-service teacher training programmes. Needless to say, students who come from rural and semi-rural areas usually do not have an English-speaking home background either. When students enter into the universities from such schools, they have difficulty competing with students who come to the university with better English language competency, even though the latter group may comprise less than 5% of the total student population. These students from rural and semi-rural backgrounds make up a large majority of the students at the Faculties of Arts/Humanities/Social Sciences. Among them, however, are the talented singers, dancers and other types of good performers we mentioned before who perform poorly only in English language-related activities. It is from this group that most student union leaders emerge and the class dimension in the universities in South Asia is manifested in language attitudes related to English. Those who speak English, have English-speaking backgrounds and/or come from popular urban schools are subject to more ragging/hazing due to hatred and envy of the students from the lower classes who are typically poor performers in English.

Language acquisition stages of the English language learner

As we have discussed in the previous chapters, South Asian English language learners lack confidence to speak English and may become comfortable in their poor learner identities, come to terms with their insecure L2 identities and accept the (not)possible selves (that are limiting them) and/or may find ways to retaliate against others in the language learning process due to their inadequacies in L2. Needless to say, these attitudes, at the social, individual and personal levels have contributed to creating and reinforcing LAA in learners, both inside and outside the English language classroom and in the larger society.

The English language learners in question, after about ten years' worth of English language learning, readily admit that they lack confidence to speak English because of the language attitudes that exist in their society. In this postcolonial South Asian context, it is little wonder that English language education fails to obtain the desired results in spite of numerous policy changes and initiatives. Given this, it is important to examine the state of language acquisition among the large majority of English language learners.

According to studies, learners go through five stages in second language acquisition. They are (a) pre-production (silent), (b) early production, (c) speech emergence, (d) intermediate fluency and (e) advanced fluency. The following section discusses the general features of an ordinary learner in second language acquisition and those of low proficiency learners in South Asia who have studied English for over a decade.

Stage 1: Pre-production (silent)

General features of ordinary learners at this stage

Those who are at this stage have about 500 words in their receptive vocabulary but are silent in the classroom. Some may repeat phrases after the teacher but are unable to produce any language on their own.

In ordinary circumstances, that is, among learners who are beginners in English language learning, they will listen attentively and they may even be able to copy words from the board. They will be able to respond to pictures and other visuals. They can understand and duplicate gestures and movements to show comprehension. Total Physical Response methods work well with them. English language learners at this stage usually require repetition of instructions to carry out tasks in English (Hayden, everythingesl.net).

General features of learners with poor proficiency

In our specific South Asian scenario, we find that learners with years of English language learning history behind them are often still stuck in this silent period. They may even have more than 500 words in their receptive and productive vocabulary. They will also repeat after the teacher but may not listen attentively. They are able to copy words from the board. However, no amount of vocabulary building seems to help them to produce language in an ordinary teaching–learning session. In spite of their years spent in English language instruction, they simply go through the same cycle over and over again while they remain in the same silent stage even after they reach the undergraduate level.

Stage 2: Early production

General features of ordinary learners at this stage

According to research, this stage may last up to six months. During this stage, learners will develop a receptive and active vocabulary of about 1,000 words. Students can usually speak in one- or two-word phrases. They can use short language chunks that have been memorized, although these chunks may not always be used correctly.

General features of learners with poor proficiency

As per our study conducted at the University of Colombo, Sri Lanka, students belonging to levels 1 and 2, the two lowest proficiency groups, are expected to have a vocabulary of 2,000 words upon reaching level 3. This standard is set for them to reach after having studied English for two years at the undergraduate level (needless to say, this is in addition to their primary and secondary education). This shows that in terms of vocabulary (number of words), most undergraduates are still in the early production stage or even lower. Some of them can use short, memorized language chunks, but not always correctly.

Stage 3: Speech emergence

General features of ordinary learners at this stage

According to experts, by this stage, students will have developed a vocabulary of about 3,000 words. They are able to communicate with simple phrases and sentences. Also, they can ask simple questions that are not always grammatically correct. In addition, they are able to comprehend simple narratives with the support of the teacher and visual aids. They will also be able to do some content work with teacher support.

General features of learners with poor proficiency

Those undergraduate learners at this stage will have a similar capacity in regard to vocabulary even though it is not always used in the correct context. Sometimes learners may use vocabulary in a totally incorrect way, manifesting their lack of usage in favour of the memorization of the meaning of English words in their mother tongue. This may happen with keen second language learners as a result of having tried a variety of ways to learn/speak English over a decade who finally resort to learning words in English from a dictionary and memorizing the meaning in their mother tongue. The other features of an ordinary second language learner will generally be present in the undergraduates with low proficiency who can nevertheless be found in the speech emergence stage.

Students who belong to the next two, higher, stages of intermediate and advanced fluency are very few in number and this is represented in our study.

Nevertheless, their presence was felt as they showed a higher level of fluency during the interviews that were conducted for the study.

Stage 4: Intermediate fluency

General features of ordinary learners at this stage

English language learners at the intermediate fluency stage are said to have a vocabulary of 6,000 words that they actively use. They try to use more complex sentences in their speech as well as in writing. They do not hesitate to express opinions on matters. They will ask questions to clarify doubts in class. English language learners in the intermediate fluency stage will be able to study other subjects in the medium of English with a good deal of teacher support. They will be able to comprehend English literary texts with their increasing ability. Research shows that these students will use strategies from their native language to learn content in English.

However, their writing at this stage will have many errors due to the complexity of the grammar and sentence structures found in the English language. Many students may be translating their written work from their native language. Students in this stage will be able to understand more complex concepts presented in English.

Features of learners in the intermediate fluency stage with issues in relation to speaking English

The general features of learners in the intermediate fluency stage in terms of vocabulary and the ability to write complex sentences, study in the medium of English, etc., are present among the group of learners in our sample. However, what they lack is the confidence to express their opinion, to ask questions or to clarify doubts. Often, a teacher may find them after class waiting to ask questions when no one is present, or with a close friend. If a teacher asks them a question during the class, they will hesitate and either utter a fragmented idea or resort to complete silence. This shyness and feeling of inadequacy may disappear over time, at least in the English language classroom, if the teacher approaches this type of learner tactfully. If the teacher adds to their existing fear/shyness, LAA may increase and the student may resort to complete silence in the classroom.

At the interviews we conducted, we found that some students who could be categorized in the intermediate fluency stage were very vocal and had a satisfactory command of the language. However, as they themselves admitted, 'We only feel safe to talk with you as you will not laugh at our mistakes.'

Stage 5: Advanced fluency

General features of ordinary learners at this stage

Cummins (1981) states that students may require 5–7 years to develop Cognitive Academic Language Proficiency Skills (CALPS) in a second language.

According to Collier (1987) and Klesmer (1994) it takes at least five years for students to catch up with native speakers in the academic aspects of L2. Therefore, learners at this stage may have near-native fluency in their ability to perform in English language even though they may need support from the teacher at the beginning of this stage in both speaking and writing.

Features of learners in the advanced fluency stage with issues in regard to speaking English

We came across very few learners in this stage who are reluctant to speak due to FLA and LAA. However, many of those few students stated that they did not want to speak in English and were more comfortable using mother tongue because society would think of them as trying to 'show off' if they spoke in English. Therefore, we can see that societal attitudes, not necessarily shyness or fear that others may laugh at them or their mistakes, still result in a lack of confidence to speak English among South Asian learners with advanced fluency.

The significance of the comparison between the two types of English language learners, i.e. the ordinary English language learners and the learners represented in the sample from our study (with the most highly proficient learners eliminated) is in the finding that the vast majority of these students with a long history of English language learning are still in the lowest stages of second language acquisition and cannot be thought of as 'passing' from one stage to another in the usual manner. Instead, they have been 'stagnating' in the lowest stage/s for many years without being able to move up to the next level in spite of the efforts from teachers as well as learners themselves. It is said that the early production stage will usually last for about six months, and to reach the last stage, advanced fluency, it is estimated that it will take 4–6 years. Unfortunately, as stated before, these students have been learning English for over ten years and many of them have not even reached speech emergence stage. Also, one may come across learners who struggle with repeating what the teacher says, which is indicative of a lower level than an ordinary second language learner with 4–5 months of English language learning.

This is mainly due to the language attitude issues that have been ignored throughout the students' language learning histories as we discussed in Chapter 4. The process we presented, in which existing language attitudes affect the language learner's language performance in a linear process, essentially brings learning to a standstill. The language attitudes prevalent in society towards the English language and its speakers weigh on the language learner in his or her attempt to produce it (primarily in spoken form) and influence the societal response to the language learner's attempt. When this response is negative and manifests itself in mockery, overcorrection, etc., the learner develops LAA which produces a lack confidence to speak English. As a result, the learner shapes his already existing language attitudes into negative attitudes towards the English language and its speakers due to his or her negative experiences. The same negativity is often self-directed towards his own English language speaking ability and this is projected onto English language learning as a whole. The totality of such a process is that learners, in spite of being in an English language classroom, have basically given up on learning English.

As stated elsewhere, this analysis is not meant to downplay many other factors such as poor language teaching, lack of facilities, etc. (discussed below), that affect English language education. However, our effort is to encourage the language planners, policy makers, curriculum designers, teachers, etc., to be aware of the crucial role that language attitudes play in our post-colonial South Asian societies and of the need to recognize its ill-effects on learners.

Understanding power relations

Our sample of students represents the large majority of rural and semi-rural English language learners in India, Pakistan, Bangladesh and Sri Lanka and the results are not in accord with the language acquisition stages discussed above when related to the number of years spent by these learners in second language acquisition. As we have said, the vast majority of learners have been 'living in' the silent stage or the early production stage and occasionally in the speech emergence stage for years without 'passing' on to the succeeding stage. It is said that covering basic interpersonal communication skills (BICS) can be acquired in six months to two years and CALPS in five to seven years, but these do not appear to apply to the students in our sample. This is because in the environment in which these learners find themselves, the study of English is different from ordinary (ideal) second language teaching–learning, like the environment in which Cummins carried out his study that led to his developing the BICS–CALPS theory among migrant students learning French. The main differences can be thought of in terms of (a) the quality of English language education the learners in question receive during their schooling, which can have a strong impact upon their English language acquisition, and (b) the societal attitudes related to English language that affect the learners in South Asian societies. In short, the quality of English language teaching during schooling, and the power play between the 'representatives' of English as the former colonial master's language and the rural/semi-rural masses, affects English language learning in South Asia.

It can be argued that low performance in English and remaining in the early stages of language acquisition despite a long history of learning English are due to poor English language education and a lack of facilities for English language education. We do not deny this, but our claim is that learners' lack of confidence as a factor is not a minor issue and it should not be neglected. What manifests itself in a lack of confidence to speak is often extended into the other aspects of English language learning and produces the overall poor performance in English language found in South Asia. Even where top-notch facilities are found in some schools and some students do perform well in English, the majority are unsuccessful. Likewise, the fact that a large majority from each country stated that they wanted to improve their speaking skill most of all and that they were either too shy, scared or both to speak English because of societal attitudes is indicative of a major context-specific problem in South Asia that must be addressed. Our sample also does not include the many students who do not qualify for undergraduate education. Therefore, we can somewhat safely assume that most of those who are unable to get into a university are also unable to perform in English as well. After all, if a large proportion of those who are 'smart enough' to be selected to the universities are negatively affected by language attitudes and are reluctant to speak English, there is a high probability that the larger percentage who do not qualify for university may be even more severely affected by the same.

Out of the sample that we interviewed, almost everyone from all four countries reported that their society is not supportive of speaking English in that people will laugh at the learners for making mistakes or think that the learners are trying to 'show off' and this creates LAA that manifests itself in a lack of confidence to speak in English in spite of speaking English being their most desired skill.

Although the ability to speak English seems to be a far-fetched dream for most of the students in South Asia in spite of their desire to do so, a large majority of respondents viewed those who spoke English well favourably. Interestingly, these favourable dispositions have some significant differences from country to country, even though all four countries were former British colonies that gained independence during the same period.[3] Students from Pakistan, India and Bangladesh viewed those who spoke English well as more 'intelligent' whereas students from Sri Lanka viewed them as belonging to a 'higher class' with better education facilities. In addition, students in India used words such as 'stylish, smart, beautiful, classy and graceful' to talk about people who spoke English well. Bangladeshi students saw English as a 'weapon' which was similar to the '*kaduwa*' (sword) notion in Sri Lanka, and those who spoke English well were considered to be 'influential and educated' people. While all of these 'call words' for English and its fluent speakers call for a separate study, it is noteworthy to mention that the association of 'intelligence' with English was not found among the Sri Lankan undergraduates. This could be attributed to the higher literacy rate in Sri Lanka (98%, the highest in South Asia) when compared to her South Asian neighbours, which has clearly differentiated access to English and access to education or intelligence. In contrast, in the other South Asian countries, owing to their lower literacy rates (India, 72.2% in 2015; Pakistan, 58% in 2017; Bangladesh, 72.76% in 2016) as literacy is associated with access to education and those who are literate may be considered educated and therefore may tend to be viewed as more intelligent. Interestingly, given the association of English with education in these countries, it is not surprising that one of the terms most associated with their perception of locals who spoke English is that they were considered 'literate'.

In the interviews and on the open questionnaires on which students could write anything related to their English language learning/speaking experiences, the call words for English and phrases they used to express their views were highly significant.

It must be noted that neither the questionnaire nor the interview questions mentioned 'confidence' or a lack of it. That word was carefully avoided to allow the respondents to express their own feelings with their own chosen words. Interestingly, respondents themselves frequently used confidence along with other words/phrases/utterances/sentences and the frequency with which anxiety related words appear in the sample shows the strength of the power play between the English language and society in post-colonial South Asia (see Chapter 3).

Power words were associated with those who speak English well, in contrast to what learners perceive themselves as being able to do. For instance, those who speak English well are seen as being able to 'handle any situation', which is in contrast to a learner who wants to speak in English 'without showing' his or her 'face'. The recurrent reference to being 'nervous' when trying to speak English has been uniformly noted among the young generation in all four South Asian nations. Learners feel 'inferior' when speaking in English, while seeing others who speak English as having 'awesome personalities' and as 'more refined'. This is another instance where the power play is very prominent. It is as if the perceived power emanating from those who speak English overwhelms the English language learner and creates the very anxiety which manifests itself in a lack of confidence to speak the language and it is apparent that learners who are overcome by anxiety to use a language in its primary form, speaking, are affected in the language learning in general.

It is also interesting to note that the presence of representatives of the colonial master's language is not always physical, but can also be imaginary, understandably, due to negative experiences in the learners' English language learning history as discussed before. Also, the power play, very interestingly, takes place in the presence of complete 'non-representatives' of the colonial master's language as well. For instance, in Pakistan and Bangladesh, learners reveal that they are afraid and are shy to speak in English because those who do not speak English at all would laugh at them if and when these learners try to speak in English. One student in Bangladesh blatantly said that when he spoke English others would ask him, 'You are a Bangla dog. Why are you barking in English?' The reference to 'dog' may symbolize the lowliness and the non-English speakers' recognition of being a Bangladeshi as somehow lower than being an Englishman, hence he is sarcastic towards the learner who speaks English, the colonial master's language. The learner is said to be trying to elevate himself. Also, it could be interpreted in a context which is specific to Bangladesh as well: Bangladesh is built upon a language and is a predominantly monolingual society; our interactions with Bangladeshis reveal that they are very passionate about their language, a similarity as we perceived as being shared by Sindhis in Pakistan. They take great pride in their native language and in speaking it. Therefore, the Bangladeshi non-English speaker may not like to see another Bangladeshi (the reference to a dog may also denote familiarity) speak English to show off – denoted by barking in English – and may be reminding him of his roots with 'You are a Bangla dog …', which has to be given more power than the foreign language. Whichever the connotation is, the expression is pregnant with language attitudes.

How can the responses of the learners when speaking with the native speaker be interpreted? The ease, enthusiasm and the confidence with which they interacted revealed that there was not any anxiety in them. The power dynamics that are described above seemed to not be valid at all. The live representation of the colonial master's language, the white man with an American accent, was not feared at all, but liked! This was most obvious with students from Bangladesh and Pakistan, Sindhis in particular. Some possible readings would be that learners are aware of the non-judgmental environment they are operating in; also there was no long-term effect in speaking with a stranger and the possibility of experimenting with English speaking with a native speaker of English in a non-learning setting may also have contributed to the enthusiasm. In hindsight, we question whether the very idea of speaking with a 'legitimate owner of the language' makes learners more confident and enthusiastic so that LAA does not occur. This area clearly merits further investigation.

It is evident that in other cases learners experience anxiety about speaking English as a result of the power dynamics related to the English language and its speakers. The language power dynamics are expressed via language attitudes, which learners are both aware of and affected by. As a result, they experience anxiety and, as the study reveals, for some it is FLCA only and for some others it is LAA, which may include some elements of FLCA (excluding test anxiety) as part of it. The effects of this anxiety can be long term, as MacIntyre (1995) explains in discussing the psychological process that anxious learners go through:

> Anxious students are focused on both the task at hand and their reactions to it. For example, when responding to a question in class, the anxious student is focused on answering the teacher's question and evaluating the social implications of the answer while giving it. To the extent that self-related cognition increases, task-related cognition is restricted, and performance suffers. Anxious students therefore will not learn as quickly as relaxed students.
> (p. 96)

Given the stages of language acquisition that the learners are in, it can be argued that the lack of confidence to speak English due to the anxieties they experience has been projected onto other language domains such as reading and writing. This is not to disregard the effects of poor teaching, the lack of facilities for English language education and their effects on learners, but to bring into focus the importance of recognizing the context-specific features of learners and the needs that arise from such contexts vis-à-vis English language education. As MacIntyre (1995) puts it, '... the effects of anxiety may be more complex than has been implied by Sparks and Ganschow (1991, 1993a, 1993b). If anxiety arises during learning then anxious students will perform poorly because they have learned less' (p. 96).

The adverse effects of not rectifying anxiety-related problems in English language education by considering the context-specific nature of the learner could very well be one of the main reasons for the poor results in English language education in South Asia and why students are stuck in the lowest language acquisition stages.

This does not mean that the stages of second language acquisition and the theory of BICS, common underlying proficiency (CUP) and CALPS are inaccurate. They remain valid in terms of describing the features of learners passing through each stage and the skills second language learners acquire gradually. What can be disputed is the time it takes to pass through these stages and to acquire the said skills, and a generalization of the environment/social context in which the teaching–learning process takes place.

The findings of this study are in line with some of the criticisms on the conversational/academic distinction that has been made by Edelsky et al. (1983), Rivera (1984), and Martin-Jones and Romaine (1986) in regard to Cummin's theory. One of the major criticisms is that Cummin's theory reflects an autonomous perspective on language, ignoring locations and power relations. The findings of this study put forth a similar argument not only in contrast to Cummin's theory, but also against the generalization of the stages of language acquisition in terms of duration. Otherwise, the study supports the descriptions of learners found in each stage of second language acquisition with some minor deviations as discussed above, and supports fully the order in which they acquire the basic communication skills and the higher order cognitive skills.

Language Attitude Anxiety as a projected element

There are three domains into which LAA is projected in the post-colonial South Asian English language learners' life: (a) from the outside society into the English language classroom and vice versa, (b) from speaking English to learning English in general and (c) from the history of the learner's English language learning to the present.

The LAA that learners experience as a result of the attitude changing process they go through as described in Chapter 4 (Figure 4.1), both inside and outside the language classroom, influences each other. The LAA learners experience inside the classroom is projected onto their English language use in the outside society and vice versa causing them to lack confidence to speak English in these settings.

LAA can also be projected onto other areas of language learning and performance. For instance, if a learner is overcorrected by a teacher or made to feel low due to their incorrect pronunciation, he or she will not be keen to speak in front of the teacher again. The learner may not be regular in attending the class. Then he or she will miss out and tend to neglect written work given by the teacher. Eventually his or her overall performance will suffer. 'Students who experience negative affect and who are frightened by oral evaluation are not likely to exhibit positive attitudes toward language class ...' (Phillips, 1992, p. 22).

One can argue that this is common to other subjects. However, our sample consists of predominantly undergraduates and we made an attempt to exclude groups with high English language proficiency. In all four countries, those who get into a university are considered academically excellent. However, a vast majority of the learners in our sample are not proficient in English in spite of their overall academic excellence. Among them, a very significant percentage expresses their desire to speak English and their reluctance to do so. If those who are academically proven to be outstanding students feel that they are 'not good enough' in English, there is a very high probability that the vast majority who do not pass the university entrance examinations have even lower proficiency in English, which contributes to the overall failure of English language education over the past 70 years in these countries.

If it were poor teaching, a lack of facilities, etc., that has played the biggest role in the failure of English language teaching, one must ask why poor teaching, a lack of facilities and the like do not affect the learners in their other subjects? This leads us to believe that most of these learners fail to learn English because of a projected LAA that stems from negative experiences in their English language speaking and learning history.

Language attitudes are difficult to measure, as are any attitudes in general. However, we believe that living in a particular context, be it a country, region, area, as a learner, teacher and a researcher we have a better understanding of the general colour of attitudes in South Asia and that we have a very specific, sharp and intuitive knowledge of it that is difficult for others to understand. Having said that, we have made this attempt to present our findings in order to help others understand the relationship between the language attitudes of a society and their effects on English language learners. We have also attempted to link the problems related to language attitudes to the unsatisfactory performance in English language education in the post-colonial South Asian region. We have not gone into a very heavy statistical analysis in analysing our data but have tried to present the evidence in a more qualitative framework, considering the abstractness of the main variable, 'language attitudes' in our study. Given the inherently qualitative nature of language attitudes and the vast range of perceptions that learners have in regard to the English language, we believe that a more quantitative approach wouldn't have been able to capture the variety of English language attitudes that are found in South Asia.

Also, with our preliminary 'hunch' that there is much more than what is apparent affecting English language education in our countries, we have designed our data collection tools to distinguish between Foreign Language Classroom Anxiety (FLCA) and what is not FLCA, which we have labelled as LAA. Accordingly, we attempted to delve deeply into the learners' psyche through interviews and encouraging free expression, which we believed loosened their tongues in the way we anticipated. As we have mentioned before, students believe that they lack confidence to speak English and this is attributable to LAA affecting their ability. This is an important finding, as according to Bailey, 'What they believe may be more important than any external reality' (1983, p. 86).

One may argue, by looking at the quantitative nature of most studies related to language anxiety available, that our study may need more support in terms of figures and numbers. Notwithstanding this, we want to emphasize the human element in the language attitudes described in our study, as Phillips (1992) aptly says:

> ... rejecting any association between anxiety and performance based on insufficient statistical evidence seems to ignore the human element within the anxiety/language learning framework. Why does the question of their relationship still seem so intriguing on an intuitive level? It is because ***anxiety is important from a psychological/attitudinal viewpoint***, if only modestly supported by statistical data.
>
> (p. 20)

We would like to end this chapter by noting that what learners believe is more important than any third-party description of the external reality and that anxiety is important from a psychological/attitudinal viewpoint. Learners believe that they lack confidence to speak English and LAA causes this lack of confidence. Therefore, LAA has to be eliminated with an approach that is more psychological than linguistic.

Conclusion

This chapter details the features of the language learners in terms of social, mental and educational constructs. Learner identity, possible selves and the language acquisition stages are used to better understand the learners' problem with a lack of confidence to speak English and how that lack of confidence seems to project its effects into English language learning in general. Also, the power structure within which the learners operate is discussed in relation to their responses towards their history of speaking and learning English.

Notes

1 Herein, 'Who spoke English "well"' does not necessarily mean someone whose English is like that of a native speaker or even a fluent local speaker; it may simply mean someone who spoke 'some' English but spoke 'well' in the eyes of the frightened learner. The higher the perceived fluency of the speaker, the greater the fear that is created in the learner.

2 There may be instances where some learners pick up after being ridiculed in instances that are listed above and start performing better. However, such cases are rare.

3 Even though Bangladesh was created in 1971, it was East Pakistan before and Pakistan gained independence in 1947, at the same time as India followed by Sri Lanka in 1948.

References

Bailey, K. M. (1983). Competitiveness and anxiety in adult second language learning: Looking at and through the diary studies. In H. W. Seliger and M. H. Long (Eds.), *Classroom-oriented research in second language acquisition* (pp. 67–102). Rowley, MA: Newbury House.

Bernstein, B., & Solomon, J. (1999). Pedagogy, identity and the construction of a theory of symbolic control. *British Journal of Sociology of Education*, 2(2), 265–279.

Burke, P. J. (2006). Identity change. *Social Psychology Quarterly*, 69(1), 81–96.

Coll, C., & Falsafi, L. (2010). Learner identity. An educational and analytical tool. *Revista de Educación*, 353, 211–233.

Collier, V. P. (1987). Age and rate of acquisition of second language for academic purposes. *TESOL Quarterly*, 21, 617–641.

Cummins, J. (1981). The role of primary language development in promoting educational success for language minority students. In California State Department of Education (Ed.), *Schooling and language minority students: A theoretical framework* (pp. 3–49). Los Angeles: Evaluation, Dissemination and Assessment Center, California State University.

Edelsky, C, Hudelson, S., Altwerger, B., Flores, B., Barkin, F., & Jilbert, K. (1983) Semilingualism and language deficit. *Applied Linguistics*, 4(1), 1–22.

Ellis, R. (1985). *Understanding second language acquisition*. Oxford: Oxford University Press.

Ellis, R. (2008). *The study of second language acquisition*. Oxford: Oxford University Press.

Foote, N. N. (1951). Identification as the basis for a theory of motivation. *American Psychological Review*, 16, 14–21.

Granger, C. A. (2004). *Silence in second language learning: A psychoanalytic reading*. Clevedon: UK: Multilingual Matters.

Horwitz, E. K. (1988). The beliefs about language learning of beginning university foreign language students. *The Modern Language Journal*, 72(3), 283–294.

Johnson, T. R. (2011). *Foreign language learner identity: A sociocultural perspective*. The University of Texas at Austin, unpublished MA dissertation.

Klesmer, H. (1994). Assessment and teacher perceptions of ESL student achievement. *English Quarterly*, 26(3), 5–7.

Koay, J. (2018). What is learner identity? EduMaxi. *Journal of English for Academic Purposes*, 33, 119–120. Dankook University. Retrieved from: http://www.edumaxi.com/what-is-learner-identity/

MacIntyre, P. D. (1995). How does anxiety affect second language learning? A reply to Sparks and Ganschow. *The Modern Language Journal*, 79(1), 90–99.

Marcus, H., & Nurius, P. (1986). Possible selves. *American Psychologist*, 41, 954–969.

Martin-Jones, M., & Romaine, S. (1986). Semilingualism: A half-baked theory of communicative competence. *Applied Linguistics*, 7(1), 26–38.

McDonald, V., & Mitsutomi, M. (2005). Factors in learning second language and culture. *Academic Exchange Quarterly*, 9(2), 56–68.

Norton, P. B. (1995). Social identity, investment, and language learning. *TESOL Quarterly*, 29(1), 9–31.

Norton, P. B. (2000). Identity and language learning: Gender, ethnicity and educational change. Harlow, UK: Pearson Education.

Osguthorpe, R. T. (2006). Learning that grows. Current developments in technology-assisted education. Retrieved from http://www.sustainicum.at/files/projects/289/en/additional/learning%20that%20grows.pdf. Accessed 24 May 2019

Phillips, E. M. (1992). The effects of language anxiety on students' oral test performance and attitudes. *The Modern Language Journal*, 76(1), 14–26. Retrieved from: http://www.jstor.org/stable/329894. Accessed 16 July 2018, 10:34 UTC.

Preston, D. R. (1989). *Sociolinguistics and second language acquisition*. Oxford: Basil Blackwell.

Rivera, C. (Ed.). (1984). *Language proficiency and academic achievement.* Clevedon, England: Multilingual Matters. Retrieved from: https://knoema.com/atlas/India/topics/Education/Literacy/Adult-literacy-rate; https://profit.pakistantoday.com.pk/2017/05/26/literacy-rate-falls-by-2pc-economic-survey-2016-17/; https://www.dhakatribune.com/bangladesh/education/2018/03/21/unesco-bangladesh-literacy-rate-reaches-time-high-72-76-2016

Sparks, R., & Ganschow, L. (1991). Foreign language learning difficulties: Affective or native language aptitude differences? *Modern Language Journal*, 75, 3–16.

Sparks, R., & Ganschow, L. (1993a). The impact of native language learning problems on foreign language learning: Case study illustrations of the linguistic coding deficit hypothesis. *Modern Language Journal*, 77, 58–74.

Sparks, R. L., & Ganschow, L. (1993b). Searching for the cognitive locus of foreign language learning difficulties: Linking first and second language learning. *Modern Language Journal*, 77, 289–302.

6 Fight fire with fire

Introduction

Finding the point for intervention to build confidence is as important as identifying the problems associated with language attitudes. The way to defeat Language Attitude Anxiety (LAA) involves finding the strategic point to intervene and eliminate it. Since LAA manifests in a lack of confidence to speak, the best approach to tackle LAA is by building confidence. The approach we recommend for doing this is mainly psychological and works by using habituation and exposure to scenarios in which learners speak in English. Thus, the course that we have designed to build learner confidence requires special material and teachers who are specifically trained to teach in the course.

The remedy

We believe that rectifying measures to help English language learners who are affected by LAA in post-colonial South Asia should take into consideration the results of our analysis. The cyclical nature of language attitudes development (discussed in Chapter 4) is helpful in this respect, because it makes space for intervention to steer the cycle of language attitude formation in a positive direction. Learners are affected by societal language attitudes that filter into their consciousness as society reveals its attitudes towards the language learners when they attempt to use English in spoken form. These attitudes are revealed in the 'mockery', 'making fun' and other forms of ridicule that have a negative impact on the way learners establish and shape their own attitudes towards the language and its speakers. As a result, learners also form negative attitudes towards their own speaking ability that may be extended to their English language learning in general.

Developing a platform to strategically intervene is as challenging as analysing the process of how language attitudes change. However, our attempt of intervention occurs at a stage where there is a clear manifestation of these attitudinal changes taking place in English language learners: that is the stage at which we notice the lack of confidence to speak English in their fears/shyness/uncertainty with hesitation/stammering, etc.

As discussed, this lack of confidence is generated by LAA as a reaction to societal language attitudes. In other words, LAA acts as a bridge between societal negative language attitudes in society and the inside of the language classroom. We believe that it is at this juncture that the intervention needs to take place. In metaphorical terms, the bridge that is being constructed must be destroyed in a way that builds learners' confidence to speak English. This can be accomplished by using speaking activities and encouraging speech, the language skill which almost all the learners across countries desired the most.

The required language attitudinal change, that is, to change learners' negative attitudes towards their own speaking ability (and then learning) will result in positive language attitudes, thereby eliminating LAA while building confidence to speak English. Once this is accomplished, learner positivity, rather than negativity, will be projected into other areas of English language learning. Changing language attitudes needs to be viewed as part of the cyclical process that is discussed related to language attitude development in Chapter 4 so that learners are steered away from negativity and towards positivity. By building confidence to speak English within the four walls of the classroom, learner positivity can be projected outside the classroom. From a position of confidence, learners become less hesitant to speak English both inside and outside the classroom. This initial confidence also acts as a foundation upon which we further develop learners' language abilities while developing the confidence that has already been instilled.

The need to build confidence

The lack of confidence to speak English is present inside the English language classroom as well as outside it. Therefore, building confidence in the learners to speak English both inside and outside the language classroom is the challenge we face. Initially, for teachers in South Asia, this may look like a far-fetched dream, but we have had success in developing a course, 'Confidence Building to Speak English' that aims at the classroom level and that has produced good results.

First and foremost, the negative attitudes of learners towards their own speaking ability need to be transformed into positive attitudes in order to eliminate LAA. It is a truism that changing the attitudes of an entire society is incredibly difficult. In contrast, it is easier to change the attitudes of an individual learner. In fact, it is relatively easy to change the attitudes of an English language learner towards his or her own English-speaking ability simply by emphasizing speech activities and letting the learner's ability to speak in these activities 'speak for itself'. Learners already have a great desire to speak English and all they lack is the confidence to do so. Therefore, building confidence to speak English is our most compelling need, and fulfilling it is our first step towards making learner language attitudes positive.

The approach we suggest to build confidence is mainly psychological and partly methodological. If confidence in speaking English is built by using speaking, the skill learners most desire to improve yet are most vulnerable in using, the confidence building process will be stronger and longer lasting. This built confidence must then be maintained and further developed in subsequent English language courses.

The basis for the remedial measure needed to approach the learners is in the understanding that the learners already have LAA compounded with complex learner identities, conflicting roles and frustrating possible selves in regard to English language learning and its uses. Also, the relationship they have with speaking English is of a love–hate variety. Thus, any rectifying measure must be well planned and executed by personnel specifically trained to cater to a target group with these characteristics. It is worth quoting MacIntyre's (1995) opinion in this regard:

> One area in which both the cognitive interference model of anxiety and Sparks and Ganschow's (1991, 1993a, 1993b) linguistic coding deficit hypothesis converge is in the remedial action suggested to address language learning deficits. In both cases, it is suggested that attempts to reduce language anxiety may require some skills training as a supplement to anxiety reduction strategies in order to compensate for deficiencies created by anxiety arousal, native language problems, or both.
>
> (p. 97)

The 'Building Confidence to Speak English' course we have designed consists of very specific 'skill training' in its teaching methodology along with material that is tailor-made for learners with the aforesaid features.

Our view that the anxiety related to language learning is more serious than previously thought is also shared by Phillips (1992), although LAA is not identified in her work:

> ... in today's proficiency-oriented classroom, teachers must continue to view foreign language anxiety as a serious problem to be confronted in the effort to encourage students to further their education in foreign languages.
>
> (p. 22)

The initial step in 'confronting' the serious problem of anxiety must be taken within the domain of English language teaching–learning itself. Even though Phillips suggests that the most effort should be directed at encouraging students to further their education in the foreign/second language, our view is that the effort should be directed towards projecting the confidence to speak English from inside the classroom to the environment outside the classroom, as well as from speaking in particular to language learning as a whole. In this way, the learner will not have any hesitancy about his or her further education in English and English teaching in the region will become more successful.

The number of studies that have been carried out in regard to foreign language anxiety is evidence that many learners experience some level of foreign language anxiety. However, studies on the shyness and/or fear of being ridiculed in society and the uncertainty this causes among English language learners in the post-colonial South Asian context and the relationship between this anxiety and societal language attitudes are very few, with most of them limited to the classroom setting. The type of remedial actions to be taken is also rarely, if ever, presented in the form of a well-planned curriculum.

Fight fire with fire: using the fear factor to eliminate fear

As the saying goes, 'Fight fire with fire'. To get rid of fear, shyness, and uncertainty in regard to *speaking English*, we must assume that *speaking itself* would be the best way to counter it. It is also wise to focus on the speaking skill as it is what the large majority of students most want to learn. Therefore, 'A Confidence Building Course to Speak English' has been developed with the objective of building student confidence to speak English through the use of speaking activities. The underlying principle is that eliminating the fear factor requires use of the activity that causes fear in order to habituate the learner and progressively reduce anxiety by gradually exposing the learner to the very activity that causes their anxiety. At the same time, it embeds the idea that speech will act as the catalyst to build confidence to speak and learn English. The approach is psychological because the lack of confidence, fear, shyness and uncertainty are psychological states. It is also assumed that if students are immersed in an environment which involves the production skill, speaking, they will not feel so much fear/shyness/uncertainty as they will be used to speaking English and listening to it during the immersion process.

The psychology of the approach

According to Shpancer (2010), a practising clinical psychologist, the experience of anxiety/fear-related feelings is the result of arousal in the nervous system. Some people are afraid to use elevators, some fear darkness, etc. The reason may be traced to some negative experience they had in relation to an object, a person or a particular incident. The American Psychological Association (APA) in its Clinical Practice Guidelines explains these situations:

> When people are fearful of something, they tend to avoid the feared objects, activities or situations. Although this avoidance might help reduce feelings of fear in the short term, over the long term it can make the fear become even worse.

According to Shpancer (2010) and as per everyone's general experience, when we avoid something that scares us, we tend to experience a sense of failure. Every time we avoid a feared object or situation, our anxiety gains strength while we lose some of our confidence. Every time we avoid the feared object or situation, we accumulate another experience of failure. This adds to the already existing failure, confirming our weakness.

English language learners in post-colonial South Asia experience LAA as a result of negative experiences in their language learning/speaking history, which causes a lack of confidence to speak English. As a result, they are scared/shy/uncertain about speaking English. This anxiety manifests itself in the language classroom in front of teachers and peers, as well as outside the classroom, in front of friends, outsiders, etc. Some learners are hesitant to speak anywhere in front of anyone. As such, they tend to avoid people who speak English and contexts and situations in which English is spoken. This causes the anxiety to remain novel, which arouses their nervous system in the way it was explained in clinical psychological terms. Avoidance not only maintains learners' anxiety but magnifies it. Shpancer (2010) says that finally, avoidance takes over and eliminates practice completely. He says, 'Without practice it is difficult to gain mastery. Without mastery, confidence is less likely to rise.'

The remedy is habituation. In clinical psychology, this principle is used in anxiety treatment. Merriam-Webster Dictionary defines habituation as 'the diminishing of an innate response to a frequently repeated stimulus'. The Glossary of Psychology (in AlleyDog.com) describes it as follows:

> As humans, we get used to things. Something that is new and incredibly exciting can become boring. This tendency to have decreased responsiveness to something is habituation.

According to Shpancer (2010), habituation refers to the fact that nervous system arousal decreases after repeated exposure to the same stimulus. Simply, it means that familiar things become less exciting over time.

In the 'Confidence Building to Speak English' course, learners are habituated to speaking in English, for 3–4 hours a day over 3–4 weeks, without undue concern for the accuracy of their speech. In other words, learners are continually exposed to spoken English every day over a period of time. Shpancer (2010) views exposure as the 'most potent medicine' known to psychology, particularly for anxiety treatments. The APA in its Clinical Practice Guidelines identifies exposure therapy as 'a psychological treatment that was developed to help people confront their fears ... Exposure therapy helps break the pattern of avoidance and fear.'

Shpancer (2010) states that exposure scares people. However, as one faces fear it starts to decrease as one becomes habituated. As time goes by and the effects of habituation begin to manifest themselves with continued exposure to spoken English and the practice of speaking English in the classroom, the learners' initial hesitation, fear, nervousness gradually diminish.

In order to make learners less fearful in the beginning, the mechanism the 'Building Confidence to Speak English' course adopts is one in which the initial activities incorporate miming. This means that learners are not expected to utter a word, but only to listen to the teacher and mime accordingly. In our experience teaching this course, this has been proven to be a very effective means of breaking the ice. In these activities learners get to act and enjoy themselves and most begin to lose their sense of fear by focusing on the miming activity, which starts the course out with a bang. Exposure to English language in spoken form is then gradually increased throughout the course.

APA Clinical Practice Guidelines further state:

> ... in this [exposure] therapy psychologists create a safe environment in which to 'expose' individuals to the things they fear and avoid. The exposure to the feared objects, activities or situations in a safe environment helps reduce fear and decrease avoidance.

Just as psychologists create a safe environment to expose the patients to the objects they fear, the confidence building classroom is turned into a 'safe zone' where learners speak English and English only. The safe zone for building confidence is created within the four walls of the classroom and facilitated by the teacher to be a friendly approach, using carefully designed materials. The characteristics of a 'safe zone' are discussed in detail in Chapter 8.

Psychologists view exposure as effective in reducing anxiety on four different levels: (a) physiological, (b) psychological, (c) behavioural and (d) emotional (Shpancer, 2010).

Exposure is recommended as better than avoidance at a *physiological level* because habituating the nervous system is considered a physiological antidote to anxiety (ibid.). On the *psychological level*, confronting fear/shyness/uncertainty instead of giving in to it leaves a person with a sense of achievement. Likewise, every time learners speak/respond in English, they confront their own fear/shyness/uncertainty and gain power; their LAA loses strength. For instance, learners may feel, 'Now that I have to speak English, let me do it even though it is not easy.' Every time this occurs, learners gather courage and accumulate evidence of their ability to cope with speaking English. In order for this to happen, the safe zone in the classroom must operate at all times. Likewise, the teacher's role (which has been changed – see Chapter 8) in following the teaching methodology that has been designed for the course is of paramount importance.

On the *behavioural level*, habit formation takes place as learners confront their fear/shyness/uncertainty and begin to develop and master skills. When learners are exposed to speaking English on a daily basis, they begin to develop their speaking skills, maybe at a slow pace and to a low level at first, but as they gain some control over their use of the language to carry out the assigned activities, they begin to feel that their chances of failure diminish and this in turn reduces the number of reasons for anxiety.

Exposure is helpful at an *emotional level* as well. Shpancer (2010) observes that many anxiety issues have a *fear of fear* at their core. For example, English language has its own phonetics and phonetics themselves are neither dangerous nor scary. What usually puts the learners off is the sensation of fear that has arisen from overcorrection by teachers in regard to pronunciation; for example, the mispronunciation of the sound /p/ instead of /f/ is common because such sounds are absent in their mother tongue. However, when learners are exposed to situations where they have to speak English and where only English is spoken in a safe environment, they soon become habituated to the sounds and begin to lose the fear of fear that was caused by previous overcorrection. At the same time, they improve their emotional literacy because staying in the terrain helps them learn how to navigate, manage and work within an environment in which the fear of fear has been neutralized (Shpancer, 2010).

Exposing learners to an English language speaking environment is not simple. Especially if learners have been overloaded with negativity in their previous English language speaking and learning histories and have habituated themselves to avoidance over the years. It is not easy to get these learners to speak English or to get them used to an English-speaking environment. However, one definite advantage the teachers in the 'Building Confidence to Speak English' course have is understanding that these learners (a) are genuinely very keen to be able to speak English and (b) aware that avoiding speaking English does not help to get them anywhere they intend to go. So, unlike many patients the psychiatrist meets in his or her clinic, learners in the English language classroom are well aware of the disadvantages of avoiding speaking English and tend to respond willingly while forgetting their short-term discomfort and looking at exposure as a valuable long-term asset. It is therefore of the utmost importance that exposure is given in the right dosage, in the right environment and by the right person. Carefully designed and sequenced material, taught by teachers rigorously trained in specific teaching techniques and strategies, is essential to address the potential challenges of exposing learners to situations in which only English is spoken.

Exposure has proved successful, directly or indirectly, for most of the positive improvements achieved in the treatment of anxiety. In clinical psychology, the use of exposure as therapy is considered helpful in several ways. The APA Div. 12, Society of Clinical Psychology (as cited by APA Clinical Practice Guidelines) describes these as follows:

a Habituation: Over time, people find that their reactions to objects or situations that cause fear decrease.
b Extinction: Exposure can help weaken previously learned associations between the feared objects, activities or situations and bad outcomes.
c Self-efficacy: Exposure can help show the client that he or she is capable of confronting his or her fears and can manage feelings of anxiety.
d Emotional processing: During exposure, the client can learn to form new, more realistic beliefs about feared objects, activities or situations, and can become more comfortable with the experience of fear.

Learners in a classroom who are exposed to the English language in its spoken form over a period will begin to lose their fear/shyness/uncertainty due to habituation and their ability to speak English will gradually increase. As exposure gives them more opportunities to engage in speaking activities, their previous negative experiences will gradually be forgotten because the new experience of speaking English differs from their previous experiences. These new experiences are facilitated by teachers who are trained not to correct learner utterances, not to demand 'correct' answers, not to make learners work and perform individually, etc. (see more details in Chapter 8. When learners respond to the new classroom activities, they realize on their own that they are able to perform in English (even if it is not at a very high level) and this gives them the courage to cope with their lack of confidence. They become familiar with confronting their fear/shyness/uncertainty in regard to speaking English. Eventually, there will be not be an anxious arousal of the nervous system when learners are faced with situations in the classroom among their teachers and peers, as habituation leads to familiarity.

Psychologists believe that with anxiety, the only way out is through. For instance, Shpancer's (2010) view is that:

> If you're anxious about spiders, you will have to handle spiders. If you're scared of the elevator, you will have to ride the elevator repeatedly. If you dread talking in class, you will need to start talking in class. This is not easy to do, since confronting your fear will produce a lot of initial anxiety. You will have to stay in the feared situation and stay with the heightened fear response until it begins to subside, which it will, because it must by design.

The 'Building Confidence to Speak English' course has been designed to achieve a specific objective, i.e. to build learner confidence to speak English by exposing learners to English via a step-by-step process through which they become habituated to speaking, extinguish previous negative experiences and develop positive attitudes towards speaking English by increasing their self-awareness and helping them to face their fear of speaking English.

Conclusion

An analysis of the problem of LAA enables us to create a platform where we can intervene strategically to remedy the problem. Learners' lack of confidence is a manifestation of the effects of LAA. Therefore, building confidence to speak English is the best intervention to address the problem. The fear of speaking is addressed in the confidence building course by using speaking to build learner confidence with specially designed material and specifically trained teachers with a proper understanding of what is required to teach this type of learner. Our course uses a psychological approach in which habituation is the main method of eliminating LAA.

References

MacIntyre, P. D. (1995). How does anxiety affect second language learning? A reply to Sparks and Ganschow. *The Modern Language Journal*, 79(1), 90–99.

Phillips, E. M. (1992). The effects of language anxiety on students' oral test performance and attitudes. *The Modern Language Journal*, 76(1), 14–26. Retrieved from: http://www.jstor.org/stable/329894. Accessed 16 July 2018, 10:34 UTC.

Shpancer, N. (2010). Retrieved from: https://www.psychologytoday.com/blog/insight-therapy/201009/overcoming-fear-the-only-way-out-is-through

Sparks, R., & Ganschow, L. (1991). Foreign language learning difficulties: Affective or native language aptitude differences? ***Modern Language Journal***, 75, 3–16.

Sparks, R., & Ganschow, L. (1993a). The impact of native language learning problems on foreign language learning: Case study illustrations of the linguistic coding deficit hypothesis. ***Modern Language Journal***, 77, 58–74.

Sparks, R. L., & Ganschow, L. (1993b). Searching for the cognitive locus of foreign language learning difficulties: Linking first and second language learning. ***Modern Language Journal***, 77, 289–302.

https://www.alleydog.com/glossary/definition.php?term=Habituation

https://www.apa.org/ptsd-guideline/patients-and-families/exposure-therapy.aspx

7 Experimental course design and material

Introduction

In this chapter, the development of the experimental curriculum design for confidence building is discussed in terms of theoretical perspectives. These include the suitability of Basic Interpersonal Communication Skills (BICS), Common Underlying Proficiency (CUP) and the Cognitive Academic Language Proficiency Skills (CALPS) theory of Jim Cummins (2000a) as an overarching theory for the complete curriculum. This experimental curriculum has three courses in its developmental sequence, as subdivided by us, and is explained with illustrations. The course under discussion in this book, 'Building Confidence to Speak English', the first among these, is discussed at length, including: the use of speech as a catalyst to build confidence to speak/learn English; the use of Austin's Speech Act Theory, first discussed in his lecture series in 1955 (Austin, 1975) and as developed by Searle (1969) and further advanced by Bach and Harnish (1979) and Crystal (1994) for selecting speech functions. The application of Speech Act Theory in developing the material is presented with examples. The use of activities along with their potentials is detailed as discussed by Dubin and Olshtain (1987) in their book on course design. The sequencing and gradation of activities is analysed by juxtaposing Dubin's and Olshtain's activity potentials with Bloom's taxonomy (Bloom, 1956). Also this chapter demonstrates how repetition of speech acts in an ascending order of difficulty can reinforce a particular speech function. Next, examples of teaching material are given that highlight each of the said features. The chapter concludes with the related logistics of the Building Confidence to Speak English course.

The overarching theory and the sub-divisions of BICS, CUP and CALPS

The BICS, CUP and CALPS theory of Cummins (2000a) is the overarching theory for the entire curriculum design and it has been selected by considering the developmental sequence of the learner language. According to Cummins (1979), it takes a student about six months to two years to achieve BICS and 5–7 years for CALPS. However, in post-colonial South Asian countries such as

India, Pakistan, Bangladesh and Sri Lanka, a large majority of students, especially those from rural and semi-rural areas, are unable to utter a single comprehensive sentence in English after a decade of English language learning in the school system.

The context specificity of South Asian post-colonial English language learners is such that they lack confidence to speak English. As explained in the previous chapters, Language Attitude Anxiety, a psychological complex, can lead to poor performance in English both in its spoken and written forms. However, performing well in English is required for everyone at the undergraduate level in order to be a competent graduate today. Therefore, a carefully planned and gradually sequenced curriculum is required to lead students towards mastery of the language through a step-by-step process until they reach the levels needed for academic and career purposes. The follow-up on the Building Confidence to Speak English course leads students towards the type of English language proficiency required for higher studies. These more advanced courses namely, the Narrative-based Course and the English for Academic Purposes (EAP)/English for Specific Purposes (ESP) courses are developed with the Building Confidence to Speak English as their foundation (Figure 7.1).

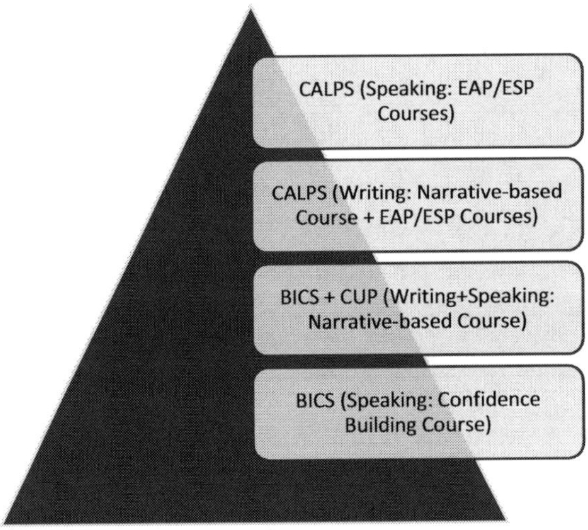

Figure 7.1 Structural design of the complete curriculum in terms of theoretical perspectives (with adaptations to Jim Cummins' Theory – 2000a[a]). BICS – Basic Interpersonal Communication Skills[b], CUP – Common Underlying Proficiency, and CALPS – Cognitive Academic Language Proficiency Skills.

a Jim Cummins' BICS, CUP and CALPS theory (2000a) discusses the skills a learner acquires and makes use of in the process of learning a second language.

b The Confidence Building Course aims at making use of the existing BICS of the learner (while developing them further).

c The Narrative-based Course aims at using Common Underlying Proficiency (CUP) between mother tongue and English language to develop BICS writing so that students are given the chance to transfer the skills, ideas and concepts that they learnt through stories in their mother tongue to English.

Theoretical linkages among the courses

At the end of the confidence building course, learners have achieved some level of BICS. They are able to communicate with their peers in English, especially in regard to the type of utterances needed for carrying out activities in the classroom. Also, one can hear occasional utterances, such as jokes, from learners outside the English language classroom amid the constraints placed on them by learner identity, role conflicts, etc., which were discussed in previous chapters.

The Narrative-based Course operates with CUP in mind. By making use of these underlying principles that are common to both the learner's mother tongue and English, we underscore the assumption that stories have concepts common to all languages and that reading stories in English will be supported by these common underlying concepts (Cummins, 2000b). When learners are given the chance to read story books, some of which are required for the course, and others which are chosen by the learner, the chances for CUP to operate are increased.

The EAP/ESP courses are developed for Cognitive Academic Language Proficiency (CALPS) to take place while traces of the Narrative-based Course are still lingering in them. For example, in EAP courses, lesson materials are designed in such a way that the lessons begin with a small narration thematically related to the subject/discipline that is being used for content.

Thematic linkages among the courses

A tightly knit curriculum with well-defined linkages is required to address the issues pertaining to English Language Teaching in post-colonial South Asian societies. With the large majority of students being unable to perform in English, we face a bleak picture, and with most of our students lacking confidence to speak English, these linkages cannot be only theoretical, but must also be thematic in terms of themes related to 'confidence'. This must be established and reinforced through the curriculum (Figure 7.2).

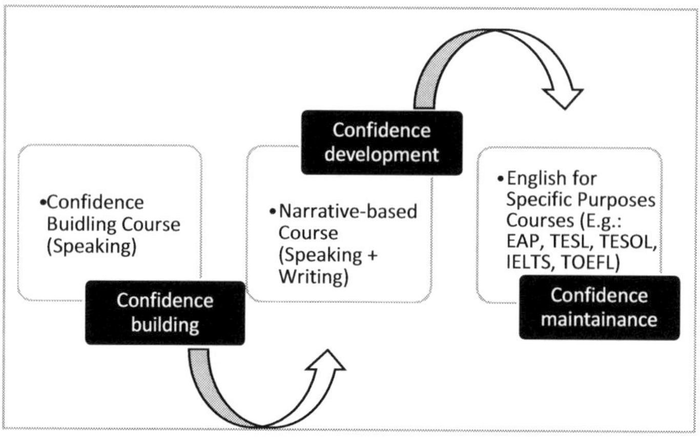

Figure 7.2 Structural development of the three courses along the theme of 'confidence'.

Throughout the Building Confidence to Speak English course, learners' most desired skill, i.e. speaking, is used to help learners eliminate Language Attitude Anxiety in order to speak English. In so doing, learner *confidence is built* in order to help them begin to speak English. The Narrative-based Course is designed with the use of stories, as the name suggests, and through these stories we improve English language proficiency while their built *confidence is developed.* Once learners pass this stage, it is expected that they have achieved some mastery of the language. Then the courses EAP and ESP are introduced. With these courses, English proficiency is further improved and the built and developed *confidence is maintained.*

Other possible linkages

Within the aforesaid structures, other linkages are not only possible but essential. For instance, there has to be a linkage in terms of teaching grammar and structures. In the Narrative-based Course, we teach some of the active voice (the simple, continuous and perfect) sentence structures while the perfect continuous and its parallels in the passive voice are taught in the ESP/EAP courses. At the same time, selected, basic parts of speech sections (e.g. regular and irregular nouns and verbs) can be taught in the Narrative-based Course while more advanced structures, such as main and subordinate clauses, may be taught in the ESP/EAP courses.

Moreover, linkages in terms of content, difficulty levels of tasks, etc., also have to be maintained in order to produce a tightly knit curriculum with well-articulated goals. This in turn will help measure output in terms of these linkages.

The Building Confidence to Speak English course

The structure

The structure of the confidence building course consists of material production, teaching methodology and assessment. For the material design, Speech Act Theory (Bach and Harnish, 1979; Crystal, 1994; Searle, 1969) is used along with principles of gradation and the sequencing of activities. As for the teaching methodology, techniques based on Cooperative Language Learning (CLL) are developed; they are discussed in detail in the chapter on methodology. Assessment is performance-based with students acting in groups to perform stage plays (Figure 7.3).

The material

The material for the Confidence Building Course has been developed using Speech Act Theory (Bach & Harnish, 1979; Crystal, 1994; Searle, 1969) that classifies all speech functions into five categories: Declaratives, Constatives, Commissives, Representatives and Directives. All of the speech activities in the set of modules belong to one of the above categories and represent a speech function. In addition, all of them serve the function of basic interpersonal communication.

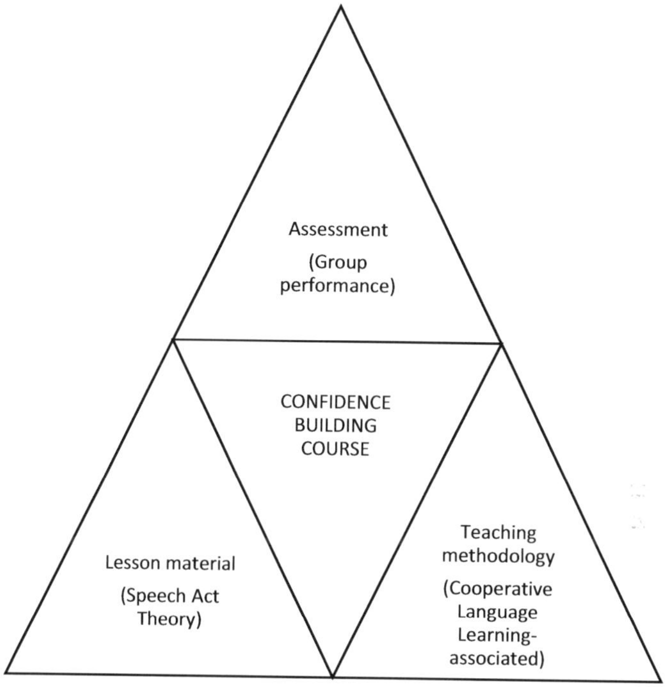

Figure 7.3 Internal structure of the Building Confidence to Speak English course.

The Communicative Potential Development and Cognitive Potential Development scales (Dubin & Olshtain, 1987) are used to measure the activity potential in the lesson materials. The sequence and gradation of activities within a module and between modules comply with the stages of the two scales. The Cognitive Potential Development scale, in its many stages, is juxtaposed with Bloom's taxonomy (Bloom, 1956). In other words, students, in the process of achieving a higher level of cognitive skills development, are made to go through a step-by-step developmental process which is similar to that professed by Bloom in his taxonomy.

The use of Speech Act Theory for selecting content to teach speech

Speech Act Theory

In general, speech acts are acts of communication. To communicate is to express a certain attitude and the type of speech act being performed corresponds to the type of attitude being expressed. For example, a statement expresses a belief, a request expresses a desire and an apology expresses a regret (Bach & Harnish, 1979).

As an act of communication, a speech act succeeds if the audience identifies, in accordance with the speaker's intention, the attitude being expressed. For philosophy of language in particular, the theory of speech acts underscores the importance of the distinction between language use and linguistic meaning (PRAGMATICS and SEMANTICS – the meaning of words and sentences). Statements, requests, promises and apologies are examples of major categories of communicative illocutionary acts (the intention of a speaker in saying a particular thing, e.g. naming, threatening, warning or promising, as opposed to the literal meaning of the words spoken): constatives (statements), directives, commissives (making a commitment, threat) and acknowledgments. Bach and Harnish (1979) use this nomenclature.

1 *Constatives*: affirming, announcing, answering, classifying, confirming, denying, informing, predicting, reporting, ranking, etc.
2 *Directives*: advising, asking, begging, dismissing, excusing, instructing, ordering, requesting, permitting, suggesting, urging, warning, etc.
3 *Commissives*: agreeing, guaranteeing, inviting, offering, promising, swearing, volunteering, etc.
4 *Acknowledgements*: apologizing, condoling, congratulating, greeting, thanking, accepting, acknowledging (an acknowledgement), etc.

Another more elaborative classification of speech acts is presented below.

Crystal (1994) details the following classification of illocutionary speech acts that one can perform while speaking.

1 Representatives: the speaker is committed, in varying degrees, to the truth of a proposition. For instance, to affirm, believe, conclude, deny and report. The following examples illustrate this point.
  E.g.: (a) The earth is flat. (b) Chomsky didn't write about peanuts. (c) It was a warm sunny day.

In all the above instances, the speaker represents the world as he or she believes it is.

2 Directives: the speaker tries to get the hearer to do something. For example, to request, challenge, insist, command, advise and suggest.
  E.g.: (a) Could you open the door, please? (b) I suggest you take a taxi. (c) Don't go too far.

The examples above illustrate that the speaker tries to make the world fit the words through the hearer.

3 Commissives: the speaker is committed, in varying degrees, to a certain course of action. For example, to promise, refuse, pledge, guarantee, vow or swear, a threat or an oath.
  E.g.: (a) I will be back. (b) We will not do that.

The instances shown above point out that the speaker undertakes to make the world fit the words through the speaker.

4 Expressives: the speaker expresses an attitude about a state of affairs. For instance, to congratulate, excuse, thank, deplore, apologize and welcome.
E.g.: (a) Congratulations! (b) I am really sorry.

These sentences indicate that the speaker makes words fit the world of feeling.

5 Declaratives: the speaker alters the external status or condition of an object or situation solely by making the utterance. For example, to resign, sack, appoint, name, christen, sentence (in court), bid (at auction), declare war, pronounce someone husband and wife.
E.g.: (a) Priest: I now pronounce you husband and wife. (b) Referee: You are out.

One can say in these cases that the speaker changes the world via words.

Speech activities in the course materials are planned and prepared to meet the above functions of language. There are some listening activities as well and some of them require students' passive listening only. However, reading and writing skills are only incorporated sparingly into the confidence building course. This is in keeping with the main objective of the course, i.e., to build confidence to *speak* English by not giving any significance to writing. This will be further discussed under the chapter on teaching methodology.

Sequencing and gradation of activities

Activity (workout) potentials

Speech activities are measured and graded according to the two scales recommended by Dubin and Olshtain (1987). They discuss the assessment of activities, which they call workouts, in terms of two potentials: communicative potential and cognitive potential.

As they present them, 'Workouts are language using and language learning activities which enhance the learner's overall acquisition process, providing planners and teachers with a variety of ways through which to make this process engaging and rewarding' (p. 96).

The activities are woven around the functions of speech as given in Speech Act Theory.

a Communicative potential development scale – stages
From 1 (most interactive) to 7 (least interactive).

1 New information is negotiated
Includes expression of, reaction to and interpretation of new information. For example, most workouts for small groups if the interaction among members of the group is in the target language.

2 New information is expressed

For example, making up a questionnaire, writing a letter of composition, giving an oral report, leaving a taped telephone message or a written message, providing information to someone else.

3 New information is used or applied

For example, writing a letter in response to an advertisement, filling out a form, answering a questionnaire which requires objective replies, organizing main ideas in a logical sequence, strip-story activities, gathering information outside of class or from peers.

4 New information is transferred

For example, filling in a table or a chart, completing a graph, putting indicators on a map, copying information.

5 New information is received but there is no verbal reaction

For example, communicating with a physical response such as drawing a picture, following a route shown on a map, following instructions to construct something.

6 No information is processed; focus is on form

For example, mechanical operations such as ordering, combining, adding, deleting, substituting; practicing a dialogue which has been memorized; reading aloud with attention to pronunciation.

7 New information is received (exposure only)[1]

For example, listening to a song, hearing a story read aloud, watching a TV program, or any extended listening period activities that do not require a physical response (p. 99).

We can see that at the least interactive level, there is exposure only and that at the point (5) level, new information is received but there is no verbal reaction expected. As the communicative potential is developed, more transferring, application and expression of new information is expected with the negotiation of new information at the peak. The goal of selecting and sequencing speech activities according to the scale is to help students reach this level gradually.

This can be achieved in a number of ways: for instance, with a student population that is very weak in English language proficiency, the goal of achieving the highest interactive communicative potential, i.e. the negotiation of new information may not be achieved by the end of the activity. Instead, one can aim to achieve this level by the end of the week, month or even by the end of the course if necessary. In the latter case, each activity can cater to achieving one level of communicative potential at a time.

For example, one can begin a chain of activities with a listening task where students are exposed to the language but a verbal reaction is not required. Instead, learners can listen to the teacher and mime; or a worksheet can be given with 'fill in the blanks' as an assigned task to be completed as pair work; only then gradually moving on to more interactive activities. Conversely, with a relatively higher language proficiency group, the highest level of communicative potential can be aimed for at the end of each activity with steps in between being used to cover the other stages that come between the least interactive and the most interactive.

Lesson materials preparation should also be carried out with special attention given to the sequencing and gradation of the activities in terms of communicative potential at a social level, for instance, initially with tasks that involve individual involvement in accomplishing a simple task, say, listening to a song; and gradually with tasks that involve pair work and group activities where learner interaction with peers is expected to be at the maximum level.

b Cognitive potential development scale – stages

Dubin and Olshtain (1987) present a scale to grade and sequence activities in course material with a view towards developing the cognitive potential of the learner. It spans from low (7) to high (1), with memory as the lowest in cognitive potential and evaluation as the highest.

1 Evaluation

Making a judgement of good or bad, right or wrong, valuable or useless, according to standards designed by the learner.

For example: writing a critical review of a book, play or TV program.

2 Synthesis

Solving a problem that requires original, creative thinking.

For example: working with a group on large-scale project such as planning and producing a class newsletter, a play, a panel discussion, etc.

3 Analysis

Solving a problem in the light of conscious knowledge of the parts and forms of thinking.

For example: playing a board game (dominoes, checkers) or a card game (gin rummy) in which choices must be made among known possibilities.

4 Application

Solving a life-like problem that requires identification of the issues and the selection and use of appropriate generalizations and skills.

For example: taking part in a simulation in which the issues to be resolved are known and understood by the participants although the outcome will be determined through the group interaction itself.

5 Interpretation

Discovering relationships among facts, generalizations, definitions, values and skills.

For example: taking notes at a lecture, then using one's own notes to answer evaluative questions about the content of that lecture.

6 Translation

Changing information into a symbolic form or language.

For example: reading information in a text, then scanning to find specific facts in order to put the correct data in a chart, map or other graphic display.

7 Memory

Recalling or recognizing information.

For example: reading a passage in a text then answering comprehension questions which ask about specific details in the text (p. 100).

The scale identifies activities with the lowest cognitive potential and those with the highest potential with five stages between the two extremes. The stages of the cognitive potential development scale closely resemble Bloom's taxonomy (Bloom, 1956).[2] The gradation and sequencing of activities within a module and between the modules that were designed for the confidence building course comply with the cognitive potential development scale.

The blend of these two scales, namely the communicative potential and cognitive potential developmental scales, is reflected in individual activities and their gradation and sequencing in course materials. The starting point of the two scales in terms of the difficulty level of activities is decided by the language proficiency levels of the target student population. For instance, with a comparatively low proficiency group as the target group, the course may start with a listening task which involves exposure only, as is found in the communicative potential scale. Corresponding to that, a simple activity involving repetition (memory) of some phrases in the listening text may be given as group/pair work. Gradually, sequencing and gradation of activities can be done with an incremental increase in difficulty levels corresponding to both scales, with activities that increasingly demand higher cognitive skills until learners reach the final stages, i.e. evaluation.

With building confidence to speak English as our main objective, materials are designed with these two developmental potential scales in mind, predominantly in relation to speech activities. As such, listening, and particularly reading and writing, are given the least attention in 'negligibly small dosages'. With building student confidence as the pivotal point around which speech activities are clustered, the two scales used in designing and sequencing materials are exploited mostly in pair and group activities. The inevitable by-product of giving learners Basic Interpersonal Communicative Skills (BICS) comes through the use of activities that are designed to give students more exposure to day-to-day conversational skills.

An example activity from a module of the course, 'Building Confidence to Speak English' is given below.[3]

Example excerpt of a module/teaching material

Module 4

Activity 1 – getting to know more about others
Time: 40 minutes
Procedure:
Step I: Find out information about group members and report it to the class.

- i Get into groups of 4–5.
- ii Find answers to the questions given below.
- iii First ask the questions from the group members.
- iv Note down the number of 'Yes' and 'No' responses separately.

Questions:

- a Do you live in Maharagama?
- b Do you like to wear bright colours?
- c Do you like western music? Do you like to listen to western music?
- d Do you like soft drinks?
- e Do you like small children?
- f Are you afraid of flying?
- g Do you like dogs?
- h Do you like ragging?
- i Do you like social service?
- j Would you like to live in a country that has snow?

Step II: Find out information about your classmates and report it to the class.
Time: 40 minutes
Procedure:

- i Work in the same groups.
- ii Take two questions from the above list and go around the classroom asking the questions from all the other students.
- iii Then come back to your group and put everyone's answers together and draw a graph.
- iv In groups, present your findings to the class. Look at the graph and describe the findings.

    E.g.: One student lives in Maharagama. Eight students like to wear bright colours. No one likes ragging.

Step III: Look at the graph and write a report.
Your teacher will help you if necessary.
*Note that this excerpt is taken from the fourth module. (See Appendix A for a complete module.)

Analysis of the activity in terms of the communicative potential development scale

Step I: Step I takes place within a small group of four or five. Students are required to ask ten simple questions with the same question word at the beginning (except for Qs f and j). They are made to repeat after the teacher so that they learn to use the appropriate intonation (and pronunciation) to ask these questions while working in their small group. Students then ask the same questions verbally from their group members. The answers they get are also in the verbal form. They translate the responses into numerical form. As per the communicative potential development scale, this level falls somewhere between 5 and 4.

Step II: In order to carry out this task, students will have to go round the class asking two questions, which by now they are very familiar with. The same sentence structure (asking a question) is being repeated over 24 times.[4] By the time they complete asking the questions to 24 students, their communicative potential has increased to level 1 from an interaction perspective, i.e. their interaction with others has increased. However, since there is no negotiation of meaning among the members, this is limited to the aspect of communicating with many people at a very low level.

When they come back to their groups after gathering information from the entire class, their communicative potential has developed to level 3, in that new information is used or applied.

When they transfer the data they collected into one sheet by providing the information each of them gathered and when they report their findings to the class, as a group, they look at the graph they drew while reporting. Now their communicative potential has increased to level 2, as new information is expressed.

Analysis of the activity in terms of the cognitive potential development scale

Step I: Students ask questions verbally from group members first and then the whole class. The answers they get are also in the verbal form. They translate the responses into numerical form and this is, as per the cognitive potential development scale, one of the lowest stages, i.e. level 6, translation.

Step II: When the students gather information from their group first and then from the entire class, they synthesize the data to make the graph. This is at stage 2 on the scale. When they present the report to the class, there is an analysis of the graph and at the same time, an evaluation (stage 1) of the class profile in terms of the areas covered by the questions.

Repetition of speech acts in a hierarchical order

The incremental use of language items (phrases, utterance, etc.) that are required to carry out basic interpersonal communication is maintained throughout the lesson materials in their design, sequence and gradation.

For example, modules two and three have fewer questions and require students to give yes or no answers, while modules five and six have tasks that require students to give reasons for preferring certain activities while also giving yes or no answers to questions. Thus, the repetition of asking for student likes/dislikes is arranged so that the speech act of 'asking' (a directive) is reinforced while reasoning is introduced.

In addition, a phrase every day (discussed under teaching methodology) is given to the learners to carry out their group work. Teachers are asked at the teacher training sessions to make learners repeat such communicative phrases every day until learners are able to use them habitually.

Familiar content of learner contexts

The dialogues, situations for simulations and other instances where speech acts are performed are selected carefully to produce lessons that learners can relate to their immediate environment. The use of pictures to make students create and narrate stories is an important part of this material. Pictures like the one given in the figure below are used in the Building Confidence to Speak English course at the Faculty of Arts, University of Colombo. These pictures are not from an environment alien to the learners but are depictions of close-to-heart contexts that are mostly rural and not too distant from their day-to-day experiences in academic life or their lives in the village.

The example pictures that are given in the figure show two typically rural and semi-rural experiences from the 'developing world' (Figure 7.4). In the first, a policeman is chasing a 'thief' (assumed). This is commonplace in villages in countries like Sri Lanka. The situation is made farcical by adding the actual thief bathing, while fully clothed. The well, the attire of the man, the surroundings

Figure 7.4 The use of pictures related to learners' immediate background/environment (Illustrator – Upul Siriwardana).

and the activity of taking one's bath in a well using a bucket is a typically rural and not very privileged background. Such pictures in the confidence building classroom help learners relate to the experience easily. This in turn brings them closer to English language learning.

The other picture is about the plight of the students in the developing world today. They are supposed to run a rat race, from dawn to dusk. They are made to carry a heavy load of books and cram for examinations. After school, they are made to go for extra tuition classes conducted either by the school itself or private tuition institutes. Students in countries like these come home exhausted in the evening only to face the same thing the next day.

Module structure

1 Detailed instructions

The whole idea of a course aimed at building confidence in the English language classroom was novel even to Sri Lanka when we piloted the course in 2009. Novelty continued to find its way into the course throughout the stages of goal setting, material designing, defining teaching methodology and planning the assessment. Thus, the new process of introducing an entirely different set of modules/lesson materials was introduced.

This 'different type' of module makes a difference to the teachers as well, as there is no teacher's guide as is found in a stereotypical course. The modules/materials contain detailed instructions for both students and teachers as to how to go about an activity and as a result, there is no need to provide teachers a guide on how to get the work done. Moreover, these instructions are in very simple English. (See the example activity above.)

The overall aim of the course is to build student confidence with speech activities. Teaching other skills is a by-product. Detailed instructions are given in the modules to achieve the following objectives:

a To promote self-learning to help develop student confidence.

When detailed instructions are given in the modules, students are aware of all the steps in the procedure to finish an activity. It is expected that eventually they will be able to perform the activities as per the guidelines given in the modules without depending on their teacher, although they may need teacher's support at the initial stages in reading and understanding the guidelines. However, teachers are advised to 'give instructions to carry out a task' rather than to 'read' them out.

b To be compatible with the teaching methodology for the course, which is centred on CLL that advocates cooperation among students.

CLL requires students to work together in groups to accomplish a task. To develop cooperation, students need to know what is expected of them in a given task, so that collaborative reading and comprehension are promoted when the teacher's instruction may not be clearly understood by each and every member of the group.

c To avoid competition

When students work in groups with instructions at hand, they can always refer to the lesson materials for further clarification in carrying out the task. When they do not understand certain parts of the instructions given, they can seek support from their peers first without having to go to the teacher. Therefore, the kind of competitive setting that can emerge from individually listening to the teacher and following instructions does not arise. A counter argument could be made that a competitive environment is important in the classroom to motivate the students. Yet, considering the main aim of the course is to build student confidence by making them speak in English, cooperation, rather than competition, should be promoted. This also helps to create a safe zone within the four walls of the classroom for the students to use the language.

d As the target student population is a low level, near-similar ability group, it is expected that they would support each other in understanding the process of learning with detailed instructions.

For the confidence building course, a lower level, near-similar ability group is desired (as discussed under related logistics) to manifest its multi-facetedness and support learning. This is because the teaching methodology that is designed for the course is associated with CLL (as discussed in the chapter on Teaching Methodology), which requires group work and peer support. When the instructions are difficult to understand, support from a peer whose language proficiency is slightly higher than theirs can come in without making the lowest proficient learner feel low.[5]

This in turn supports Krashen's (1981) hypothesis about an effective input as i + 1, that is, an input slightly higher than what the learner already possesses. By combining the lowest English language proficiency learners with a slightly higher level, it is assumed that such a i + 1 input is made available in the language classroom.

e The transparency of the instructions would make students feel that learning a language is a process in which their own interaction with the material is important.

The teaching–learning process in the developing world today is usually one of a *spoon-feeding* nature, in which the teacher is the most important figure in the classroom with the 'spoon' in his or her hand, feeding information to students instead of creating a *learner-centred* teaching–learning process. The manifestations of such a spoon-feeding environment in the second language classroom include: the teacher reading out the instructions already given in the book/exercise to students; hiding or not reading out (not necessarily in the negative sense) some segment/s of the instructions in the teacher's guide, so that students are made to feel that there are some parts of learning that should be known to the teacher only and that the learners need to wait for them to be disclosed by the teacher; the lecture method; giving out all of the to-be-required vocabulary and language structures before learners need them to carry out a task, meaning that students do not have an opportunity to 'feel the need' of what is required for a given situation. In contrast to this, detailed instructions given to students in a simple and straightforward manner make them feel the need to read the instructions to carry out the task. Thus, the need to interact with the materials and the skills needed to be responsible for their own learning are created together. Such a process has an additional effect: it automatically accustoms students to reading, which most teachers complain that their learners do not do.

f The transparent nature of instructions will make them feel that the teaching of English is directly related to their learning of English.

English has been distanced from rural and semi-rural learners in the South Asian countries in a number of ways: making learners feel that British or American English is 'the goal' they need to aspire in learning to speak in English; giving them the idea that any mistake committed in spoken English is a crime (thereby giving them the warped notion that making mistakes in their own mother tongues is something to be proud of); the general attitude that anything from the West is superior and what is theirs (South Asian) is inferior and the superiority of all things western is always unlikely to be grasped by inferiors, etc. In such a context, teachers of English and the teaching of English is often looked at as something like a river to cross; a colossal river to go towards an entity that is both superior and far away, and the rural student experiences this. Therefore, apart from teaching English in a novel way, there is a challenge to bring the English language and its teaching closer to the learners in a post-colonial South Asian context. One way to achieve this is to make the learners feel that teaching English and learning English are not distinct and distant discourses, but parallel and close. The detailed yet simple instructions in the lesson materials, it is assumed, may make the teaching–learning endeavour more transparent, thereby making students feel that even the teaching English is within their reach, thus narrowing the existing gap.

g To limit learner expectations of teacher intervention in learning, so that they will feel responsible for their own learning. This in turn will make them feel confident as they are entrusted with responsibility.

As discussed above, the spoon-feeding nature of South Asian education has made learners depend on the teacher to such an extent that any 'learner-centredness in the teaching approach is just limited to documents. When detailed instructions are given directly to the learners, there is very little to expect from the teacher in order to carry out the task. In that situation, students feel that they have been entrusted with the responsibility of reading and following the instructions by themselves where necessary, because they are capable of doing so.

h Teachers are compelled to follow the instructions without skipping some steps in them.

Teachers are humans and by nature, there is a tendency to skip or overlook certain steps in the instructions, when and if they are given in a teacher guide. When the detailed instructions are given to students, teachers are compelled to work with students by facilitating each step.

2 Simple language and content format

The language that is used for instruction as well as content is very simple so that learners with low proficiency in English are able to comprehend it with minimum support. Lengthy instructions in paragraph style are completely avoided. In order to achieve clarity, instructions are subdivided into steps and each step is a stage in which learners come a step closer to completing the task. Also, each step has instructions given in one line/sentence, so that the complete instructions for a given step are given in a couple of sentences.

3 The reference to the teacher as 'your teacher'

In the instructions, the reference to the teacher is given as 'your teacher' to make learners feel close to the teacher who teaches English to them. This is a silent attempt to create a sense of bonding with the teacher and is a subtle mechanism to connect them with English language learning. Instead of 'Get the help from *the* teacher, if needed', 'Get the help from *your* teacher, if needed', may bring the teacher closer to the learner. With about 10–15 lesson modules for the course with 'your teacher' appearing regularly, it is expected that a healthy bond is encouraged and sustained throughout the course, contributing to creating the safe zone that helps learners build confidence to speak English by bringing the teacher and the teaching of English close to the learners.

Related logistics

1 A class must not have more than 25 students in it.
2 The course should run every day for a minimum of two hours (three hours per day is most effective).
3 The course duration should be a minimum of one month (maximum three months).
4 A language proficiency homogeneous group is preferred (or near-homogeneous, e.g. the lowest and the next lowest).
5 If they are mixed ability groups, then the lowest and the highest proficiency groups should not be mixed together. It has to be lowest and the second lowest. The highest proficiency groups may not even need their confidence to be built after all!

Reasons

When the learners who belong to the lowest English language proficiency groups are mixed with the highest (this happens in random grouping or in mixed ability groups), the learners in the lowest proficiency category feel threatened. Also, the learners with the highest proficiency levels tend to dominate. Therefore, the expected 'safe zone' will not be created in such a classroom.

On the other hand, if/when the teacher caters to the lowest group, the highest group may feel bored. If the teacher keeps up with the speed of the highest group, the lowest will be left behind. Either way, learners in general are disadvantaged. Even though for some language courses, mixed ability groups may be helpful, for the confidence building course random or mixed-ability groups are detrimental to the aim of building confidence to speak English.

Also, learners with a high proficiency in English when mixed with lower proficiency groups may tend to laugh at the mistakes of the lower proficiency learners, thus creating a similar situation where the initial root cause for the lack of confidence is being repeated in the classroom and destroying the whole objective of the course.

Conclusion

The chapter discusses the overarching theory and the sub-divisions of BICS, CUP and CALPS in a curriculum that aims at developing the English language proficiency of weak learners. It establishes the linkages among the courses of this curriculum in terms of theoretical and thematic linkages and other principles such as grammar and vocabulary. The next section of the chapter details the Building Confidence to Speak English course in terms of its structure and materials production by using the theoretical principles of Speech Act Theory. In addition it also discusses the sequencing and gradation of activities that underlie two different activity potentials, namely, Communicative and Cognitive Potential Development and their scales. An excerpt of teaching material from the Building Confidence to Speak English course at the Faculty of Arts, University of Colombo, Sri Lanka is presented along with analysis of the activities in terms of the communicative and cognitive potential developmental scales. The need for the repetition of speech acts in a hierarchical order and the use of content familiar to learner contexts are emphasized. Also, the module structure is discussed at length under the significance of giving detailed instructions in modules and the importance of simple language and a simple format in the modules. The chapter concludes with a note relating to logistics that are crucial for the confidence building classroom.

Notes

1 The examples given are for reading and writing activities as well and not exclusively for speech activities. Since this is a direct quote, we have not omitted any examples. However, for the confidence building course, we have used the workouts that are relevant for speaking only.

2 The authors acknowledge that the cognitive potential scale was adapted from Benjamin Bloom's *Taxonomy of educational objectives* and Norris Sanders' *Classroom questions: what kinds?*

3 This excerpt is taken from the fourth module of the Building Confidence to Speak English course at the Faculty of Arts, University of Colombo, Sri Lanka where we are

the curriculum designer for the course and the academic coordinator for the lowest proficiency group of First Year undergraduates who scored 0–35 marks at the placement text. For a complete sample module, see Appendices.

4 Student number in a class for the Confidence Building Course is limited to 25. This is discussed at the Teaching Methodology section.

5 As the researcher witnessed in the English Language classrooms in the Faculty of Arts, University of Colombo, Sri Lanka in 2009 when the course was piloted and in the successive years, students belonging to two proficiency groups, i.e. Level 1 (lowest) and Level 2 (second lowest), peer support in accomplishing a group activity has been a major feature.

References

Austin, J. L. (1975). *How to do things with words.* Cambridge, MA: Harvard University Press.

Bach, K., & Harnish, R. M. (1979). *Linguistic communication and speech acts.* Cambridge: MIT Press.

Bloom, M. (1956). *Taxonomy of educational objectives.* New York: David McKay.

Cummins, J. (1979). Cognitive/academic language proficiency, linguistic interdependence, the optimum age question and some other matters. *Working Papers on Bilingualism*, 19, 121–129.

Cummins, J. (2000a). *Language, power and pedagogy: Bilingual children in the crossfire.* Clevedon, England: Multilingual Matters

Cummins, J. (2000b). Second language acquisition: Essential information. Retrieved from: http://esl.fis.edu/teachers/support/cummin.htm

Crystal, D. (1994). Words Worth. *Times Higher Education*, 11, 34.

Dubin, F., & Olshtain, E. (1987). *Course design: Developing programs and materials for language learning.* Cambridge, UK: Cambridge University Press.

Krashen, S. D. (1981). *Second language acquisition and second language learning.* Oxford: Pergamon.

Searle, J. (1969). *Speech acts.* Cambridge: Cambridge University Press.

8 Teaching methodology and the role of the teacher

Introduction

This chapter discusses in detail how Cooperative Language Learning (CLL) is used as the main component in the teaching methodology for the course. The techniques of CLL are discussed in at length alongside the discussion of the psycho-social features of language learners. These details are examined in relation to the teacher's role in the confidence building classroom. In addition, other techniques that are used in devising a specific teaching methodology for the confidence building course are also discussed. For instance, error correction, the demand from individual learners for performance, homework, etc. that are found in an ordinary language classroom that can create Language Attitude Anxiety (LAA) in the language learners' mind are analysed along with remedial techniques. The teacher's shift from an 'ordinary teaching position' to that of an observer who 'overlooks' the errors and mistakes found in student speech is emphasized. The necessity to create a 'safe zone' and the essential components of this safe zone are discussed along with the role of the teacher as the sole authority responsible for creating that safe zone. The potential challenges for teachers and the process-oriented nature of the approach are discussed against the backdrop of the necessity for teachers to be trained to use the confidence building course; this includes training on the teacher's authority, role and awareness creation in regard to language attitudes and student needs.

The psychology of the post-colonial South Asian language learner

It is apparent that a large majority of South Asian language learners are affected by some form of language anxiety. Some may experience foreign language anxiety only, whereas others may also experience LAA. As discussed in the previous chapter on understanding the learners, the psychological complexities of the learners and the influence of society in creating them cannot and should not be ignored. Therefore, we believe that any attempt to resolve the psychological dilemmas of the learners should be addressed at the social level, starting from the English language classroom, the smallest unit of society in which societal influences can be controlled. The society of the English language classroom can be controlled in terms of the material and the teaching methodology, all of which should be geared towards eliminating LAA and building student confidence to speak English.

In our opinion, the teaching methodology that is best suited for this purpose is predominantly based on CLL principles.

Cooperative Language Learning

The principles of CLL, as the name denotes, promote cooperation. The main features discourage learning and performance at the individual level. In their English language learning histories, learners experienced fear/shyness/uncertainty about their English language performance resulting in LAA. The outcome is a lack of confidence to use English at an individual level when speaking with others. Therefore, any rectifying measure should begin with making them feel safe and comfortable enough to speak English. In other words, the strategy should not make learners feel threatened and/or isolated in the classroom. In order to create such an environment, it is necessary to use a teaching methodology that has cooperation as its core guiding principle. To this end, as Phillips (1992) states:

> ... encouraging a relaxed atmosphere in the classroom may be a first step in alleviating anxiety related to oral testing. In fact, several approaches to language learning have been developed that attempt to counteract the debilitating effects of anxiety by providing a low-stress environment where students may work cooperatively in the learning process.
>
> (p. 20)

The aim of our course is to build learner confidence through speech activities. The best reason to select CLL is therefore that it is 100% compatible with the overall aim of the confidence building course. It involves a lot of group and pair work to help create an active and safe zone for the learners to speak in English.

CLL is part of collaborative learning (CL). According to Olsen and Kagan (1992),

> Cooperative learning is a group learning activity organized so that learning is dependent on the socially structured exchange of information between learners in groups, in which each learner is held accountable for his or her own learning and is motivated to increase the learning of others.
>
> (p. 8)

Cooperative learning is based on the communicative aspects of language and its learning. Therefore, it is built upon some principles which comply with the interactive nature of language use. Communication is the primary purpose of language.

1 Most speech is organized as conversation.
2 Conversation operates according to certain agreed upon sets of cooperative rules or 'maxims' (Grice, 1975).

3 One learns how these 'maxims' are realized in one's native language through casual, everyday conversational interaction.
4 One learns how the maxims are realized in a second language through participation in cooperatively structured interactive activities (p. 8).

CLL is supportive of both structural and functional models as well as the interactive model of language (Olsen & Kagan, 1992). In addition, CLL is based on the theories of developmental psychology and social interaction, especially those of Piaget (1965) and Vygotsky (1962) who emphasize social interaction as central to learning. CLL promotes activities based on Bloom's Taxonomy (1956) for developing critical thinking in the learner. CLL's emphasis is on cooperation, rather than competition, in learning (Kagan, 2009).

Goals of CLL

Some of the main goals of CLL are listed below:

1 To provide a naturalistic language acquisition environment
2 To pay attention to particular lexical items, language structures and communicative functions
3 To allow learners to develop successful learning and communicative strategies
4 To enhance learner motivation
5 To reduce learner stress and build confidence (Richards & Rodgers, 2001).

To achieve these goals, CLL emphasizes maximum use of cooperative activities through pair and group work. The group learning activities are organized in such a way that

> ... learning is dependent on the socially structured exchange of information between leaners in groups and in which each learner is held accountable for his or her learning and is motivated to increase the learning of others.
> (Olsen and Kagan, 1992, p. 8).

According to Olsen and Kagan (1992), some of the key concepts related to CLL are positive interdependence, individual accountability, group formation, social skills and structuring and structures.

Principles of CLL

1 Positive interdependence

Positive interdependence is present when the answer to the following questions is 'yes':

a What hurts one member hurts all?
b What helps one member help everyone?

- c Is everyone's contribution is needed to complete the task?
- d Do learners feel a spirit of mutual support within the group? (Richards & Rodgers, 2001, p. 196).

2 Individual accountability

This involves group as well as individual performance. The tasks do not allow 'free riders' but group members who perform before peers or class.

3 Group formation

Random groups or pre-designed groups with 4–5 members will ensure learners interact with each other. It will allow group members to interact with each other well. It is also important to assign a specific task to each member so that there is equal participation and positive interdependence (Richards & Rodgers, 2001, p. 196).

4 Social skills

It is important to assign tasks to each member with clear instructions in terms of time and turn taking to make them feel equal.

5 Structuring and structures

This refers to ways of organizing student interaction and the different ways in which student are to interact and perform, e.g. Round Robin (Richards & Rodgers, 2001, p. 197).

Characteristics of CLL

1. Learners work together in groups in order to reach common goals.
2. Learners benefit from sharing ideas rather than working alone.
3. Learners help one another so that all of them can reach some measure of success.

How does this (CLL) differ from traditional methods? In traditional methods, the following features can be seen.

1. Learners work individually.
2. They may work competitively.
3. Learners are generally concerned with improving their own grade.
4. Goals are individualistic rather than group-centred (Richards & Rodgers, 2001).

One can see that by its nature CLL completely contrasts with traditional methods. The theoretical perspectives of CLL underscore three major perspectives: the motivational perspectives, social cohesion perspectives and cognitive perspectives involved in cognitive developmental aspects and cognitive elaboration (Richards & Rodgers, 2001).

Elaboration of each of these perspectives gives a clear idea of how they work in a classroom setting: in regard to motivational perspectives, individual goals can be achieved only if the group is successful. Therefore, learners help each other partly because it benefits them as individuals. However, the individualistic element is buffered by the next perspective, i.e. social cohesion, which brings out one of the inherent characteristics of humankind, i.e. team spirit; individuals help each other because they also want others to win and because they care about the group. Cognitive perspectives involve developmental aspects whereby learners discuss, argue and hear others' views in order to complete a given task. Cognitive elaboration takes place as learners have to engage in restructuring and explaining concepts and ideas to others, since group achievement depends on such discussion activities.

The critical variables

Olsen and Kagan (1992) state that language acquisition is determined by a 'complex interaction of a number of critical input, output and context variables' (p. 15). He also states that cooperative learning has a dramatic positive impact on these critical variables.

When students engage in group activities, they constantly interact with each other at their existing level of language proficiency. This may be the first input they receive and may not always be grammatically correct and appropriate to the context. The teacher's input comes in either form of indirect correction (of the inaccurate use of student language, if any) or as instructions. Both of these input types are important as the former is at a level of comprehension by the peers and the latter as the accurate and appropriate input by the teacher.

As stated, the main disadvantage of an input by peers over learners is that it may lack accuracy due to the fact that students use the language structures and vocabulary they have already with them in the target language. The remedial measure we suggest is controlled use of language structures with teacher intervention. As a facilitator, the teacher can intervene, tactfully, where correction of pronunciation, vocabulary and sentence structures are required. This is further discussed under error correction, teacher's role.

According to Olsen and Kagan (1992), language acquisition is fostered by output that is functional, communicative, frequent, redundant and consistent with the identity of the speaker. Cooperative learning is an ideal situation for communicative output. The language functions embedded in the activities found in the lesson material of the confidence building course allow learners to perform similar speech functions which are communicative in nature. This is because performing a speech function has to be carried out either in a group or as part of pair work. In addition, the activities are sequenced and graded in the lesson materials in such a way that continual repetition of the same speech function while gradually increasing the difficulty level is maintained throughout the course so that the output is frequent and redundant. Most importantly, because learners are encouraged to speak, even with all their flaws, learner output is consistently allowed to improve in line with learner identity as there is no force or compulsion for learners to speak or speak accurately and fluently during the teaching–learning sessions. At the same time, gradual elimination of LAA allows the learners to develop ambitious possible selves in relation to speaking English.

The context in which students learn the language is conducive to the language learning–acquisition process: they need to communicate to accomplish goals; there is peer support on the basis of sameness; the cooperative structures of the activities demand speech; the incentive to praise and encourage others is embedded in the process and interdependency requires the consideration of others' views.

Grouping and groups

It is important to have 20–25 students in a class, as exceeding 25 will be unmanageable for the teacher who has to work with each group in carrying out activities. Fewer than 20 will be insufficient to help learners develop their communicative potential with a good level of interaction with peers, while monitoring five groups with four to five members in each group is relatively easy to manage effectively.

Each class should be composed of learners with similar proficiency levels in English. Mixed-ability groups will create problems as the learners with higher proficiency levels will dominate the groups and those with lower proficiency levels will feel threatened as a result. Such a situation will work against the sole aim of the Building Confidence to Speak English course. Also, the teacher will have to cater to at least two different types of learners in terms of teaching pace and this will make the higher proficiency groups bored with the lessons while the lower proficiency groups are challenged beyond their capacities.

Teachers can make small groups in a couple of ways: by putting learners into groups of four to five for each task/activity and changing the members of a group a few times a day or by assigning group members to a particular group for each day. In this way, learners get to interact with the whole class. It is not advisable to have permanent groups. Learners should be able to interact with everyone without getting into the habit of either becoming dominant in the group or becoming a free rider, both of which must be discouraged in a cooperative setting.

The advantages of small groups

Students find it much easier to talk to a peer in a small group instead of speaking in front of the whole class and they have more opportunities to communicate in small groups at the developmentally appropriate level. The immediate feedback that students give to one another in cooperative group settings also leads to better acquisition of vocabulary and forms. There is less chance of self-consciousness and anxiety than we find in the traditional classroom. The 'threat of having to do it all alone' is completely absent when learners go through the process of accomplishing a task by sharing their knowledge, skills and assigned responsibilities with the other members of their small group. Also, when learners have to produce speech output in an activity, which is the most frightening step of all for South Asian learners, this burden is shared by everyone in the group and initial anxiety is minimized.

We find that materials prepared under the theoretical perspectives discussed in the previous chapter with necessary adaptations (localization and personalization), help in achieving the main aim of the course, i.e. building student confidence (via speech activities). The aim of the course and the objectives of CLL are quite compatible because the latter promotes cooperation rather than competition, aims at developing critical thinking and is designed to develop communicative competence through socially structured interactive activities. In our experience, after two to three weeks of complete immersion in the confidence building course, students become more at ease with the speech activities given to them and help each other in their groups to accomplish the tasks assigned to them.

As the course builds the confidence of learners, they begin to acquire the language in an environment which is conducive to language acquisition as the need for meaningful responses arises to accomplish their speech functions. The confidence building environment inevitably bonds itself with second language acquisition and cooperative learning by means of the 'natural marriage' put forth by Kagan and Olsen (1992).

The safe zone

As the findings of this study show, learner fear/shyness/uncertainty manifests in a lack confidence to speak English, whether inside or outside the classroom, with some learners unable to use English anywhere. Some learners experience only Foreign Language Anxiety (FLA) while others experience LAA as we discussed. The bottom line is that they do not feel 'safe' to speak or even to attempt to speak and utilize the language knowledge they have already acquired. While no one is able to change the dynamics in the society outside the classroom in which learners feel anxious, it is possible to alter the dynamics in the 'small society' that exists in the English language classroom itself. These can be changed so as to create a zone in which learners do not experience the same negative emotions they say they go through in speaking English in society. This zone must give them safety from the 'potential threats' they fear outside the classroom.

This 'safe zone' in the English language classroom in which learners feel secure will build their confidence to speak English. This safe zone should be devoid of anything the learners are afraid of or uncertain about. The interviews in this study reveal that there are a number of elements that discourage learners from speaking English in the language classroom: overcorrection, grammar rules, individual tasks, mandatory performance, etc. During the teacher training sessions, these causes of anxiety are emphasized and all of them are 'banned' in the Building Confidence to Speak English course. In fact, during the training sessions that we have conducted, we asked teachers to act like their students do in their classrooms. This role-playing exercise helps to illustrate the challenges that all teachers face in trying to maintain the safe zone. These challenges are brought to the notice of everyone involved in the training and the best remedial measures are discussed so that the safe zone is created and maintained.

The following are three sample activities found in any typical South Asian English language class. The features of the safe zone in the Building Confidence to Speak English course are discussed using them as the context, highlighting the 'do's' and 'don'ts':

Example scene I

TEACHER: Hello everyone, good morning/afternoon! I am your new English teacher. My name is Ajantha. I want all of you to introduce yourselves to your new friends. Now, you (pointing at a student, most likely one in the front row), start and introduce yourself please.

STUDENT A: I am A. I am from *Kanthale.*[1] I am twenty years old. (Old is pronounced as /Ɔlɗ/)

TEACHER: It is not /Ɔlɗ/. It is /aulɗ/. Say it again, /aulɗ/; repeat, 'I am twenty years /aulɗ/.'

STUDENT A: (A is a little taken aback but repeats) I am twenty years /old/. (Not with complete accuracy, but better than the previous effort.)

TEACHER: Good. You can practise it later /aulɗ/ and not /Ɔlɗ/. Okay, now you (pointing at the student next to A)!

STUDENT B: I am B. I am from *Madawala.*[2] I am twenty-one years ... (hesitates, looks at the teacher and then looks at the rest of the class helplessly).

TEACHER: Yes (encouragingly), I am twenty-one years ... what?

STUDENT B: (Stammers and with a lowered voice) I am twenty-one years /Ɔlɗ/.

TEACHER: /aulɗ/ and not /Ɔlɗ/. Yes, repeat. Again. Not quite. Again. /aulɗ/, /aulɗ/. Remember. Now the next one please!

STUDENT C: (Cringes in his or her seat and is reluctant to get up from the chair.)

Example scene II

A teacher is reading out a story. Once the story is read, the students are given a worksheet to fill out on vocabulary related to the story: synonyms and antonyms. The teacher gives a specific amount of time to carry out the activity. The teacher sits at her table for a while and then walks around monitoring. Some learners immediately act on the work; some others look completely lost; while the majority fall somewhere between these two extremes and spend their time looking around, whispering to their neighbours, peeping at their work sheets, copying from each other, etc. The ones who started immediately (a minority in every class) run to the teacher quickly with their answers. Those who looked lost now look blank while others may ask a few questions from the teacher and their peers in an effort to complete the task.

Example scene III

Students are given a group activity which is to be presented in front of the class. The time given for the activity is also communicated to the students. When the time is finished, the teacher asks learners to stop working and get ready to present. The ones who are forward, with 'good' proficiency (a minority in every class) will get up quickly. Those who are weak and 'not so good' will hesitate. Then the teacher's usual intervention is something like:

'You (pointing at a student), yes, get up and present your answers please. Come on!' 'Okay, good.' 'Next you (pointing at another).' 'Oh come on, why are you so hesitant?' (Other students laugh.)

Characteristics of the safe zone

The safe zone that is created in the Building Confidence to Speak English course has the following features:

i No individual work
ii No individual performance
iii No error correction
iv No grammar teaching
v No performance is mandatory
vi No homework
vii No mother tongue
viii Other strategies *(a phrase a day, sitting down with learners at their level)*

It is very important to delve deeper into the torture chamber that is usually referred to in non-spatial terms as the 'English period' and in spatial terms as the 'English language classroom'. Adult learners with many years of English language lessons and the undergraduates with over a decade of English language learning history behind them come to the university only to be placed in a lower proficiency group than they expected, coming to understand that their marks at the placement test for the university English course are low and that their English is not satisfactory. All through their English language learning history, they faced situations like those we discussed in the example scenes above. However, they come to their new English class expecting a different learning system, a system that gives them more freedom to learn. At the same time, they come into the system determined to rectify all the issues they faced learning English in the past. This is especially true in regard to undergraduates, as being able to get into university is something to be proud of and the learners come with a sense of pride. Yet these expectations are soon to be destroyed as there is nothing in the university that is any different from the 'English period' in their schools. It is disheartening for the students to realize that the situation is just an extension of what it was and it hurts their sense of pride to think they are likely going to fail to learn English yet again. Any learner with some history of English language learning is destined to be disappointed in the post-colonial South Asian English language classroom.

The following section discusses the features of the safe zone and the teacher's role in further detail by locating them in the example situations given above.

No individual work

Example II shows an ordinary lesson on vocabulary. The task looks simple but to a low proficiency language learner the activity may be very difficult as it has to be accomplished alone. When teachers assign individual tasks, the learner has to face two challenges: (a) to navigate finding their answer/s alone and (b) finding the correct answer/s alone.

This may be very demanding for a learner who is not proficient in English as carrying out a task is a process involving many steps. There is room for learners to feel insecure, lonely and isolated in dealing with the task in front of them. This is worsened for the weak learners when they see learners who are able to promptly begin working on the given task. More often than not, learners in post-colonial South Asian societies do not seek help of their teachers when they encounter difficulties. Some students may pretend to be hard at work, all the while not having a single clue as to how to go about completing the task!

This is why the Building Confidence to Speak English course completely does away with any activities that require learners to work individually in the English language classroom. Instead, the teaching methodology is designed with CLL techniques that promote small group activities and the activities themselves are specially designed to be performed in small groups or pairs. This is to make learners feel secure in carrying out a task/activity where the responsibility is shared. The idea that underscores making learners 'feel secure' is more important than anything else. When learners get to perform in small groups, some of the negative elements that would be borne by the individual learner alone are now shared by the group. Some of these are given below.

1 If learners do not understand or are unclear about the process for a given task, their *ignorance* is shared.
2 If there is a step that is not understood by many in the group, their *unawareness* is shared.
3 If learners feel uncertain about their answer at the end of a task, the *uncertainty* is shared.
4 If learners lack knowledge of a concept that is required to do the activity, the *lack of knowledge* is shared.
5 As a result of all these, if the task outcome is not up to the expected level, even the *sub-standard nature* of their response is shared, although performance is more likely to be better because there are more opportunities for the learners to get issues clarified by another student or by going as a group to the teacher during the learning process.

It is important to note that irrespective of their age, it is inevitable that learners will feel *ignorant*, *unaware* and *uncertain* and that they *lack knowledge* if they are to carry out tasks alone and produce some outcome individually. As a result, individual learners feel insecure in the English language classroom. When they feel that others share their ignorance, uncertainties, etc., they realize that it is not only he or she who is 'not so good' at English, but there are many others like them. This makes them feel less inadequate and builds a sense of solidarity in the classroom.

In order to create the safe zone that is required to build learner confidence, learners need to be protected from any feeling of being 'unsafe' in the classroom. In other words, everything that creates a sense of insecurity in them has to be avoided. One sure way to do this is to assign learners to work in pairs, small groups and occasionally as a whole class so that they are never isolated at any point in carrying out an activity.

TEACHER'S ROLE

In order to make learners feel secure, the teacher should, at all times, ensure that learners are assigned to pairs, small groups or engaged in large group activities. The lesson materials include activities designed for small groups or pair work. These strategies to create the safe zone are to be strictly adhered to so as to produce the desired outcome, confidence building. The teacher should make sure that learners sit facing each other and are able to share their notes, if any, and accomplish speaking activities together as a group without leaving anyone unnoticed, neglected or ignored.

No individual performance

Examples I and III show what can happen in an ordinary English language classroom where learners are required to perform individually.

In a very good case, the learner will get up in the class, willingly, without hesitation. In a good case, the learner will come to the front of the class without much reluctance. In a not-so-good case, the learner will hesitate only to be prompted and pushed by the other group members to present in front of the class. In the worst case, the learner will refuse even to get up! And they will look down, avoiding the teacher's gaze, cursing themselves for looking up to meet the teacher's eyes in the first place.

If the class is a mixed-ability group, there will be three or four students who are eagerly waiting, some with raised hands, for the teacher to say, 'Yes, you!' However, let's look at the rest of the class, the large majority of learners. They will look like animals about to be slaughtered; fear-stricken faces, avoiding the teacher's eyes, heads bent, eyes glued to the book; if checked, their heart rate will be 144 heartbeats per minute; not knowing when the worst will occur, but knowing that their fate will be to be tormented in front of the class, surely, sooner or later. All the experienced teachers know this. Most of the teachers, who were themselves students once upon a time, will remember this too. Yet, the torture continues.

The safe zone that needs to be created in the confidence building classroom should be free of all of these tormenting mechanisms that are found in the 'ordinary' English language classroom in the South Asian region. The demand to speak in English in front of the class is very challenging for learners who are weak in English and who come from rural and semi-rural backgrounds. Demanding individual performance is extremely challenging for weak students. They are fear-stricken at the thought of being ridiculed by peers, frustrated by the teacher's overcorrection, tormented by negative experiences from outside the classroom and weighed down by their unpleasant learning histories. As they step into a new English language classroom, they may still be negotiating and coming to terms with their learner identities and role conflict issues related to English.

It is therefore essential not to demand individual performance from learners in the confidence building classroom.

TEACHER'S ROLE

When learners are assigned group tasks (or pair work) to be completed within an allocated time, the teacher should walk around, going from group to group monitoring and observing, offering help when required. Once the time to perform arrives, the teacher can ask for volunteers first to come forward *in groups*. In our experience, at the initial stages, only one or two groups will volunteer. However, as time goes by, teachers will barely be able to handle the number of volunteers! This is because the performance is produced by the groups, rather than individuals. In the safe zone, the teacher should ask the learners to present only in groups (as per the instructions in the lesson material), while paying attention to other features such as no error correction, etc. (discussed below). When this occurs, learners become very eager to perform in front of the class. Teachers are not expected to point to a particular group demanding performance either. Instead, the teacher can use simple methods such as saying, 'Okay, group one came first, now how about the next.' Or, 'Group four presented first, great! Would their neighbours care to go next?' without making it compulsory for group two or five to come forward next.

Another tip to increase the effectiveness of the teacher's role is to avoid sitting in front of the class, dominating the ground where performance takes place. Instead, the teacher should sit with the other students in the class, being part of each of the different groups for a period of time, blending into the audience's domain. When learners realize that there is no overpowering authority looming over their performance, they feel less inhibited. Also, if the teacher sits with the group who performed immediately before the group that is presenting, it will boost the courage of the groups as they take it as an unspoken acceptance/reward from their teacher for their performance.

No error correction

A typical English language class in the South Asian region will have a 'self-introduction' session on the very first day. There can be exceptions, but it is likely that the teacher will want to know the names of the learners in his or her class and at least their ages and where they are from. Example I shows what these sessions usually look like.

The scenario could be slightly better or worse or depending on the English teacher's demeanour, as some teachers are known to be friendly while others are seen as 'terrors'. The first scene is in fact, an example of both individual performance and error correction, both of which we discourage in the Building Confidence to Speak English course. The situation of the poor learner having to perform alone, standing, maybe in front of the class, is worsened when the teacher starts correcting errors. The vulnerable position of a learner, small or grown up, standing in front of the class, getting corrected by the teacher after every third or fourth spoken word is something that we, the practitioners in the field, should never forget, along with the position of the audience, waiting to be chosen at any moment to take the place of the 'now-being-slaughtered'! Given this, it is not surprising that learners are absent as often as possible, dislike the English period, sit as far as possible from the teacher, counting the minutes until the English period is finished and are jubilant when the class is over.

In our view, these negative experiences, most probably repeated frequently throughout their history of English language learning, have created two types of English language learners in the South Asian sub-continent: one who has given up on learning English and the other who is deathly afraid of and completely shuns speaking English.

The teacher MUST NOT intervene and correct learner mistakes, whether in groups or as individual performers when speaking, while the learners are in the process of accomplishing a task or on the performing stage. Instead, teachers should ignore errors or recast them correctly and point them out at the end of the lesson in general terms without making any individual learner or group of learners feel singled out or discouraged.

This is initially a very difficult part to play for the teachers, because they are used to correcting learner errors whenever they hear them. Our advice for them is 'just ignore it' and keep listening, so that the learner will continue speaking in English. It is necessary to remind the teachers every so often during the teacher training sessions that building learners' confidence in speaking English, not improving their language proficiency, is the principal objective of the course.

Two significant experiences in regard to the implementation of this 'no error correction' rule are worth noting. The first was at the pilot course in 2009; a very experienced elderly teacher was heavily critical about this 'newly introduced technique' and demanded to know how the students would 'learn' if their errors were not corrected. For the trainer, one of the youngest members of the staff, whose PhD was only very recently obtained, it was not at all a pleasant encounter to train teachers with 30–40 years of teaching experience who were not keen to adhere to these 'seemingly baseless' rules. Nevertheless, our response was enough to overcome this resistance: 'We have been correcting their errors over ten years in their schooling and still they are in Level 1' (the lowest proficiency group).[3] Secondly, after eight years of running the course at the Faculty of Arts, University of Colombo, Sri Lanka, we were baffled when a teacher reported an observation that a student contributed to a discussion: in 2016, at one of the teacher training sessions where teachers shared their tricky experiences and success stories in teaching the course, one teacher said that a student in her class asked her why the teacher would not correct any mistake that the students made! Ever since then, teachers have been advised to inform students around the third day of the course that their errors will not be corrected during this course but will be corrected in the next, 'Narrative-based Course to Learn English'. It is expected that by about day three (after six to nine contact hours), learners will be familiar enough in the new setting and that the teachers will have made themselves friendly enough to share such 'secret' techniques with their students. Also it was felt that the assurance that their errors 'will eventually be corrected' should be given, so that they will not be disappointed, because no matter how much they say overcorrection scares them, learners also expect teachers to 'teach' something.

The significance of these two narratives paves the way for an important discussion. Learners in South Asia expect teachers to correct them even though it has proven to be counter-productive. As the study shows, not only are learners aware of its negative effect but they are outspoken about it as well. One of the reasons for their fear to speak in the classroom was that teachers would correct the students constantly and this causes them to become 'unsure' of what to say next. Nevertheless, the students have been conditioned by their learning histories to such an extent that they have difficulty recognizing other ways of 'teaching'. This shows the stereotypical teacher figure as presented in the South Asian classroom and the student acceptance of it. The *guru* knows everything and the *guru* should correct student mistakes. In addition, it reveals the spoon-feeding nature of teaching in the South Asian education system, in which students expect teachers to give them everything related to passing examinations and teachers are comfortable in trying to meet student expectations. In such a context, the role of the teacher figure in the confidence building course poses a challenge to both parties. On the one hand, for South Asian students, it can be disheartening to learn from a teacher who does not correct mistakes. On the other, it is not easy for the teacher to break out of their typical role. The latter difficulty is represented by the question the elderly teacher asked, which implied an inability to conceive of English language teaching taking place in such circumstances. This gives us insight into the dogmatic nature of South Asian teaching in general and how teachers have taken it to heart that correcting students is the main role of a teacher and that it must be done at every level.

TEACHER'S ROLE

When the learners perform in their small groups or walk around the class, asking and answering questions, the teacher's task is to sit with them in their small groups or also walk around and take part in their activities, as another group member, helping them when necessary. Also when learners are supposed to present their work in front of the class, the teacher is just an observer like the other learners, sitting with them as part of the audience. When learners make mistakes in pronunciation, grammar, word order, etc., the teacher is not supposed to intervene and correct them. It is in fact 'prohibited' for teachers. For instance, if, after completing the group activity, a learner raises a hand and announces enthusiastically, 'We ready!' usually followed by a repetition of the same from the entire group, the teacher can simply join that group, raise her hand too and declare that, 'We are ready!' Invariably, the entire group will follow suit.

The significance of such a seemingly small gesture on the part of the teacher, joining the group, in addition to repeating the statement (correctly), is that the sense of belonging the learners share with the rest of group will be stronger and they will feel that the teacher is included in their team. This in turn, will make them feel closer to the teacher who is their *English* teacher, which will help them to develop a sense of closeness to the subject of English itself. This is projection, the opposite of the anxiety-related phenomena that we discussed earlier.

The reasons given by learners for disliking English and developing a fear of speaking English stem from a variety of reasons that have been discussed earlier. For the poor learners who may come into the classroom with such negative experiences *vis-à-vis* English language learning, the teacher joining their group to repeat what they uttered is itself not only a form of 'acceptance' but also 'inclusion' into the 'English-speaking circle'. This makes the learners feel proud and may leave them with a sense of achievement. This sense of achievement can and will be projected to the next level when they perform in front of the class. Again, it is the teacher's sole responsibility to take them to the next highest level. How should the teacher do this? Ignoring all the errors the learners make when they perform, appreciating their performance and encouraging the other groups to applaud them are some of the best strategies.

The teacher can appreciate everything pronounced accurately by complimenting, e.g.

Wow! You got it all correct!
Very good, indeed!
Very clever all of you!
Outstanding!
(Applause)

Also, the teacher can appreciate everything the learners perform in front of the class, regardless of their accuracy, by using phrases of encouragement, e.g.

Good performance!
Clever!
Wow!
(Applause)

It is worth quoting one of the Indian students in the sample who has taken pains to describe an experience while speaking English to show how any kind of support, even mere clapping *after* a speech performance, can make learners more confident:

> Once while I was new at my spoken English class, there was a debate going on. When it was my turn to speak I was nervous but somehow I speak with my broken English. The other [sic] present in the room were better than me, but still they supported me and clapped for me at the end of my speech. This incident gave me a lot of confidence and thus made my learning much easier.
> (Student code I-261)[4]

Some way to signal approval for the learners' speech performance is necessary from the teacher, their peers or both. The teacher should therefore encourage others to applaud every group after their performance without making any reference to any errors that were committed, so that learners, in spite of their awareness of their 'poor English', remain confident enough to perform again.

Teachers can compile all the errors made by the learners during their group activities and group performances to talk about them in general, at the end of the class. This is because pointing to an individual or a particular group to correct their errors may result in embarrassment for the learners, causing them to feel threatened or humiliated, which will hinder the confidence building process.

In our experience of teaching the course, we realize that 'no error correction' is one of the most effective strategies for contributing to the maintenance of the safe zone. As a result, not only does the eagerness to perform increase to the point where soon there is no reluctance at all to run to the front of the class, but there is also a notable improvement in student performance in terms of using the language in a trial and error manner.

No grammar teaching

Another strategy advocated in the confidence building course is not teaching grammar. During the pilot programme in 2009, this was met with many raised eyebrows. It was interesting to realize exactly how much importance is given to the grammar component in teaching English when the burning question came from all quarters, from coordinators, teachers who taught in the course and others who were not even connected to the course but had only heard of it: 'Aren't you going to teach grammar in this new course?' The answer was a clear 'No.' Upon reflection, it seemed to us that it was unheard of to develop a new course to teach English that did not teach grammar.

The reasons for not teaching grammar in the Building Confidence to Speak English course are:

1 By the time the undergraduates enter the university/college, they have about ten years' worth of English language learning history behind them. This is common to all four countries studied, namely India, Bangladesh, Pakistan and Sri Lanka. The undergraduates in the South Asian region have learned

English as a second language throughout their school career, in some cases from grade one and in others from grade three.

During the entire duration of their school careers, they learn English grammar as a compulsory component along with other skills such as reading and writing, accompanying a minimal amount of listening and speaking. In short, with a typical English language learning history in the sub-continent, learners' will have already learnt a good amount of English grammar. The problem is that they hardly put (or get to put) any of that grammar into actual practice, i.e. with spontaneous speaking or writing. The examinations at each grade are in writing in all four countries. Unfortunately, neither the grammar knowledge manifested in the written paper nor their performance at the examinations is satisfactory, as most of the students do not pass the English written examinations.[5] This was discussed in detail in the background chapter.

Therefore, teaching grammar once again is futile without giving them a platform to use it, a platform that they did not have during their school career. Speaking is an area that has been neglected or under-emphasized, as none of the four South Asian countries have a formal system to test spoken English at term or year-ending examinations. Nor is speech formally assessed at national level examinations such as the university entrance examinations.

2 When the students were asked to choose their most desired skill in learning English, an overwhelming majority opted for the speaking skill and this has remained unchanged *vis-à-vis* the Sri Lankan ELT scenario from 2008 to 2018. In the larger South Asian region, with students from India, Pakistan and Bangladesh, the preference is the same. Other than one or two respondents out of more than 4,500 respondents from four countries, no students reported a desire to learn more grammar in the 'any other' preferred category that was given as an option on the questionnaire.

3 It is worth mentioning that many Bangladeshi students explicitly stated in their responses that they had enough grammar taught to them throughout their schooling and during their undergraduate days and that they need less emphasis on grammar and more emphasis on speaking English.

4 The failure of commonplace English language courses is that they are a bundle of everything: a little bit of speaking, plenty of reading and writing, some listening, some vocabulary and a good amount of grammar. With these courses, over the past 70 years of English language teaching in the region, we have not produced the desired results. This is what inspired us to 'invent' something different and more focused on actual learner needs instead of what was 'assumed' to be necessary by teachers and course developers.

Even though grammar is not ***taught*** explicitly in the confidence building course as a discrete unit, there is grammar in the confidence building course that is to be ***acquired*** by students while engaging in tasks/activities.

The researcher perceives the teaching of grammar to students during and after schooling under a common 'grammar component', whether it is done deductively and inductively, as being like pouring water into an upside-down pot. Teaching all the grammar points long before students feel the need to use them is futile as their minds are not ready to absorb them. Even though the learner may understand the rule and how and when to use it at the time of learning it, one cannot guarantee that they will retain that knowledge when the actual need to use it arises. The effort made to teach grammar may seem to have been utilized well as learners may answer some questions related to the grammar point taught, mostly in written form, at the end of the lesson. However, more often than not, they will fail to use it spontaneously. For instance, outside the classroom, in a general conversation, answering a question that requires 'flew' as the answer, which has been taught under 'past tense formation of irregular verbs', a learner may say 'flied' despite having given the correct answer on the grammar test at the time it was taught. (We are certain that teachers have more and better examples.) In addition, the overall results after 70 years of English language teaching in the entire South Asian region do not give us a satisfactory outcome when the large majority, especially those who come from rural and semi-rural areas, are performing poorly (in grammar) in written national examinations as well as being unable to speak a word of English when they are spoken to. (See Chapter 2 on background.)

TEACHER'S ROLE

The detailed instructions given in the lesson materials (see the chapter on Course Design) involve simple grammar structures. For instance, 'Your teacher will help you with the necessary language structures and vocabulary.' Teachers are not supposed to teach the grammar points, which they usually 'assume' are required by learners to carry out the task, but are instead supposed to wait until the need comes from the learners. In other words, when learners are engaged in a particular activity, in groups, they may have questions as to how to express a certain idea in a particular form. Teachers are expected to walk around the class, going from one group to the other, attending to such learner requirements.

When a small group needs a certain language structure (e.g., a grammar point) to express its members' views, the teacher should give it to *that particular group only* and then may come to the board and put it on the board specifically for that particular group's use and for others *only if and when they need it*. The teacher is not supposed to make it a general teaching point and teach everyone as to how to use it and its structure, assuming (wrongly!) that it is everyone's perceived need. The teacher should leave it on the board till the activity is over. At the end of the activity, the teacher may go back to the structures that are on the board (which are there as a result of learners' needs) and highlight them.

Students are made to feel the need for grammar structures (this is also valid for vocabulary) and are given the structures on their own request, which will occur based on their own perception of the needs that arise when they are at work. Such a stance underscores the ideology that learning grammar is not an end in itself but a means to an end. This approach is more effective for a course that aims at building confidence to speak English.

The detailed instructions also include the following sentence: 'You may use the following language structures' whereby students are given examples of simple sentence structures that may be required to accomplish a given task. Teachers are advised to be open to more structures of similar nature when learners suggest/request them or struggle to form their own. Teachers are given the freedom to suggest their own, yet the collection of structures that appear on the board should not be too many (no more than five) so that it will not be overwhelming for the learners if/when they try to use all of them in one exercise.

This strategy should not be misunderstood as *teaching* grammar. This is not and should not be the case. Teachers are not expected to explain why, for instance, the verb takes a singular form or the auxiliary verb is found at the beginning of a question, etc., when the structures are given on the board. Instead, one can make learners repeat after the teacher a few times to practise and learners can use these structures in their group performances as they are given in the lesson material. What is crucial to remember is that when the requirement for a particular structure comes from a particular group, then the repetition is only for the group that asked about the sentence structure and not for the whole class. This is done to help these particular learners with the sentence structures they feel they need to carry out a particular activity. In so doing, the teacher helps the learners to *acquire* grammar to use in a meaningful manner.

This stance in regard to grammar and its (non)teaching is underscored by the idea that post-colonial South Asian English language learners with years of English language learning history behind them already possess sufficient knowledge of grammar rules in order to carry out a simple conversation related to their day-to-day communication (Basic Interpersonal Communication Skills – BICS) and do not need more grammar lessons. Instead, what the learners need is an occasional gentle reminder of the grammar they are already acquainted with at some level and a platform to put that knowledge into practice while feeling safe enough to make mistakes in their practice.

Performance is not mandatory

In the Building Confidence to Speak English course, student performance is not mandatory. They engage in activities in pairs, small groups or as a whole class. Once they complete the task/activity assigned to them in pairs or small groups within the allocated time frame, some activities require them to present their results in front of the class. However, it is stated very clearly in the instructions, 'Present it to the entire class, if you would like to do so.' This means that if a pair or a group *does not feel like* performing, they can opt out of presenting in front of the class.

TEACHER'S ROLE

After working at a given task/activity, learners are usually expected to speak in their groups at the end. However, teachers are not supposed to make performance compulsory. If a group shows some reluctance to get up and perform, then the teacher should move on and wait for another group to volunteer without making any negative remarks. The instructions in the course material state that 'Volunteers can perform', so that learners do not feel any kind of anxiety when thinking about compulsory performance, which is the case with most low proficiency groups.

Once the learners understand that their teacher is not going to (op)press them to perform in front of the class, they start to feel relaxed and begin to volunteer to come to the front of the class without any hesitation. In the case of a group that shows reluctance to perform in front of the class, the teacher can simply move on to the next group of volunteers. When the next group gets up from their seats to perform, the teacher can praise them by applauding them or making a positive remark such as 'Wow, clever group!', 'You are very keen!' etc. This not only encourages the group that is ready to perform but inspires the other groups to want to perform as well.

The objective of the *no mandatory performance* rule is to create a relaxed atmosphere in the English language classroom so that learners will enter the classroom, work in groups and pairs, and leave it with relaxed minds. These relaxed minds will gradually start to perform wonders. In 2009, when the Building Confidence to Speak English course was piloted, we allocated time for each activity, allotting what we thought was a generous number of minutes for each group performance. In the second week of the course, teachers asked us to allocate more time as everyone in the class wanted to perform and the time allocated was not sufficient. This was corroborated during our class observation: every time we went into a class, we had to seek permission from a group of students since they were the ones in front of the class, in the middle of a performance, relishing their position at the centre of attention. In addition, it was hard to find the teacher as he or she was usually lost among the audience!

No homework

In order to create a relaxed, stress-free environment both inside and outside the English language classroom, the confidence building course does not require learners to do any homework. Instead, all of the activities are completed during class time and learners leave at the end of each session without feeling burdened by homework as they have been accustomed to throughout their schooling and in the university. During their schooling, students have always been bombarded with homework of some sort to work on in every subject, including English, while as undergraduates the students are constantly pressured to complete assignments and meet deadlines in their subject-streams. Our programme is meant to be a radical break from the status quo. This is why it should differ not only from the learners' previous English language learning experience, but also the way they learn other subjects, which is why the confidence building course does not require homework. This is yet another special feature of the course that helps to create a safe zone for learning and speaking English.

TEACHER'S ROLE

Teachers are expected to be careful not to fall back into their old habits by inventing some homework with the best of intentions to aid the learners in improving their proficiency. Homework is not required during the confidence building course, precisely because the primary aim of the course is NOT to improve English language proficiency. *No homework* is relaxing for the teachers as well, as they do not have to waste valuable class time to check whether learners have done their homework. Learners are not burdened with having to do homework after classes and they don't have yet another reason for skipping the class altogether because they failed to do their homework or to feel embarrassed when the teacher enquires about homework that they did not complete. One particular experience we had at the University of Colombo, Sri Lanka, is noteworthy here. During our weekly teacher training sessions, when we reminded the teachers about the no homework policy, one teacher said that some of her students actually asked for homework! She wanted to know what to do in such a case. This goes to show that South Asian learners are so accustomed to a set of patterns in teaching and learning that any divergence from these set patterns is seen to disorient some students. In order not to disappoint such learners, teachers can be creative and give those who ask for homework some kind of work to be completed at home. For instance, one can ask them to read a small story book, to listen to the English news bulletin, talk with someone in English for a few minutes, etc., which the teacher can easily check the next day without having to take away from the time allocated for group activities. Teachers need to check on such homework as informally as possible, so that others who did not ask for it will not feel left out. Also, those who ask for homework should feel that their enthusiasm is rewarded.

No mother tongue

Another very important characteristic of the confidence building course is that classroom instruction is exclusively in English. The idea behind such a stance is that it is not required for learners to understand (or for teachers to make learners understand) 100% of everything the teacher utters in the classroom. For instance, learners may only comprehend 5–7% of the teacher's instructions on the very first day of class, partly due to their unfamiliarity with the teacher's use of language, accent, etc. However, as the days go by, learners will gradually be able to comprehend ever more of the teacher's language as they become accustomed to the teacher's expressions and his or her body language. This supports the idea that learning is a gradual process and that learners should be given an opportunity to go through this process where they get the opportunity to guess the meaning of words, make mistakes in guessing and understanding and actively take part in classroom activities. Also, when there is no mother tongue instruction and the 'English only' principle prevails, learners are encouraged to speak in English at whatever level they are capable of. In addition, the principle of 'no error correction' helps learners to speak in English without being conscious of any potential mistakes they may make in speaking exclusively in English.

TEACHER'S ROLE

Teachers are advised to use simple language in classroom instructions and to be ready to adjust to the lowest proficiency groups. Moreover, teachers can make use of body language and visual aids (e.g. simple drawings on the board) to support their instructions in English.

The learners' low proficiency will lead them to switch back to their mother tongue quite often. The teacher has to be with each group taking part in the activities, not as a teacher, but as a group member with higher language proficiency able to help whenever the learners face a stumbling block (related to lack of comprehension or not having the vocabulary to express themselves, even in 'broken' English). For instance, when learners try to adjust their chairs to form small groups, the teacher may hear a phrase equivalent to 'move your chair a little please' in the learner's mother tongue. In such cases, teachers are advised to give the equivalent phrase in English and make the entire group repeat it several times so that they can use the phrase then and there.

An utterance everyday

Considering the low proficiency level of the learners, it may be too ambitious to expect them to speak English at all times during their group activities. A very important strategy in the confidence building classroom to support the no mother tongue principle is to give learners a simple English phrase to use every day during their activities.

TEACHER'S ROLE

Phrases can be taken from the learners' needs. Teachers, while walking among the groups, may hear the learners speak (most likely in their mother tongue) from which phrases can be picked out and translated into English. Some of the commonly used phrases may be written on the board and the teacher can have ALL of the learners repeat the phrase a couple of times. It is also good to get the learners to copy it into their notebooks so that they can always go back to their 'phrase bank' to speak English. Teachers need to be conscious of what learners are speaking about in class so that the most frequently used utterances (in mother tongue) are picked out and given in English translation. Some repetition of the phrases can be accomplished in drills. After about a week or so, the teacher can go back through all of the phrases that have been given and get learners to repeat them several times so that learners will remember the phrases and their pronunciation.

It is advisable to give one phrase/utterance per day instead of bombarding students with many. If the phrases learners use in mother tongue while communicating with other group members can be translated and given back to the learners, it will be more effective as they have shown a need for the phrase in the context of their immediate use. However, teachers are advised to give the English translation of the utterance only to the particular group that used it in mother tongue. It is also good to get only that particular group to repeat it several times so that the group will be able to utilize it for their immediate use. The teacher needs to understand that a phrase that is useful for a particular group may not be useful to another group, even while they are working on the same group activity. Therefore, instead of creating a common teaching session around one particular phrase/utterance required by a single group, it is advisable to pick one commonly used utterance as the 'phrase/utterance for the day' and get everyone to repeat and write that particular phrase while restricting questions about any particular phrases to the group that needs them. As the days go by, the teacher can ask the learners to give an utterance (in mother tongue) that they feel they need so that the teacher can give the English equivalent. Some of the most common phrases that learners require to carry out group activities are given below:

Show me your answer please!
Is this correct?
What do you think of this?
I am not sure.
I think you are correct.
That sounds good!

Kagan and Kagan (2009), Kagan (2011) speaks about gambits, i.e. useful phrases that are needed for a team to work together effectively. They could include ways to ask for help, check for understanding, disagree politely, encourage effort, etc. However, in contexts where English is a foreign/second language and among learners who are weak in English and/or hesitate to speak in English, gambits can be made use of in classroom communication in English and English only. Kagan and Kagan (2009), Kagan (2011) identifies three types of gambits: paraphrasing gambits, gambits for politely disagreeing and positive affirmation gambits. Some examples are given below:

PARAPHRASE GAMBITS: So what you're saying is ..., All in all ..., If I understand you correctly ..., You said ..., In other words ..., So you mean that ..., To sum it up ..., Let me rephrase that ..., In a nutshell ..., Let's remember ..., I can see it that way ..., On the other hand ..., etc.

GAMBITS FOR DISAGREEING POLITELY: That would be great except ..., I don't see how ..., One problem is ..., Actually ..., I'm afraid ..., That's good. Another thought is ..., etc.

POSITIVE AFFIRMATION GAMBITS: Wow! I really like that! That's awesome! You rock! Excellent! Super-duper job! Way to go! Great job! I wish I had thought of that!

Sitting down with learners at the same level (of chairs/benches)

The teacher should get out of his or her central position in the classroom as this is very important for helping the learners to feel safe in the English language classroom. As we discussed before, in the South Asian region, the teacher is a figure who is revered; this is reinforced when the students see the teacher as the central figure in the classroom. Needless to say, this poses a problem for student-centred teaching in the confidence building classroom. The teacher must therefore go to the periphery and allow the learners to come to the foreground. Another tip to encourage this is to sit with the learners at their level on the same benches or chairs the learners occupy, or at times, just below them, bending a little. Teachers will find their students a little embarrassed initially as they are not accustomed to this practice and may even try to get up from their seats. The significance of this simple gesture on the part of the teacher helps to free the learner from the mindset that the teacher is the sole authority who is both unchallenged and unchallengeable. It is this mindset that creates an aura around the teacher and emphasizes the teacher's role as a 'mistake-catcher' and 'corrector'.

TEACHER'S ROLE

In the many roles a teacher is expected to play in the confidence building classroom, including acting as a monitor, facilitator, group member, etc., the teacher is advised to sit with learners in their groups and on the same level or even a slightly lower level. This makes the teacher less of a looming presence watching over the classroom. Whenever a group is presenting, the teacher can sit with the group that just finished their presentation, in one of the chairs/benches and simply be a part of the learner community. Also, when explaining or giving specific instructions to a particular group, the teacher can bend down or sit with the group so that he or she is not perceived as an imposing figure. Even if learners show some level of discomfort with the teacher's newly found 'humility', they will also feel less threatened by and friendlier with the teacher.

Potential challenges for teachers

The duties expected of teachers in the confidence building classroom are different from the duties found in an ordinary classroom. While maintaining the features of the safe zone as discussed above, it can be very demanding for the teacher to instruct, to monitor, to act as a group member in four or five groups and at the same time, to cater to different types of needs that arise, etc. Also, with low proficiency groups, having to repeat the same instructions and questions may be exhausting. At times, having to change the input to a level that is comprehensible to the learners may be taxing. There can be instances where unprecedented occurrences may make the teaching even more challenging. We report below three particular incidents as examples so that challenges can be viewed in realistic terms. They emphasize the importance of a teacher's constant conscious effort to maintain the features of the safe zone and to tackle unforeseen incidents that require on-the-spot improvisations.

Incident I: We were invited to run the Building Confidence to Speak English course in a popular school in Colombo, Sri Lanka, to junior secondary students.

Every Monday, for two hours, we trained the teachers to teach the next four days of the week, after school. As usual, we did some teacher observation sessions while teachers were at work.

We went from class to class, and sat with the teachers and students for about half an hour or so. What we saw in one class was absolutely shocking! The teacher was sitting in the centre of the class, having made her students sit around her in a circle, while she was explaining everything in the lesson material to them as if it was a reading comprehension lesson. She was also using some amount of mother tongue in her effort to explain the content.

Obviously this is quite unacceptable in the confidence building class: students are not supposed to sit in any other way other than in small groups or in pairs; the teacher is neither supposed to preach and/or spoon-feed the students nor is she required to be in the centre; the activities are not meant for listening or reading comprehension but are for actively doing while speaking; the teacher is not supposed to explain anything using mother tongue, etc.

The challenge is that teachers in the South Asian region often fall back into their old habits: the usual way they teach comes back to them despite being exposed to new methodologies and advancements in the discourse. Very sadly, after many years of experience in interacting with teachers in various capacities, we have come to the stark realization that some teachers simply do not care!

Incident II: Another similar incident was reported during the time the course was piloted. A teacher approached me to tell me that her students asked her why she was not prescribing any grammar book or teaching any grammar. This was because their friends' English teacher not only taught them grammar but had shown them a particular grammar book to buy. On investigation, it turned out that what was reported was correct. This again shows that teachers may not only fall back to their old 'teaching habits', consciously or unconsciously, but also, in order to feel that they are teaching, revert to teaching grammar too. Also, it shows reluctance on the part of the teachers to embrace anything new, letting go of the old and the habitual.

These two incidents may make us look at teachers through a tainted lens. Notwithstanding this, teachers should take responsibility for their actions if they want to see some improvement in their learners' English language proficiency and are sincere in their efforts. A common lamentation that comes from teachers of English in rural or semi-rural South Asia is that their students are not keen, they do not have the conducive environment to learn English, their parents are not educated, etc., implying that over 10–20 years of teaching English these teachers always get the same type of students. However, this prompts the inevitable question, 'Couldn't the blame lie, not with the students, but with the teacher who has been the same over 10–20 years?' Teachers need to be open to new ideas, supporting experimental teaching–learning and ready to improve their teaching with innovative methodologies, with awareness and sincerity.

Incident III: Teachers need to be prepared for the unexpected. While using the speech functions that are required for BICS, accompanied by the use of pictures related to learners' rural and semi-rural settings for storytelling, the need for proverbs, or idiomatic expressions that are close to learners' background may arise without warning. When learners turn to their teachers for these, they may not be able to find the equivalent on the spur of the moment.

We remember one incident when the Building Confidence to Speak English course ran for the first time; students were asked to create a story by looking at a picture (with a man who has fallen into a pit while stealing bananas, in the middle of the night). One teacher, in the middle of his teaching, rushed to us and asked, 'What is the equivalent to the idiom in Sinhala, *puhul hora karen dane*?' (meaning: a thief who has stolen ash pumpkin is revealed by the ash on his shoulder).

It was a tricky moment: the teacher did not want to show his students that he could not find the equivalent; as for the course designer, this was something unexpected. It should be noted that it is not always possible to find equivalent phrases between languages in relation to their particular subtexts, nuances, idiomatic expressions and proverbs as there may not be equivalents at all and/or even when there are, realistically speaking, the equivalents may not come into our heads immediately.

In this case, we struggled to find an equivalent, unfortunately to no avail. Then, it dawned on us that it was not necessary. We advised the helpless teacher, 'Ask them to say, "This is what happens when you do bad deeds; *puhul hora karen dane*. You see?"'

Later, every year at the teacher training sessions, we refer to this particular incident as a potential challenge and ask the teachers not to hesitate to 'sandwich' the phrase/term in mother tongue in between two English sentences or phrases. This in fact serves as a positive point to achieve the overall objective of the course in a number of ways: we put learners at ease by showing them that they can use words and phrases from their mother tongues while speaking in English, if the context is understood by the parties involved in the conversation, without having to sweat over finding the equivalent in English; also, we bring the English language another step closer to the learners; we show that the English language does not and need not represent only stereotypical English culture.

The process-oriented nature of the approach

The confidence building classroom operates with a process-oriented approach in two aspects, both of which are geared towards eliminating LAA: the features of the safe zone focus on making the learners go through the process of using the language; the activities are designed and sequenced according to two scales, namely, communicative and cognitive potential developmental scales, which contribute to the process of learners going through a step-by-step development. The purposes of sequencing of activities in the lesson materials and the characteristics of the safe zone must be thoroughly understood by the teachers.

The safe zone is the exact opposite of an ordinary classroom. The ordinary classroom in post-colonial South Asia has produced learners who experience anxiety when speaking English. Such a classroom is characterized by a set of features: learners work and present alone for the most part; teachers either translate every word/phrase into the mother tongue of the learners or the classroom language is the learners' mother tongue; teachers correct learner errors as soon as an error is committed; speech activities are rare and performance is mandatory whenever they are taught. Often the teacher points to the students to present; grammar teaching is given the utmost importance and learners are given heaps of homework, some of which is never checked. Teachers expect a tangible output at the end of each lesson/day. All in all, these features contribute to a product-oriented approach in teaching.

On the contrary, the safe zone of the confidence building course has none of these features. In fact, the safe zone operates on contrary principles. First and foremost, the whole course involves speaking in English and writing is extremely sparse. As discussed, there is no individual work or performance, no performance is mandatory, there is no error correction, almost no mother tongue, no homework, no grammar teaching, etc. Most importantly, no tangible output is expected at the end of each lesson/day in any form. Also, learners may present in pairs, small groups and even as part of the entire class. As emphasized, performance is voluntary as learners go through the process under the teacher's monitoring and supervision. If peer cooperation at work is observed, visible output is not required. Such a stance underscores a very important principle: the approach is process oriented and not product oriented.

As discussed earlier, the Building Confidence to Speak English course has a sound psychological approach. LAA is a social construct, which has to be fully comprehended as a process in itself that has been created and perpetuated over many years in the learners' lives. To beat LAA, speaking English, the most feared skill is used. Ironically, it is the skill that is most desired as well, which helps it act as a remedial measure. Psychology professes habituation to be the best rectifying measure and exposure the best technique to use for habituation, while a safe environment is conducive for habituation to maximize its effect. The English language classroom is converted into a safe zone where all the features that are present in the ordinary classroom setting and produce and aggravate LAA are avoided. Exposure is given gradually, in increments. Thus, the learning process is inherent and an immediate tangible product is not sought. This process-oriented nature of the approach is manifested by (a) the materials and their design, with carefully sequenced activities aiming at a gradual communicative and cognitive potential development of the learners, and (b) a teaching methodology that discourages teachers from looking for an immediate visible output.

Initially, teachers may find it frustrating to speak only in English where they find blank faces staring back at them when instructions for an activity are given. However, with a lot of body language, simple audio-visuals (e.g. quick sketches on the board) and repetition, teachers themselves will find that the learners are 'picking up' the language over time. An important warning is that teachers should not expect the learners to understand everything that is being said to them. Our advice is that the teachers should expect their learners to understand only 5% of what is uttered by the teachers on the very first day. On the second day, with a little familiarity, learners will be able to catch about 7% of what is said to them. As the days go by, learners will start to understand almost everything that is uttered at a good pace as their familiarity with their teachers' language use, style and body language in the safe zone increases.

In an ordinary classroom in post-colonial South Asia, most teachers of English in rural or semi-rural schools and universities often resort to either translating the English instructions into the learners' mother tongue or only use mother tongue for instructions. This is because teachers expect an immediate output in terms of comprehension from their learners, while aiming at the next immediate tangible output, correct answers to the questions/activity that is being planned for the day. Learners, on the other hand, get the correct answers and are happy. Teachers are satisfied as they feel they have taught well. However, this is counterproductive as learners often prove not to have retained anything from the lesson to use meaningfully in context. One example is that the learners in Sri Lanka study passive voice sentence structures from about grade six onward but even at the undergraduate level (in the lowest proficiency group), they are unable to speak or write a single sentence using the passive voice. Most importantly, students are unable to listen to the instructions in English and figure out what to do.

In order to become confident speakers, learners need the support of their teachers. This support is to help them go through a process, in which learners get to guess, make mistakes and become confused while trying to understand the English spoken by the teacher, and to finally emerge with clarity. Thus, the 'no mother tongue' policy in the teaching methodology of the Confidence Building to Speak English course supports this process-oriented principle.

Likewise, the 'no error correction' rule, may initially make the learners look at their teachers with suspicion when they are not 'picked on' for every spoken mistake. When they begin to realize that they are not being corrected, a gradual sense of security will come over them. Having to perform is a mandatory component of the ordinary classroom, especially if the lesson is a speaking activity, and at first, learners may wait for the trauma of being picked by the teachers to get up in the English language classroom. However, the teachers' gentle approach to those who are reluctant will gradually make the learners keener to perform, especially in a context where their teachers have nothing to correct as the learners seem not to be making any grievous mistakes!

'A phrase every day' equips the learners with language to use in their English language classroom. When they accumulate phrases and sentences each day, this also contributes to a process of learning/acquiring language phrases for communication within the classroom. By the time they reach the third week of the course, learners are usually in possession of about 20 phrases/utterances that are ready for their immediate use.

The activities in the lesson materials are carefully designed and sequenced so that the stages of the cognitive and communicative potential development scales are reached gradually with incremental increases in the difficulty level.

The requirement for repetition of phrases, questions, sentences in activities reinforces the process the learners have just been through while slightly more difficult new phrases and sentences are introduced to proceed with the process of language use.

Gradually, activity by activity, day by day and with the teacher's support, learners will attain success at the next level. While speaking and being spoken to in English, learners are exposed to the English language and become habituated to speaking English in a way that is developmentally appropriate to their proficiency levels. Consequently, the fear/anxiety/shyness in speaking English will not remain novel and, as they become habituated to speaking English, this will result in decreasing the arousal of their nervous systems. Finally, LAA will gradually diminish.

The simultaneous process taking place is that of confidence building, from one activity to the next, one day to the next, as their confidence increases along with their ability to speak English. As a result, learners are given not only the opportunity to speak English but a conducive environment that allows them to be members of the 'English-speaking community' which was the 'other' they previously feared. Gradually, learners will become comfortable with their new persona, their new learner identity who speaks 'some' English without hesitation. This occurs as the learners begin to identify themselves and others around them as changeable within the reciprocal and variable relationships between learner and context (Johnson, 2011).

As discussed, these learners have been frustrated in their English language learning by what can be described in terms of a gap between two selves: the self that is competent in their mother tongue and the other self that is unable to express themselves in their L2 (Granger, 2004). This incompatibility between the fully developed L1 psyche and the emerging second language self may now be lessened as this 'new L2 self' begins to blossom. This in turn will reduce the frustration that arises due to the mismatch between the L1 and the new L2 psyche that Granger (2004) speaks about in adult learners. As a result of not being silent, instead being active in the English language classroom and being accepted in their new active capacity, the barrier that has been built between themselves and the English language (and its uses) may begin to crack. Just as a little bird cracks its shell and comes out of it to see the world, the learners, looking through their cracked shell, may start to see a new world, a world that looks safe in spite of their suspicion. It is the teacher's responsibility to give them assurance about the safety of this new world. It is important to understand the features of this learner who was silent and inside a cell for so long in the English language classroom, who now comes out speaking some English. Their insecure L2 identity, which was created as a result of numerous social forces in their lives, will still be there in some form. It is only through the unwavering support of the teacher that the learners can create a new identity in the English language classroom first that can later be developed into a more stable and assured identity that also functions outside the classroom and creates opportunities for them to aim at becoming better possible selves.

It is important to understand that learners' lack of confidence to speak English was not instantaneous, but the outcome of a process that occurred over many years. LAA is a chronic condition in psychological terms, as learners have been the victims of negative attitudes in society over many years. Therefore, eliminating LAA requires a careful, gradual and scientific approach and a consistent, coherent process.

The necessity of teacher training and its components

There are a few reasons that compulsory teacher training is required for the teachers of the Building Confidence to Speak English course: (a) the failure of the Eclectic Approach in South Asia, (b) teacher habituation, (c) the compelling need for a change in teaching methods and (d) teacher awareness of bridge building between language attitudes and language needs.

From our interactions over two decades with teachers of English language in the region, as colleagues, as teacher educators, as supervisors, as mentors, etc., we have realized that most teachers fall into at least one of the following groups with some in more than one: teachers who do not do what they say they do; teachers who do what they are habituated to doing; teachers who are not aware of current developments in the field. While teachers and teacher trainers in the western world may see this perspective as top-down and authoritarian, teachers and their trainers in post-colonial South Asia will agree with us that this is our reality.

In the history of English language teaching methods and approaches, teaching English as a second/foreign language has come a long way in terms of theoretical perspectives. From the Direct Method, Grammar Translation Method and Communicative Approaches in the 1980s to the Thematic Approaches and 5E Method, most South Asian countries have ended up using the Eclectic Method/Approach. If we ask ten teachers of English in the region, 'What is the Method/Approach you use to teach English to your students?' there are two inevitable and prompt responses from *all* of them: one is 'Eclectic Approach/Method' and the other, 'Communicative Approach'. We have found some very interesting revelations when trying to probe into these two answers further. For instance, when teachers are asked what constitutes their Eclectic Method/Approach, their answers are mostly confined mostly to two methods: Communicative Approach and the Grammar Translation Method. When asked about Communicative Approach and asked to elaborate on the way they teach grammar, their responses reveal that they usually teach the rule first and give exercises for their students to work on, a deductive method which is actually discouraged in Communicative Approach. Problem-based learning, Task-based Learning, CLL, 5E Method, etc., can contribute immensely to the English language teaching in the region if they are included in the Eclectic Method/Approach. However, we cannot see any newer methods being utilized at any level in any South Asian countries.

The Eclectic Approach/Method is a complete failure in the region. This is because most of the teachers of English are not aware of the many methods and approaches that are in use and that were used in order to select the best to teach a particular lesson. Some teachers may have heard of some methods but have no clue about the underlying principles. In our view, this is due to (a) systemic inefficiency and (b) teacher negligence. With most of our education being in the public sector, the teacher training programmes available for school English teachers in the region are mostly pre-service with infrequent and random periods of in-service training. Once the teacher trainees are absorbed into the school system, they get by with using the age-old techniques they studied during their teacher training courses. As in-service teacher training programmes are rare and not systematically organized, teachers do not have an opportunity to update their knowledge. Also, there are no proper monitoring systems for teachers in South Asian countries. Supervision is rare. Supervisors themselves are usually not competent in English. In addition, teachers in the public sector are not rewarded or punished for their performance. Private sector teachers are recruited mostly on the basis of their English language fluency (spoken) and not on the basis of any professional competence in teaching. The teacher training courses they follow are offered by private institutes that are not regulated by any government body and may not be recognized. Student feedback on teacher performance is not sought either in the private or public sector. In the absence of incentives, teachers attempting to get by while doing the bare minimum is the only outcome one can expect. Teachers are also burdened by having to complete the syllabus in order to prepare students for a common written examination. They have neither the time nor motivation to update their professional knowledge. Teachers in rural and semi-rural areas are more adversely affected by such a situation, as are their students.

In this context, it is crucial to train teachers specifically to teach in the confidence building course so that they will be well equipped with skills that are required for creating and maintaining the safe zone. In addition, the ground rules for the confidence building course are given to teachers. They are expected to read them during every teacher training session, so that they are constantly reminded of the course objectives and the special features of the safe zone (Appendix B).

As we have seen in potential challenges that are discussed above, teachers often fall back into their old habits of routine teaching. Unfortunately, routine teaching has proven to be a failure with students lacking confidence to speak English due to overcorrection, emphasis on individual work and mandatory performance, etc., as we have discussed. It must also be judged to be a failure on the grounds that most students in all of the countries studied fail the national examinations in English.

Teacher habituation results in teachers who take teaching for granted and do not look beyond a goal of making students produce tangible output at the end of each lesson, while aiming at covering a section of the syllabus every day and simply not caring about the way in which their teaching is carried out. These factors are stabilized in the teachers' mindset and continually influence their teaching. Teachers with years of teaching experience are hard to change ideologically and teachers in the sub-continent are not being challenged professionally or intellectually. In fact, teachers are treated like gods in the region, as ***gurus*** who are capable of guiding the young and old alike, in all matters relating to life, and not only teaching. Teachers acting in this role are hardly questioned in their performance even when they prove to be dull failures who do not produce the intended results. Therefore, eradicating ordinary and routine practices from their teaching is difficult. Only continuous and rigorous training can help lure them out of their regular teaching methodologies, techniques and strategies without allowing them to fall back into their old habits.

From this context of failure in teaching English as second/foreign language, the need for change is obvious. In order for the teachers to refrain from falling back into their habitual, routine way of teaching, which includes their notions of Eclectic Approach and Communicative Approach, it is important that they are immersed in a rigorous training programme on a regular basis with a strong emphasis on the methodological principles of the confidence building course. The requirement for training that is regular, specific to each activity and that contains learner actions and perspectives embedded within it becomes imperative, as such rigorous training will constantly remind teachers of the significance of the teacher's role in developing and sustaining the features of the safe zone.

The interest of some teachers in change should not be downplayed in this discussion. We have met teachers who genuinely want to improve their teaching but lack the resources to improve, although they are in the minority. Most of these teachers lack facilities and opportunities to upgrade their quality of teaching, update their knowledge and make changes to the teaching–learning process. The compulsory training included in the Building Confidence to Speak English course can contribute to helping these teachers not only in teaching the course, but also in applying these principles to their teaching in general, so that they develop student-friendly strategies for developing language proficiency in the learners. Thus, the compulsory teacher training takes teachers forward in their general development as rigorous training is considered an essential component of professional competence (Wallace, 1991).

Language attitudes create LAA. Even though it is difficult to change societal attitudes towards the English language and its speakers, teachers of English can change learners' language attitudes. As part of the larger society, teachers also have a certain way of looking at the English language and its speakers. It is crucial that we change these attitudes so that they can contribute to changing learner attitudes and take their teaching in a positive direction. Training in the confidence building course helps teachers create a different value system in regard to English language teaching and a new set of attitudes towards the English language and its speakers. Also, it helps to build bridges between language attitudes and language needs (see Chapter 11). Once teacher attitudes towards the English language are changed for the better, the ripple effect will influence the learners. The effort made by the teachers in changing the negative language attitudes of the learners and helping them to eliminate LAA is crucial for the confidence building process. It is conceivable that with increased effort, anxious students can reach the same level of performance as relaxed students (MacIntyre & Gardner, 1994) and the sole responsibility for this effort lies in the hands of the teacher.

Conclusion

The psychology of language learners is discussed against the backdrop of LAA that most learners struggle with in learning English. The need for a society where learners feel safe from competition, overcorrection and a watchdog looking for mistakes is discussed to bring out the suitability and the importance of CLL principles as the core of our teaching methodology. The English language classroom needs to be transformed into a safe zone with special features such as no individual work, no individual performance, no error correction, no grammar teaching, no mandatory performance, no homework and no use of mother tongue. All of these features contribute to making classroom language learning different from that which is otherwise ordinary and commonplace. In addition, other strategies that are used are discussed. These include a phrase every day, sitting at the same level as the learners and summing up the errors/mistakes encountered during the day in general terms. All of these strategies are important to strengthen the safe zone. The process-oriented nature of the approach is discussed in terms of the features of the safe zone and activity sequencing of the lesson materials while emphasizing the necessity of teacher training for the course and its components. The chapter ends with a note on the importance of teacher awareness creation to build bridges between language attitudes and language needs.

Notes

1 A remote area in the Eastern Province of Sri Lanka.
2 A semi-rural area in the Central Province of Sri Lanka.
3 The students who belong to Level 1 category are the weakest in their English language proficiency among the undergraduates of Sri Lanka. The total intake of undergraduates per year is about 750–800 students at the Faculty of Arts, University of Colombo, Sri Lanka. Those who score 0–35 marks at the placement test upon entry into the university are put into this category, and every year about 400–500 students (2/3 of the cohort) fall into this category. It is for these students that the Building Confidence to Speak English course was introduced.
4 Another noteworthy statement is that this particular student's most desired skill was writing and not speaking. It could be assumed that once the learner develops enough confidence to speak, that confidence is projected to the next level, i.e. to develop a desire to write in English.
5 The majority of the learners selected for this study are from low proficiency groups in regard to English language.

References

Bloom, M. (1956). *Taxonomy of educational objectives*. New York: David McKay.

Granger, C. A. (2004). *Silence in second language learning: A psychoanalytic reading*. Clevedon: UK: Multilingual Matters.

Grice, H. P. (1975). Logic and conversation. In P. Cole and J. Morgan (Eds.), *Syntax and semantics, speech acts* (pp. 41–58). New York: Academic Press.

Johnson, T. R. (2011). Foreign language learner identity: A sociocultural perspective. UT Electronic Theses and Dissertations. Retrieved from https://repositories.lib.utexas.edu/handle/2152/12463

Kagan, S. (2011). Why call on just one when we can call on everyone? San Clemente, CA: Kagan Publishing. *Kagan Online Magazine*, Spring. www.KaganOnline.com

Kagan, S., & M. Kagan. (2009). *Cooperative learning*. San Clemente, CA: Kagan Publishing.

MacIntyre, P. D., & Gardner, R. C. (1994). The effects of induced anxiety on three stages of cognitive processing in computerized vocabulary learning. *Studies in Second Language Acquisition*, 16, 1–17.

Olsen, R., & Kagan, S. (1992). About cooperative learning. In C. Kessler (Ed.), *Cooperative language learning: A teacher's resource book* (pp. 1–30). New York: Prentice Hall.

Phillips, E. M. (1992). The effects of language anxiety on students' oral test performance and attitudes. *The Modern Language Journal*, 76(1), 14–26. Retrieved from: http://www.jstor.org/stable/329894. Accessed 16 July 2018.

Piaget, J. (1965). *The language and thought of the child*. New York: World Publishing Co.

Richards, J. C., & Rodgers, T. S. (2001). *Approaches and methods in language teaching*. Cambridge: Cambridge University Press.

Vygotsky, L. (1962). *Thought and language*. Cambridge: MIT Press.

Wallace, M. J. (1991). *Training foreign language teachers: A reflective approach*. Cambridge: Cambridge University Press.

9 Assessment

Introduction

This chapter discusses assessment in the Confidence Building Course to Speak English. The student assessment at the end of the course is designed in keeping with the course objective: to build confidence to speak English. Also, it aligns with the teaching methodology in that it is a group performance in the spirit of cooperation. In the assessment learners are given the chance to perform in stage plays. It is not mandatory to grade them, if there is a provision in the administrative logistics. However, if a summative evaluation is required for grading purposes, then certain criteria are given for grading purposes. In addition, a formative assessment is encouraged on a weekly basis strictly in line with evaluating the exhibited confidence level among students while working in groups and performing in English.

Group assessment – stage plays

The group assessment that works best in this course involves using stage plays. This is because the course makes use of group activities extensively to simulate speech functions covering basic interpersonal communication skills (BICS). There are a number of advantages to be found in using stage plays as the assessment mode: (a) they allow all the members in a group to take part in the assessment together, (b) they are mostly live narratives in which actors speak and act and (c) they are the best method for bringing out the confidence to speak in English the students have acquired because performing in front of an audience requires a considerable amount of confidence.

The assessment of the course does not necessarily need to be graded as that may affect the built confidence to speak English in the learners. That does not mean that group performances cannot be graded. However, when the learner proficiency levels are low in terms of their English language ability, it is desirable not to grade them. However, if grading is required, it should be carried out in light of the course objective, building confidence to speak English.

The following description may take the form of a narrative at times, as we recollect our memories of student performances at the end of the course.

Preparation

The assessment is based on stage plays in which the whole group (of 25 students) *must* take part. Towards the latter part of the course, about a week and a half before it finishes, learners are given 45 minutes to an hour of their class time to practise a small stage play. The script is written by the students themselves and the teacher gives suggestions when necessary. Since the entire class has to be given some kind of role to play, students have to be very creative in writing the script in order to develop the plot.

Some of the course teachers suggested group songs as whole group performances. This was obviously put forth for convenience as it is not easy to get all 25 students to act in a play. However, as the course coordinator, we rejected the idea and asked every teacher to get their students ready to act in a seven to ten minute stage play. At the Faculty of Arts, University of Colombo, Sri Lanka, we usually have about 15 groups with 25 students in each group when running the confidence building course, so it is not practical to allocate more than ten minutes for each class.

By the time students have completed more than two-thirds of the allotted time for the course in speaking and performing, in groups and pairs, in front of the class, they are quite familiar with their teacher. They know that their teacher does not pose a threat to them by overcorrecting or 'watching over' them to find fault with their speaking and, as a result, the learners have developed a sense of security when speaking English. Also, group activities have bonded them together with each other and they have a great sense of solidarity at this time in the course.

The course coordinator decided not to have a competition among the group performances to select the best plays. Nevertheless, we felt it was good to keep the competitive spirit kindled and each group was advised not to share the details of their stage plays with others prior to the day of performances. Teachers were advised to keep their 'secrets' as well. This led to a high level of excitement as each group wanted to keep the others from knowing about what they were getting ready to perform. There were even instances where 'spies' from other groups were caught peeping through the doors to catch a glimpse of what was happening inside another classroom only to be chased out! In so doing, the learners sought the help of *their* teacher to find phrases such as 'Get out!' 'Go away!' etc., to chase out the spies. Such phrases were heard loudly every so often during the practice sessions.

What should be noted in this scenario is that the English language classroom, speaking in English and getting ready to perform in an English stage play were previously viewed as a torture chamber, a nightmare and a wild dream, respectively, to these students, but have now become causes of sheer enjoyment. We still remember how the teachers also got caught up in student excitement and were quite eager to see that *their* own groups performed better than other groups.

Phillips' (1992) observation about stress reducing assessment types became a reality in our case.

> Finally, certain types of tests encourage student participation without placing undue stress on the individual learner. Cooperative efforts reduce the

> competitiveness that can raise anxiety and hinder progress. Evaluations that involve partner and small group work, interviews, problem-solving, and role-plays are usually enjoyed by students and may reduce apprehension. (p. 21)

The day of the performance

This is a memorable day for the learners as well as for the teachers. One would find students very excited as they are going to perform on stage in an English play. That those who were timid and afraid of speaking English for fear of being ridiculed by others are actually getting ready to act on stage in English plays in front of an audience is not a small accomplishment, both for the learners and the teachers who taught them: learners who said they were nervous, shy, did not have confidence and whose 'heartbeat increased tremendously' when they wanted to speak in English and teachers who knew the problems of these learners so well.

From our experience in watching these plays, we must admit that it is a very moving occasion to see learners act out their village lives, bring to life some simple incidents from their village experiences or re-live folk narratives on the stage in English. The English culture and its representations have been portrayed in their minds as classy, smart, educated, handsome and stylish, and because of all these features, English seemed to be very distant from their rural and semi-rural selves. However, that distance seems to have disappeared. Instead, we get to see a group of learners talking as if they were conversing in their day-to-day life, clothed in their village attire and in thatched houses (with stage prompts). However, in the majority of such rustic episodes it is not uncommon to see the prince still desperately trying to find his Cinderella!

The silence is broken

This is a turning point where the gap between the learner and the English language (and all its representations) is very significantly narrowed. The silence that Granger (2004) said is created by the mismatch between the fully developed L1 psyche and the emerging second language self of the adult L2 learners is broken. As stated elsewhere, Granger's psychoanalytic approach to language and identity describes language as a tool for individuals to express their inner self to the world and shows that the incompatibility between the fully developed L1 psyche and the emerging second language self can be extremely frustrating for adult learners. In this case, the chance these learners get to express themselves in L2 through simple stage plays of their own devising is in itself an enormous accomplishment because they suddenly find out what they are capable of achieving. In addition to the confidence that has been built over the duration of the course to speak in English, these learners also feel a sense of pride in their public performance. Thus, the silence is broken and the wall is cracked.

The criteria for assessment

As we said, it is not mandatory to grade the stage plays and, if there is a provision in the administrative logistics that allows for ungraded assessments, it is desirable *not* to grade them. However, if the stage plays must be evaluated for grading purposes as a summative assessment, then the following must be kept in mind:

1. The course objective is to build learner confidence to speak English and NOT to improve English language proficiency.
2. What is important is group participation, NOT individual performance.
3. More emphasis is placed on trial and error in language use and MINIMUM/NO emphasis on accuracy and fluency.
4. Themes/plots are products of student creativity.
5. Stage props, etc., should be considered in grading.

The criteria for grading student performance should be based on (a) the confidence to speak English (including the confidence expressed through body language), (b) group participation and collaboration, (c) language use and its relatedness to the chosen plot, (d) the effectiveness of performance in bringing out the theme/plot and (e) stage prompts and costumes, etc.

In addition, the teacher may carry out a formative assessment during the course as well. With the maximum number of students being 25 in a class, it should not be a tedious task. The teacher can make a sheet with student names against which marks can be allocated for each student's exhibited confidence level to (a) carry out a task as a group member, (b) use English without hesitation, (c) prompt and cooperate with group members to perform an assigned task and (d) ability to come forward to perform/speak in English in front of the class. Accuracy or fluency in speaking should not be assessed as the course is geared towards achieving the aim of building confidence to speak English and NOT improving English language proficiency.

If a formative assessment can be done weekly, teachers will be able to monitor the progress of each student closely and may be able to help those who need more support to build their confidence to speak English.

Conclusion

The assessment of the Building Confidence to Speak English course is a stage play in which all of the members in the class take part. The theme/plot has to be chosen by the learners themselves and the teacher can help them with the script once the learners develop it on their own. Grading student performances is not encouraged. However, when required, grading criteria must not include English language proficiency as a measurement variable. The course objective is to build learner confidence to speak English and therefore, what has to be assessed and graded is the confidence level to speak in English. In addition, group performance has to be looked at as facilitating maximum collaboration among the group members using the English language in a trial and error manner rather than with fluency and accuracy. The other criteria for evaluation are themes/plots, stage prompts, costumes, etc. In addition, a weekly formative assessment is encouraged to assess and monitor the exhibited confidence level of students to work and perform in English as a team player.

References

Granger, C. A. (2004). *Silence in second language learning: A psychoanalytic reading.* Clevedon, UK: Multilingual Matters.

Phillips, E. M. (1992). The effects of language anxiety on students' oral test performance and attitudes. *The Modern Language Journal*, 76(1), 14–26. Retrieved from: http://www.jstor.org/stable/329894 Accessed 16 July 2018, 10:34 UTC.

10 Course evaluation

Introduction

This chapter introduces the course evaluation stages that are available in the discourse namely, pre-evaluation, evaluation during the course and post-evaluation. It discusses the last one in detail as it is the most appropriate for assessing the effectiveness of the confidence building course. Students are the main target group from whom to obtain feedback on the course while the teachers' views are sought in order to supplement the data from students. The areas to be evaluated include the course materials, content covered, teacher performance, the teaching methodology employed and the modes of assessment. These are identified in order to evaluate their efficacy in building learner confidence to speak in various locations and with different people. A sample questionnaire addressing these issues is presented in this chapter. In order to extract more information, interviews with teachers are suggested. In addition, the use of journal data and written records of teacher observation is encouraged.

Course evaluation stages

The evaluation of the Building Confidence to Speak English course can be carried out in terms of three accepted course evaluation stages: the pre-evaluation, in-course evaluation and post-evaluation stages. However, one must not be misled by ordinary course evaluation objectives that are designed for a standard course in teaching the English language or speaking skill; this course is set to build learner confidence to speak English and NOT to develop English language proficiency. Therefore, any tool that is used for the course evaluation must be designed to examine whether learner confidence in speaking English has been improved and whether the fear factor has diminished or has begun to diminish. These can be measured in terms of teacher perceptions in addition to student perspectives.

The pre-evaluation is of two types: one concerns the course material, suggested teaching methodology and recommended assessments prior to the teaching, which are checked against the course objectives; the other is related to the target students and is similar to a pre-test which determines the learners' existing confidence level to speak English in different contexts prior to the course, to be compared later with the post-test results. Pre- and post-evaluations of confidence levels are planned and the results can be compared. However, post-evaluation alone may be sufficient as learners and teachers will respond in terms of learners' status after the course and teachers are already aware of the learners' lack of confidence prior to the course. Interviews and questionnaires are good tools to assess outcomes. In addition, teacher observations, if recorded in a journal on a daily basis, are very useful to allow one to see the gradual progress of learner confidence in speaking English over time.

Pre-evaluation

The pre-evaluation that is discussed here is of the first type listed above. Prior to course commencement, as stated before, the course can be evaluated in terms of the suitability of the course materials, teaching methodology and assessment modes. This type of evaluation involves the teachers who will be teaching in the course. In addition, the views of senior students who have completed a different English course can also be sought that does not involve any feedback about teaching methodology, lesson materials or assessments, but a discussion on the suitability of the recommended strategies and tasks. Pre-evaluation involves the teachers who are going to teach the course reading through the course material while comparing it with the course objectives and activity potentials, namely, the communicative potential and cognitive potential scales. In order to do this, teachers need to be made aware of the principles that underlie the production of course materials. Teachers can be asked to give their views on the principles of teaching methodology as well as the features of the safe zone. In addition, teachers who are not going to teach the course and students who are in the final years of their academic careers can be asked to pre-evaluate the course in terms of material, teaching methodology and assessment methods against the course objectives. It is of paramount importance that they be made aware of the course objectives. However, one cannot expect much from a pre-evaluation beyond a general understanding.

The potential questions asked of the group should examine whether the material and teaching methodology are geared towards building learner confidence to speak English in situations inside and outside of the classroom with teachers, peers, outsiders, etc., and whether the assessment mode properly measures learners' ability to manifest confidence.

With regard to the second type, which is in fact simply a pre-test that involves the target student population, it is indeed possible to examine their existing confidence level in regard to speaking in English. However, since this does not involve anything specifically related to the course, it cannot be called a proper 'pre-evaluation of the course' but simply a pre-test where sections (A), (B) and (E) in the sample questionnaire given below are administered to students. As stated before, this is not essential as the need for a confidence building course emerged precisely as a result of the pre-existing diagnosis of a lack of confidence to speak English.

Evaluation during the course

According to experts, this is the most effective stage for evaluation since it leaves room for changes as per the needs of the learner, which at times are better identified while the course is running. However, since the confidence building course is planned to run for a month as an intensive course, changes, even in a newly identified area, may not be possible to implement as material editing, printing, etc., should be carried out without disrupting the course in progress. For a course that runs over a longer period of time, in-course evaluation may be even more useful.

Post-evaluation

The most common course evaluation method is a post-course evaluation. The evaluation of the confidence building course should examine the effectiveness of the course in building learner confidence to speak English in terms of its course materials, teaching methodology and assessment.

In order to see if confidence to speak English has been raised, it is important to reflect upon the situations, instances where learners lack confidence and the people with whom learners state they are unable to speak. Their responses in regard to fear, shyness and uncertainty to speak in front of 'others' both inside the classroom as well as outside should be noted. These 'others', as we have seen through our analysis, mainly include those who speak English well and those who do not speak English at all. In addition, the interviews show that foreign, native speakers are often exempted from this category of 'others' and in some cases learners show remarkable keenness to speak with them. In short, data collection is to be focused on specific locations and specific persons with whom the learners experience Language Attitude Anxiety (LAA). The course is designed to eliminate LAA through specific classroom activities, aiming at building confidence so that once LAA is eliminated, their confidence will be improved. Any mechanism for course evaluation should examine (a) learner confidence to speak in terms of location and people, (b) course materials and their content, (c) teacher performance (d) and assessment modes.

Questionnaires

The location and people

To gauge the effectiveness of the course, it is important to examine the learners' confidence to speak English with the teacher and peers inside the classroom as a first step. This is accomplished by looking at their confidence in carrying out activities with their peers, both in small group work and in tasks shared with the whole class. These activities are crucial to see whether the fear factor to speak English in the small classroom community has been reduced and if LAA has been eliminated.

The evaluation moves on to the next level where student confidence to speak outside the classroom can be checked. The situations can be small extensions of the classroom setting where the confidence to speak with a peer and a teacher is judged, but outside the classroom. In addition, student confidence in the stage performance, the climax of the course, will reflect their confidence (or lack of it) outside the classroom setting, and should be closely examined.

It is also important to check whether learners feel confident to speak with strangers as well. This may give a hint on how learners, after immersion in the course, view their possible selves. It may be possible that some, during the course, may have had encounters where they spoke English either with strangers or in situations where strangers were present, both of which they previously avoided.

Course material

Learner views on the course in terms of materials used and the various activities can be sought so that we can check whether the learner preference for speech has been satisfied with a variety of simulated situations that closely resemble their everyday activities.

Teacher performance

Another very important area is students' comments on the teacher and the teaching methodology. We discussed teaching methodology in great detail in Chapter 8, and the effectiveness of the entire course depends on the teacher and the teaching methodology. In our experience, a lot of courses, even those that are designed well with solid underpinning principles, fail due to the weakness in the prescribed teaching methodology or teachers not adhering to the recommended methodology. Our own experience, which was narrated elsewhere in the section on teacher observation about a teacher falling back into typical, outdated reading comprehension strategies to teach in the confidence building activities is worth restating. The course coordinator/designer must check whether teachers do what they are supposed to do. As stated elsewhere, we have experience in working with teachers in many different capacities for over two decades to justify the stance we take on teacher observation and checking teacher performance. Further, it has to be specifically asked of the students whether the features of the safe zone as discussed in the chapter have been created and maintained.

Assessment

Seeking learner views on the mode of assessment, e.g. the final stage performance, will complete the course evaluation process. The questions should focus on learner fears and related confidence factors, the appropriateness of and their preference for 'public' performance. In addition, teachers' perceptions on the same will enhance the credibility of survey outcomes.

The following questionnaire is appropriate to get student feedback during the post-evaluation stage. It has a Likert-type scale to collect data quantitatively. The options range from 'strongly agree' to 'strongly disagree' and it is desirable to interview a representative sample with open-ended questions along the same lines so that more elaborate student responses can be obtained.

Sample questionnaire

Dear students,

Please read the questions carefully and answer the questionnaire. Use the language you are most comfortable in.

Please indicate your level of agreement with the following statements:

A Inside the classroom

Inside the classroom	**Strongly agree**	**Somewhat agree**	**Cannot say**	**Somewhat disagree**	**Strongly disagree**
1 I am afraid to speak English with my peers/colleagues/ friends inside the classroom					
2 I have confidence to speak English with the teacher inside the classroom					
3 I am scared to perform in English in front of the class with members of a small group					

B Outside the classroom

Outside the classroom	**Strongly agree**	**Somewhat agree**	**Cannot say**	**Somewhat agree**	**Strongly disagree**
4 I am scared to speak English with peers/colleagues/ friends outside the classroom					
5 I have confidence to speak English with a teacher outside the classroom					
6 I don't have enough confidence to speak English with a stranger outside the classroom					
7 I am scared to perform in English (in a stage play) in front of an audience as part of the class					

C About the course

8 What do you think of the course duration?

a Too long
b About right
c Cannot say
d Too short
e Other (specify) ....

9 What do you think about the areas (situations, incidents, etc.) covered in this course?

a Too many
b About right
c Cannot say
d Not sufficient
e Other (specify) ....

10 What are the activities you liked the most? (You may underline more than one)

a Games
b Acting
c Dialogues
d Miming
e Other (specify) ....

11 How do you like to do activities? (You may underline more than one)

a As pair work
b In small groups of 4–5
c Cannot say
d As a whole class
e Individually

12 How do you rate the lesson materials (Modules) and their instructions?

a Student friendly
b Nothing special
c Cannot say
d Not student friendly
e Other (specify) ....

D Teaching methodology

Inside the classroom	Strongly agree	Somewhat agree	Cannot say	Somewhat disagree	Strongly disagree
13 Our teacher did not correct us when we spoke					
14 Our teacher used mother tongue in teaching					
15 Our teacher sat with us in our groups most of the time					
16 Our teacher gave us a sentence to speak in English every day					
17 Our teacher is friendly					

18 Our teacher pointed at me to come to the front of the class and present at the end of an activity.

a Always
b Sometimes
c Cannot say
d Rarely
e Never

19 Our teacher taught grammar lessons.

a Always
b Sometimes
c Cannot say
d Rarely
e Never

20 Our teacher gave us homework.

a Always
b Sometimes
c Cannot say
d Rarely
e Never

21 Our teacher pointed at our group to come and present in front of the class

a Always
b Sometimes
c Cannot say
d Rarely
e Never

E Assessment mode

On stage	Strongly agree	Somewhat agree	Cannot say	Somewhat disagree	Strongly disagree
22 I am nervous to act in a stage play					
23 I am not afraid to act in a stage play					
24 Stage plays are the best					

F Learner suggestions for improvement

25 What are your suggestions to improve the course? Write them below, if any.

i ....

ii ....

iii ....

iv ....

v ....

See Appendix D for an example of the sample questionnaire for teachers.

Interviews

Teachers and students both can be interviewed to examine whether the confidence level to speak English in the students has improved. Considering the low proficiency levels of the learners, interviews with them in English may not prove to be useful if they are not proficient enough to express their views in English. On the other hand, interviews in mother tongue may not help us gauge their confidence to speak English. However, learners will be able to express their views on the present confidence level as compared to that in the past if interviewed (even using their mother tongue).

The limitation of interviews with teachers is that they may not be able to speak about their learners' confidence to speak English outside of the classroom. However, teachers are in a strong position to evaluate students' present confidence level and compare it with their confidence in the past. Therefore, the interview questions should attempt to meet the requirements for a qualitative comparative analysis.

Journals and records

Teachers can be asked to maintain a journal, a form of a diary with accounts about their students' behaviour in daily class activities. Such written records also provide solid data at the end of the course for its evaluation. Teachers have to be advised to write even the minute details they observe in their class activities, no matter how trivial they may seem to be. This is because interesting themes and patterns are often discovered after the course is completed. We can also do things like quantify the number of students who were reluctant to speak during the first week and interpret the messages sent via their facial expressions when others presented in front of the class, etc.

In addition, the supervisor or the researcher can observe the teachers at work. She/He can maintain a record of events and account for variables relating to teacher and learner performance. These will prove to be useful when the course is evaluated longitudinally in regard to learner confidence to speak English.

Teacher observation by the course coordinator/designer

Monitoring the course procedures is just as important part as the course design. With our experience in running the course many times, it is always useful to observe a fair sample of teachers in class. For instance, when 25 teachers teach in the course, at least five of them should be observed, to give a fair understanding of the teachers' approach. Since the teaching methodology recommended for the confidence building course is the complete opposite of traditional methods, to which most of the South Asian English language teachers are accustomed, random classroom observation can be immensely helpful. This will serve two purposes: one, teachers will be more responsible in creating and maintaining the features of the safe zone, which is completely dependent upon the teacher in her teaching methodology; two, the course designer can account for student and teacher behaviour in the confidence building process, and this observation will serve as another data set to evaluate the course.

Logistics

It is important that the student questionnaire be given in the students' mother tongue in addition to English. The objective of the course evaluation is to see whether the students' confidence to speak English has been improved, not their English language proficiency. The language in which learners are most competent to express their views will capture a more realistic scenario. What we did in Sri Lanka was to give the questionnaire in all three languages used in the country (Sinhala, Tamil and English) so that learners could pick the language they were most comfortable in.

A long questionnaire may undermine students' enthusiasm (Harvard University Programme on survey research), so it is good to design a questionnaire to be filled out in 20 minutes or less. That is considered to be the maximum length for an online questionnaire before respondents' concentration declines and as a result, data quality suffers.

If a pre-evaluation of the student confidence level is carried out, the sections (A), (B) and (E) of the questionnaire can be used to collect data. The results can be compared with the items in (A), (B) and (E) of the post-evaluation.

Conclusion

This chapter details course evaluation mechanisms to be used after the course is taught. The pre- and in-course evaluations are not usually very practical in South Asia and not discussed at length. Evaluation at these stages may not contribute much in changing the course content given the fact that course objective is well identified against the need for confidence to speak English and the comparatively short duration of the course. The post-evaluation utilizes a questionnaire to collect data from students and teachers in the contexts where students show a lack of confidence to speak in English, i.e. inside and outside the classroom with teachers, their peers and outsiders consisting of 'others' in front of whom they are afraid of making mistakes. Interviews are recommended for teacher feedback while teacher journals and records of teacher observations are significant contributions for extracting qualitative data. If a pre-evaluation is conducted, it is emphasized that the confidence to speak English prior to the course is to be assessed against their confidence level after the course. In such a case, a complete course evaluation in terms of course material, teaching methods and assessment practices cannot be expected and the evaluation will be a simple comparison of the confidence level to speak in English before and after the course.

References

Harvard University Programme on survey research. Tip sheet on question wording. Retrieved from: https://psr.iq.harvard.edu/files/psr/files/PSRQuestionnaireTipSheet_0.pdf

https://www.snapsurveys.com/blog/survey-design-sequencing-survey-questions/; https://austinresearch.co.uk/working-with-clients-to-produce-shorter-surveys/#comment-3034

11 Developing language attitudes as an academic discourse

Introduction

This chapter discusses the significance of developing language attitudes as an independent academic discourse. The key concepts including examining language attitudes, analysing them in diverse contexts, assessing the effects of language attitudes and rectifying measures for the negative effects in relation to language teaching are discussed at length. Identifying language attitudes in terms of various aspects is discussed with special reference to social variables such as class, gender, public–private education and levels of education, profession, etc. An example analysis of language attitudes in the context of vernaculars is discussed with related implications. The effects of language attitudes in post-colonial South Asia are discussed along with the consequences manifested in the language learning domain as well as in the greater society. Remedial measures are suggested that involve teaching about the many diverse aspects along with the support of political movements aiming at a mass level of attitudinal change. The envisaged outcomes are discussed in light of developing teacher awareness as the main change agent in regard to language attitudes so that building bridges between languages and cultures/knowledge can be achieved.

Need for developing language attitudes as an independent academic discipline

Considering the uniqueness of the language attitudes prevalent in Sri Lanka and her post-colonial South Asian neighbours and the effect they have on language learners, it is timely to develop an independent academic discipline specifically about 'language attitudes'. This is far from an easy task for many reasons: (a) it is not easy to measure attitudes; (b) language attitudes, like any other attitude, are not static and may change over time; and (c) even if we gather data and uncover attitudes, the very sensitivity of the whole issue may complicate the dissemination of what we have learned. However, the second difficulty, i.e. the changing nature of attitudes, could be considered the most significant reason in favour of developing such a discipline as there is scope to change attitudes which are not healthy or positive contributions to the well-being of a society.

An academic discipline will help us to see language attitudes in a more correct and open perspective studied in a legitimate domain. Also, it will allow a formal, logical and systematic teaching–learning process to enable the elimination of negative attitudes and the development of positive ones. Once such a discipline is developed academically and included at the tertiary level and in professional education, mainly in teacher training programmes, the changing of negative attitudes towards languages among the next generation in the post-colonial South Asian region may be accomplished gradually and methodically.

We would like to emphasize the fact that this discourse be developed for tertiary and professional education purposes, considering the importance of imparting more positive attitudes towards languages to our younger generations.

A discourse on language attitudes may include discussion of the following:

1 Examining the existing language attitudes (in societies/regions)
2 Analysis of language attitudes
3 The effects of language attitudes on language learners
4 Remedial measures

Examining language attitudes

A study of language attitudes should pave the way for discussions on the definition of language attitudes and their nature, and most importantly, on the existing language attitudes in diverse societies towards different languages. Our study clearly establishes the power of the English language in South Asian society and the effects of the existing language attitudes in the region. These effects are due to the attitudes towards the English language and its speakers in the post-colonial South Asian region and the power dynamics that elevate English language speakers, who in turn influence the language learner directly and indirectly. Any discourse that is developed on language attitudes should take the responsibility for examining language attitudes in terms of the positioning of languages in various societies under varying dynamics.

A thorough examination of the language attitudes that exist in a society is necessary in order to understand the power dynamics associated with different languages in that particular society. Without an in-depth analysis of language attitudes, it will not be possible to obtain a complete picture of the total scenario. For instance, most western societies are unaware of the lack of confidence to speak English in South Asia due to a fear of ridicule by others in society. Instead, western academics seem to focus solely on the fear of negative evaluation by teachers and peers.

The study we carried out in a prominent university (Pennsylvania State University) in the USA on a Fulbright fellowship revealed that international students did not have native speakers of English in their circle of friends. This issue was raised in our queries about the use of remedial measures to acquire English outside the remedial English language classroom by international students. The reasons for such a situation, i.e. not having native speakers as friends, may presumably go unnoticed or classified as 'birds of a feather flocking together' and attributed to a desire be with one's fellow countrymen while living in a foreign land. However, the truth may be far from that. One of the interpretations we made was that it is likely due to the power play between the countries, which affects students in their informal settings, in that most of these students were from China and Arab countries that are in competition with the USA. The US education system is considered to be one of the best in the world and these international students came to the USA for studies because they are rich enough to afford it and not because they have any affinity for the country or its people. On the contrary, their countries are often involved in wars and power competitions with the USA. It resembles yet another type of 'love–hate' relationship between the international students and the English language in that they may not like the country, or may even hate it in extreme cases, but feel that they are compelled to learn English as the highly regarded American education they are receiving is in English. Therefore, any study on examining language attitudes needs to delve deeper into the context in which the languages operate, including the social, economic and political dynamics.

Examining language attitudes is a very challenging task. Any approach or mechanism needs to use both quantitative and qualitative data collection tools. The point of departure to examine language attitudes *must* always begin in 'hearsay'. This may sound non-scientific but is always a sure way to uncover the premises for a scientific discussion. Discovering the mere existence of attitudes towards a language and whether they are positive or negative is not sufficient either, though they are essential as the foundation of an in-depth analysis. The superior–inferior, useful–useless, prestigious–lowly divides, of the recognized–non-recognized variety, influential–neutral or hated–neutral nature of a language are some of the key binaries that reach beyond a mere positive–negative divide. It is essential to interview the linguistic community with open-ended questions so that the true colours and flavours of the existing language attitudes in that society can be well captured. As we stated in Chapter 3, our questionnaire was designed primarily for a quantitative data collection whereas the interview questions were very open-ended and elaborative to extract more detailed information along the lines of the questionnaire (Appendix C).

Some of the parameters along which the examination and analysis of language attitudes are to be carried out include, (a) as positive–negative types, (b) as independent entities, (c) in the context of other languages (e.g. English and vernaculars), (d) in the context of economic, political, etc., powers and (e) in the context of social variables such as class, gender, age, public–private education and employment sectors, education level, etc. Such analyses will help to uncover rectifying measures to make language attitudes a useful entity rather than a divisive tool among language learners in society. Considering the complexities in attitudes towards a language and its speakers, it must be stated that there is a need for very specific tools to collect data pertaining to studies on examining and analysing language attitude issues in language learning. For instance, detailed, unstructured interviews should be used in addition to questionnaires that invite quantitative analyses to examine the context-specific attitudes related to languages.

The analysis of language attitudes

In analysing the language attitudes in a particular society, it is important to do it under a variety of categories. The analysis needs to be carried out in the context of multiple languages (e.g. mother tongue and English), social variables and socio-political power where language is seen as serving the functions of an instrument of culture, political power and knowledge. It is useful to understand all of these aspects of language attitudes as discrete entities and in terms of their positive and negative manifestations in order to obtain a deep comprehension of the interplay among them in a given society and how this results in creating and perpetuating the language attitudes in that society. The following section, therefore, discusses language attitudes in their particular contexts.

In the context of social variables

Some of the rubrics to analyse language attitudes in terms of social variables are (a) class division, (b) gender, (c) age, (d) profession and (e) education level.

Class division

This is a very important aspect of analysing language attitudes in different segments of society. In other words, upper class, middle class and working class attitudes could be considered for such an analysis as class division is known to generate a variety of attitudes in any given society, not only towards languages, but also towards various social entities. As our study reveals, a class distinction is represented by being able to speak English, as well as the variety of English that is spoken, and this is creating division among language learners in society due to the presence of classist language attitudes.

Gender

Even though our study does not examine language attitudes in terms of gender, it is a credible parameter to analyse language attitudes in certain societies where gender discrimination is at a high level. The study of language attitudes based on gender may support the understanding of a perspective linked to education, employment and even illiteracy.

Age

The attitudes of people towards languages in terms of age can be used as another aspect in the analysis. For instance, taking in those of students in lower secondary and upper secondary classes in schools, learners in tertiary education in both the formal and non-formal sectors (e.g. undergraduates, postgraduates and learners in vocational education, etc.) and those who are in their middle and old age could provide an overview of the language attitudes prevalent in a country. This criterion will reveal how language attitudes are developed in communities during their lifetime as students, adults and at different stages of life, along with any shifts and changes over time.

Profession

Another analysis of language attitudes can be done with regard to professionals from various disciplines. For instance, professionals in administrative positions and the higher echelons may have a set of language attitudes that differ from those in lower positions. Also, public–private differences in the employment sector will bring out a very important dimension of the discussion on language attitudes as representing the force of their function in society. This type of analysis will help us to understand the language attitudes in relation to professional requirements.

Education level

In addition, the educational level of people will also make a significant contribution to the understanding and analysis of language attitudes. Those who are highly educated may have a set of language attitudes based on their exposure to education opportunities locally and abroad. With education qualifications obtained abroad and by travelling and being with foreign colleagues, it may be expected that their language attitudes have changed as they expanded their horizons. Also, as a medium for higher education systems, those who are highly educated may be well aware of the utility value of particular languages over others in shaping their attitudes. Those who have not obtained higher education or who were educated locally may have a set of language attitudes in direct contrast to those described above. Public–private sector variation in education would also contribute to obtain a complete picture of the language attitudes in a society.

In the context of other languages

Language attitude analysis in the context of other languages will be more challenging in a multilingual society than in a monolingual or even bilingual situation. If a society is generally monolingual, which is an extreme rarity today, the diversity of language attitudes can be expected to have a smaller impact as there may not be social language dynamics such as language competition or language hierarchies. In societies such as Canada, USA, etc., where languages such as English, French and Spanish operate on a basis of complementing each other with little or no sense of a related superiority–inferiority complex, the dynamics of language attitudes may not be as complex. This can lead to a limited understanding of how, in regions like South Asia, languages operate together in a society in more subtle, intricate and multifaceted ways. With hindsight, this could be one of the main reasons why the western scholars and academics we met in Singapore were curious and peculiarly interested in our presentation, 'Confidence building is central to speak English in Sri Lanka'. Also, it can be expected that the more linguistic diversity is coloured by hierarchical and competitive environments, the more language attitude comparisons and contrasts can be drawn that pave the way for a better understanding of the complexities attached to language teaching in places like South Asia.

A limited understanding of the complexities and dynamics of language attitudes in bi- or multilingual societies can result in a major setback in the way languages are taught. This is because the foundation of any language teaching will be weak if it fails to consider the psycho-social aspects of the language learner.

Example analysis of language attitudes in the context of other languages

We wish to further elaborate on language attitudes in the context of other languages with an example analysis. This was briefly discussed in a previous chapter. The research we carried out for the PhD examined the language policy and perspectives of English language and its teaching, as well as the perceptions of the university English language teachers in regard to the three main languages of Sri Lanka (Attanayake, 2017). The sample consisted of 22 English language teachers from three universities namely, the University of Colombo, representing the metropolitan, well-established universities in the country; Sabaragamuwa University, representing the newly established, regional universities; and the University of Jaffna, representing the universities in conflict areas.

Teachers were asked about their opinion on the standing of the English language in comparison to Sinhala and Tamil, the two official and national languages in Sri Lanka. All the teachers accepted the English language as very important and high in status in Sri Lankan society. However, they ranked the three languages in terms of (a) languages existing side-by-side, competing with each other, (b) languages placed hierarchically and (c) English as a replacement for the other two languages (Attanayake, 2017).

View of languages existing side-by-side and competing alternatively and its implications (competition)

Such a notion is due to the idea that the English language and its speakers are hostile to native cultures. However, it is paradoxical that the same teachers hold the view that without English there can be no progress.

'The perception that languages exist side-by-side and compete encompasses views of languages as "threatening" and as being "hostile" to each other in their collaborative function of communication' (Attanayake, 2017, p. 272). This is a notion that comes from and develops into language attitudes that pave the way for language learners to view a particular language as more important than another and give less value to one or the other. While such an approach may help learners get a practical and realistic picture of the status quo, it may also contribute to developing negative values and attitudes related to languages and to treat them as more powerful and therefore superior and less powerful and therefore inferior, thus perpetuating the status quo as found in our study.

While languages co-exist in a society, language competition can neither be considered progressive nor healthy for a society. Unlike competition in learning that may motivate learners, the language attitudes of people that create competition among languages do not help or motivate learners or users to learn other languages. Rather, competition may make groups of different ethnic and linguistic groups develop animosity and even hatred towards each other by creating a vicious cycle of language attitudes. This is because in a competitive environment languages are seen as intimidating and antagonistic to each other.

Languages placed in a hierarchy and its implications (power hierarchy)

In the context of the native languages, Sinhala and Tamil, English is considered to be more prestigious and more powerful. The words that are most associated with English are 'freedom', 'benefits', 'advantages', 'respect', 'power', 'prestige' and 'more useful', all of which imply the possibility of positive social encounters by way of English. This view is similar to the views of most of the South Asian respondents in our study. Also, these call words for English invite the comparative notion that the English language can offer something the mother tongues cannot. This is not only in terms of the global context, but within the local situations themselves.

According to this view, in the language power hierarchy English is seen as surpassing native languages while endowing an individual who speaks English with power and prestige. This perspective is another definite contribution to the creation and propagation of negative language attitudes towards native languages while ascribing an added superiority to the English language. The consequences are what we have been discussing at length in the previous chapters, including a lack of confidence among learners to speak the most prestigious and most powerful language, English, in the post-colonial scenario.

English as a replacement for the others and its implications (replacement)

Some held the view that English should be the 'only official language' and medium of education in the country. This perspective is often held in relation to the ethnic crisis that plagued Sri Lanka for decades.

The view that the English language should replace the native languages in education indicates that 'neither of the native languages is important nor useful in education' (Attanayake, 2017, p. 272). Also it shows the acceptance of English as an ostensibly neutral language, more specifically a mediator, in some contexts where deciding upon one language for education among many native languages has been difficult. The attitudinal perspective that can be derived from such an inference is that the English language is looked at from a neutral perspective as opposed to the native languages. This could be based on views of the relative usefulness of the languages as well.

The importance of this discussion based on teacher perceptions about languages is that it shows the ways that language penetrates beyond serving the purpose of mere communication. According to the main functions of language as an instrument of culture, a political instrument and an instrument of knowledge, along with the positioning of languages in each function in a given society, language attitudes are formed, shaped and perpetuate ideas about the status of languages and language attitudes in that particular society. In addition, the significance of the above perception patterns in relation to the co-existence of languages in a multilingual context like Sri Lanka is high with a recent history as a nation that faced traumatic experiences due to language issues (Attanayake, 2017).

Ramanathan (2005) suggests another way of looking at language related inequalities so that a better understanding of the co-existence of languages can be arrived at:

> Any understanding of English and Vernacular education has to begin first by locating them side by side (as opposed to arranging them in a hierarchy). Doing so is the first step not only in addressing language-related inequalities on the postcolonial ground but in recognizing ways in which English and the vernaculars while simultaneously divided and dichotomous from some points of view are also simultaneously overlapping and conjoined.
>
> (p. 3)

In context of economic and political power

Even though the preceding discussion on language attitudes analysis has been restricted to their relationship with other languages, it is quite obvious that the political power of a nation or a particular group also dominates the language attitudes domain as well creating the context in which languages co-exist. In Chapter 3 we discussed South Asian language policy issues in detail during the pre-independence, independence and post-independence periods. All four nations, within their countries, have been divided due to language issues in one way or another, in the past and in the present. Most of the political power struggles that have taken place in post-colonial South Asia either started because of, or manifested themselves in, language as a central issue. It is therefore important to understand language attitudes in the political domain in the correct perspective if we envisage the creation of a discourse on language attitudes as a rectifying measure to problems caused by language attitudes.

Initially, in the era of independence, it was the English language that posed a threat. Accordingly, it had to be downplayed and the concepts of nationhood and language became major symbols of nationality in the region. A common language to represent nationhood was sought at the cost of minority languages and this led South Asian nations into conflict. It was this continuous political power game along with world economic dynamics which brought English, again, to the forefront. Languages in South Asia have been caught up in this power play and various language attitudes have developed among the people of the region over time.

In addition, our study with the international student community in the USA provides another example of the economic and political dimension in the discussion of language attitudes: the negative attitudes of nations towards each other are often based on real or perceived economic and political power dynamics, attitudes that are manifested in international students who will not make friends with native speakers of English, thus reinforcing a power hierarchy which has already been projected on to the English language and its use.

The idea of a global language is relevant to the discussion at this point. How does a language become a global language? According to Crystal (1997), a language becomes a global language for one chief reason: the political power of its people, especially their military power. During the colonial period, it was the British who were the most powerful. Then the USA took over as the global power. As the English language is the mother tongue of both these nations, there was no shift of language when the global power shifted. English remains the global language and the language of the most powerful nations with the strongest armed forces.

Gramsci's (1971) definition of cultural hegemony can be applied to the hegemony of the English language and its culture to some extent. He refers to cultural hegemony as the

> spontaneous consent given by the great masses of the population to the general direction imposed on social life by the dominant fundamental group; this consent is historically caused by the prestige which the dominant group enjoys because of its position and function in the world of production.
>
> (As quoted by Lears, 1985, p. 568)

However, it is problematic to use 'spontaneous consent' along with an 'imposed' general direction. Notwithstanding this contradiction, the hegemony that the English language and its representative culture have established in post-colonial South Asia matches the definition, especially in recent times as opposed to the immediate-post-independence era where English was downplayed by the local rulers.

The theoretical framework of linguistic hegemony is closely related to linguistic imperialism. Phillipson (1992) argues that the English language achieved its dominant position as the principal world language because it has been actively promoted as an instrument of foreign policy by the major English-speaking states. Attanayake (2017) states that the language policies of the post-colonial countries serve the interest of the western powers even though they 'look' advantageous to the said countries.

Therefore, for any real understanding of the power hierarchy of language positioning and the language attitudes that emerge as a result, discussions of cultural, linguistics, political, economic and religious hegemonies must be considered in analysing how language attitudes emerge, operate and sustain themselves in the myriad complex dynamics of a society.

Language attitudes and their effects

In post-colonial South Asia, the existence of language attitudes and their effects show that the English language has been a successful competitor among the native languages, the front runner on the language ladder and as a potential replacement for native languages in education, as our analysis reveals. In the domain of world politics and economics, English is placed so highly that the language attitudes vis-à-vis English are affirmed. If analysis of other social variables such as age, gender, education level, etc., were conducted, we are positive that language attitude studies would reveal more subtle and intricate power positions of the English language in these societies. However, in the absence of open discussion and scientific investigation of language attitudes, post-colonial South Asian societies are likely to continue to perceive and treat some languages in a non-friendly or hostile manner. As such, the effects will continue to reflect on the language learners to their detriment. Our discussion focuses on one chief issue that operates as a cause as well as a consequence of language attitudes.

Status symbol

As a result of placing English at the top of the language hierarchy, an undue recognition is given to the language that goes beyond treating it as a tool for communication and knowledge in post-colonial South Asia. The English language has become a status symbol, a marker of class distinction and even a symbol of education and intelligence in post-colonial South Asian societies, as our study reveals. The scenario is even bleaker when the state of the status symbol extends to the variety of English that is spoken; Samarakkody (2001) investigated the attitudes of selected learners of English towards various local English speakers and found out that learners of English in Sri Lanka have a 'favourable disposition' towards people who speak a standard variety of Sri Lankan English. These include identifying them with better education, gentlemanly qualities, etc.

Fernando and Sivaji (2014) observe,

> ... attitudes towards pronunciation, particularly towards some of the segmental features of SLE (Sri Lankan English) phonology, have been similarly prescriptive and judgmental both inside as well as outside ELT classroom.
> (p. 18)

This is within a context where identification of two main varieties, standard and non-standard SLE, is primarily defined by variations based in phonology (Gunesekera, 2005).

Similarly, students in Bangladesh pleaded with us to teach them how to speak with an American or British English accent as they considered their own English (with a heavy Bangla accent) as not up to the standard. They even went to the extent of asking us which English was better: American or British.

In Pakistan, the non-use of Punjabi even among family members and other social circles that parallels the use of it to talk to domestic helpers is yet another instance that shows how languages represent status due to the effect of language attitudes.

We believe that a particular experience we had would be interesting to our readers: the Tamil gardener who is employed at a friend's house told me with pride that he got his little son enrolled in a Sinhala medium school and that his son is able to speak and write Sinhala very well, after two or three years of schooling. Although Tamil is also an official, national language, nevertheless it was considered more prestigious and useful to study in the language of the majority.

In some societies such as post-colonial South Asia, the effects of language attitudes take the form of pride, a reason to boast, to demonstrate superiority on the one hand, while making other people feel low, ashamed and inferior on the other. Since a language represents its culture, inevitably, the culture that is associated with a language that has a high status receives a prominent place. As a result, the cultural artefacts representing that language also gain more recognition than those of low-status languages. In the case of the English language with its high status symbol value, western culture gets elevated just as much as the English language. Thus, the representations of western culture in dress, food habits, leisure activities, etc., also become status symbols, marking out one's class distinction, education or as a symbol of intelligence.

Language pickling

Where language use is concerned, South Asian speakers of English, both the fluent and not-so-fluent, have a tendency to 'pickle' languages. Pickling is mixing words and phrases of the English language while speaking in mother tongue and 'looks like' code-mixing and code-switching but is different in its purpose and method. Unlike code-switching and code-mixing, the purpose of which is to support the conversation or, as some studies reveal, to express solidarity or fulfil a need such as compensating for a deficiency in one language or excluding others from the conversation (Esen, 2019), pickling is done to imply 'superiority', 'class', education', 'intelligence', etc., the attributes the learners in our study state that the English language is able to give them. A sociolinguistic study on the code-switching and code-mixing of Senegalese international students in Iraqi colleges reveals one reason for code-switching and code-mixing, in addition to many other reasons, that support our findings:

> Conversations that include people from different social ranks bring about code switching too because French in Senegal is the language of the educated elite.
>
> (Abu-Krooz, Al-Azzawi, & Saadoon, 2018, p. 121)

Twenty-first century post-colonial South Asians are notorious for pickling English with their mother tongues when they speak in their native language. It is known that the same scenario exists among fluent English speakers some of whom drop French words into their speech to appear '*chic*'. However, in the case of English being pickled with mother tongues in post-colonial South Asia, it is no longer merely dropping a word or a phrase. Some of the best examples are popular TV shows and radio shows in Sri Lanka, India, Pakistan and Bangladesh. The general population pickles their languages with so much English in their daily communication that some of the words and phrases in mother tongues are not remembered as the English equivalents are at the tip of the tongue.

It is noteworthy that this pickling of languages is not limited to those who speak English fluently. Those whose English spoken skills are poor tend to pickle as much as others or perhaps more. The implication of such pickling of languages, i.e. mixing English when speaking in mother tongue, by both fluent speakers as well as the not-so-fluent may be attributed to the following, which are linked to language as a status symbol, the chief outcome of the language attitudes we have discussed:

a a desperate attempt to be on par with people who speak English
b to show off a class that is otherwise not present
c a cover-up for not being able to speak English in a coherent and intelligible manner
d to pose as 'fashionable'
e in the case of fluent speakers of English, to establish one's status as a watchdog and caretaker of the colonial master's language.

At a deeper level, the use of such a mixture of languages is one of the manifestations by which people try to show superiority, in addition to embracing other related western cultural elements such as dress, food, ways of spending leisure time, etc. This may be due to the desire to get close to the 'developed other' and it is made easy by everything that the developed other represents and symbolizes when opposed to everything South Asian and local: the first world vs. the third world. Some of the binaries and reasons are listed below:

a the appealing nature of consumerism and capitalism as opposed to simplicity in living
b attractive individualism as opposed to communalism
c individual rights-based cultures vs. communal duty-bound native cultures
d freedom as opposed to family bonds, communal accountability and collective responsibility
e the fast spread of and easy access to pop culture
f weak local counter forces
g a lack of visionaries and role models in local cultures
h human nature, in that tendency to see the other side of the fence as greener/ or as sour grapes.

Effects (Penalties) and their magnitude

As a result of the language attitudes that elevate the English language and its culture, a number of penalties have to be paid in local contexts. We do not intend to discuss all the consequences at length but to focus our discussion on some of the most obvious concerns. They are essentially psycho-social in nature. Among them are (a) inferiority and false superiority complexes, (b) setting but settling to 'white standards', (c) the distortion of local value systems and (d) the loss of utilitarian value for mother tongues.

Inferiority and false superiority complexes

The inability to speak English creates inferiority complexes fuelled by learners' lack of confidence to speak English. In the post-colonial South Asian context, as discussed in Chapter 5, the vast majority of learners lack confidence to speak English, which in itself is a type of inferiority complex. In addition, as elaborated in learner identity, in regard to possible selves and most importantly in role conflict, this inferiority complex can lead to envy, jealousy and even hatred as exhibited in anti-social activities such as ragging or hazing in universities. Moreover, the inferiority complex created by the inability to speak English is often externalized as a false superiority complex upon which fundamentalism of varying sorts is built. Nationhood, for instance, is susceptible to be associated with a particular language and this is often manipulated by people who do not speak English to label those who do as anti-nationals or agents of western powers in post-colonial South Asia. Thus, incorrect and destructive notions of nationalism are developed and manifested in resistance to English.

Setting but settling to 'white standards'

On the other hand, the superiority bestowed upon the English language and upon the culture it represents sets the standard as a status aspired to in local culture. For instance, in Sri Lanka, advertisements feature people who are white. Even for the publicity campaigns in higher education, one can see images of white people being used. Our own forthcoming article entitled, 'The contribution of the Sri Lankan media to the construction, consumption and representation of white supremacy: Living white while being non-white' is self-explanatory and discusses at length the issue of locals setting 'white standards' (Attanayake, forthcoming, 2019). However, it is ironic that such standards are limited to external features such as dress, names of places and institutes, fast food, the use of images of white people, etc., and not necessarily with living up to the developed world's quality assurance in regard to actual standards. One would then wonder about the purpose behind setting 'white standards'; it is merely a way of manipulating the sentiments of the masses, who are driven by the supremacy of English culture represented in language attitudes for commercial gain.

Distortion of local value systems

As a result of 'pickling' languages, mother tongues and value systems in the local culture are distorted. Respect for parents and filial piety are fully exhibited in the Asian cultures in all behaviours relating to contact between parents and children, including our terms of address. Now, instead of the old respectful 'my dad' – *mage thaaththaa* (southern Sri Lankan usage) or *mage appachchi* (upcountry usage), new, 'pickled' terms like 'father *kaarayaa*' have come into use. This *kaarayaa* in Sinhala (mother tongue of the Sinhalese) is equivalent to *waalaa* in Hindi and Urdu, meaning 'the one', a neutral, distant and indifferent term that is used at times to imply 'the irritating' one. Likewise, my wife and my husband have been replaced by 'wife *kaarayaa*' and 'husband *kaarayaa*' denoting a lack of respect, neutrality, distance or even irritation.

Loss of utilitarian value for mother tongues

As a result of pickling, more and more English words and phrases are added to our daily communication in mother tongues. On the one hand, it creates the notion that English words and phrases are more fitting as expressions in daily communication than those of our mother tongues. On the other hand, it limits the growth of mother tongues by limiting the addition of new words to the lexicon. Adding new words to a language enriches the language by expanding its scope and utility in diverse domains. Unfortunately, pickling with English limits the invention and accumulation of new words to mother tongues, making them lose their utilitarian value.

A look at the scenario as a whole, therefore, does not support the claim that English language and the culture it represents create rich identities in the hands of the locals. Rather, they create 'confused nations' in which the English language further establishes its power in spheres far beyond its use for communication and as a source of knowledge.

Several facts that post-colonial South Asian societies need be cautious about emerging from this discussion are (a) the power that creates confused nations is more destructive to local cultures than the power of the colonial masters when they ruled the region, (b) language attitudes and cultural distortions emerging as a result of the supremacy given to the English language and its representative cultures are no longer being imposed by the west and (c) the blame for creating and manipulating confusion locally among South Asian nations lies with the locals themselves, more specifically, with the local elites and the so-called educated. Therefore, blaming the colonial masters for the present mistakes of post-colonial South Asian elites is no longer useful for our countries, especially with more than 2,500 years of freedom prior to a few hundred years under the Europeans.

Remedial measures

We do not propose that all the problems discussed in relation to the language attitude issues can be rectified by introducing into academia a discourse named language attitudes. However, a formal platform for the discussion on language attitudes will pave the way for an honest and open dialogue addressing the status quo. Learners will not be as inhibited by language attitudes in society when they are discussed openly. This will reduce the possibility of language attitude anxiety. Also, learners will come to understand through the existence of this discourse that the set standards are not always the 'best standards'. Such a discourse will give voice to those who are vulnerable to pressures stemming from language attitudes. It will also set an example for people to speak up for what they believe in.

Developing language attitudes as an academic discourse is one of the best remedial measures for the issues we have identified and this discourse can be strengthened by adopting specific mechanisms. These include (a) building confidence at every level of education, (b) promoting localized education in values, (c) promoting formal and informal discussion of language attitudes, (d) political movement, (e) needs building (as part of language attitude discourse and through English language teaching) and (f) building bridges between languages.

Building confidence at every level

It is very important to build confidence in those who are too afraid or too shy to speak English due to a fear of ridicule at every level of their education. There is also a need not only to build learner confidence but to develop and maintain it through special courses aimed at building confidence and then taking them forward to the next highest level as discussed in Chapter 7 on Course Design and Material. In addition, making learners aware that their abilities and capacities do not lie solely in their ability to use English 'stylishly', but in their overall presentation of themselves as competent people. It is equally important to teach them to take pride in every step they take in learning in general and in using English in particular. Teaching them to allow themselves to be inspired by role models who have excelled in life despite their language difficulties is another way to conceive of education differently and build their self-confidence.

Values education

Values education can be added into the formal discourse on language attitudes so that the perspectives of those who act as the 'watchdog' because they are able to speak English 'better than others' can be changed. To this end, there is a need to teach them to (a) pay attention to and take pride in *what* they speak and not *how* they speak, (b) listen to the substance of what others say and not how they speak and give respect to people according to that substance, (c) not ridicule others for their bad/wrong/not-so-fluent English, (d) not blindly grasp the cultural baggage that is coming along with the English language, (e) set values and standards carefully, (f) know one's roots, national and familial identities and to respect them, and (g) treat the English language as a tool with a high utility value, like any other language.

Formal and informal dialogues

Through a formal discourse on language attitudes, as well as open, informal discussions, debates, etc., it is possible to promote the cause of bringing language attitude issues to the forefront while criticizing the watchdogs. However, critical analysis is usually much easier in post-colonial South Asian societies when approached through informal modes rather than formal, systemic institutionalizations. At the same time, the promotion of informal discussions is triggered via a formal discourse. There is a dire need in these societies to openly criticize the self-appointed caretakers of the colonial master's language with special reference to the ways in which the watchdog acts. It is necessary to disapprove of the actions of this watchdog mercilessly on the one hand, and on the other hand pitiably: mercilessly for being so snobbish as to mock other English language learners for their efforts to speak English and pitiably for being the embodiment of a slave to the colonial mentality.

Political movement

In post-colonial South Asian societies, the support of the governing political parties can change attitude changes overnight via an organized movement. In Sri Lanka, we witnessed such a campaign a few years ago, around 2009. It came to a halt when the governing party lost power. This is a major reason for policy changes typical to developing countries. However, it was interesting to note how a mass attitudinal change was brought about. As we have discussed elsewhere, the concept of the 'sword' (popularly known as ***kaduwa*** in Sinhala) is used to describe the English language in Sri Lanka due to its power (symbolizing prestige, highness, refinedness, etc.). The movement, 'English as a life skill', with the political patronage of a Presidential Task Force came into being with the slogan, 'Speak English our way'. This campaign popularized an ordinary chopping knife (symbolizing ordinariness, rough and unrefined-ness, etc.) in place of the well-polished sword to symbolize the slogan. We remember that there were several advertisements on TV and in printed media with extremely successful athletes, cricketers, etc. whose English was 'not-so-good' but who 'managed' with a rural or ordinary Sri Lankan accent, came forward to speak to the general masses about the importance of speaking English in the way they could, most importantly without imitating any foreign, alien ways. Parallel to this media campaign, teachers of English were trained in Hyderabad, India (instead of sending them to the west for training) to become master teachers in order to train the ordinary English language teachers on their return. The programme was a massive success in terms of bringing about an attitudinal change in regard to English language speaking in Sri Lanka, even though it was perceived to be a failure in terms of the actual execution of the teacher training and promoting quality teaching at the school level. Nevertheless, as far as the discussion of developing language attitudes as a formal academic discourse is concerned, 'Speak English our way' is a good example of how the support of a political movement can work as a mechanism for changing language attitudes in a society.

Building bridges between the English language and local cultures/knowledge

The discourse on language attitudes should build bridges between the English language and local cultures and local knowledge. It is important to remember that learners are aware of language attitudes in the society and are distanced from the culture that the English language represents. Language is considered to be an instrument of culture and knowledge. It neither limits a language to representing one culture or its original culture, nor does it restrict to disseminating local knowledge. Therefore, the language attitudes discourse should bring about a dialogue on the necessity to use the English language to discuss and make use of local cultural artefacts that are close to rural and semi-rural learner experiences while disseminating the related knowledge. This by no means justifies language pickling or any of the other associated impacts that have been discussed above or contradicts our stance on 'Penalties and their magnitude'. Considering the problems relating to language attitudes that elevate English culture and western knowledge over the local and distance learners from learning the language, the use of English to discuss local cultures and knowledge can be used to bridge the gap. Language attitudes discourse needs to cater to this requirement, which should be further enhanced by teaching English in such a way that material design and teaching methodologies can be enriched via local traditional ways and means. One simple example would be that in the Building Confidence to Speak English course, we use pictures of rural settings for learners to describe them and develop stories. The Narrative-based Course to Learn English that follows also makes use of traditional story-telling techniques to retell local stories.

Needs building

A discourse on language attitudes requires to include building needs for students to learn English. Once the needs to learn English have been built, learners will transcend the language attitudinal issues and will be able to perceive their ability to speak and use the language with a clear focus geared towards their future betterment. This can be accomplished by including it into the language attitudes discourse via English language courses.

Our initial study in 2007 with undergraduates from two faculties, namely the Faculty of Management and the Faculty of Arts in three universities reveals that students of the Faculties of Arts usually do not have a clear focus as to why they need English: their reasons for learning English are scattered over a variety of areas with vagueness as a core feature, manifesting a lack of focus. For instance, some want to learn English because it is 'an international language' or because it is 'useful' or 'important'. The same views are expressed by a large majority of learners in the current study (see Chapter 3) with vague reasons given, such as 'because it is an international language', 'can communicate better', etc. for preferring to develop skill in English. Considering the students in the sample of the first study, i.e. Arts students who are the large majority in every university in Sri

Lanka and whose English language proficiency is lower than any other student groups studying in other faculties (For instance, out of about seven to eight hundred students, about 2/3 belong to the lowest category, Level I, in the Faculty of Arts, University of Colombo every year.), this lack of a clear focus about their need for English may be a reason for poor performance.[1] In contrast, when there is a clear and specific need for English in student life, especially if it is related to their future careers, the reasons for learning English become more specific and focused. The study we carried out for our PhD shows that 'students in faculties that offer core subjects with a career bent in them exhibit a clear career motive for learning English' (Attanayake, 2017, p. 260) and are at a satisfactory level of English language proficiency whereas, those who study in the Arts subject streams, due to the possibility of them getting into any variety of career opportunities, usually show lack of a specific purpose in learning English and are poor in English as well.

The student sample in the current study, i.e. those whose English language proficiency is not high, further supports a potential positive correlation between the need to learn English and the ability level to perform in English, in that vagueness about their need for learning English may be a major reason for exhibiting a low proficiency in English. This area clearly merits further investigation.

Needs building for learning English will not only help learners have a clear focus to learn English, but also develop new and challenging ambitions in learners' lives as well. Every year we ask this particular question from the lowest proficiency group we get to teach; 'what is your ambition in life?' It is very interesting to see the answer; out of 25 students, about 23 (in certain years 24) state, 'I want to be a teacher'. One would wonder as to what is unusual about this answer. In Sri Lanka, teachers get three months of paid holidays per year, have no work on weekends and their working hours are limited to five hours a day, all of which are not possible in the private sector or in other government professions (other than teaching in private institutes that require a very good command in English). In addition, to be a school teacher does not require a proficiency in English (other than for a teacher of English, for which separate institutes, namely Colleges of Education are established) as interviews are conducted in their mother tongues. Moreover, teachers are entitled to a pension. Even though the pay may not be very high, teaching in Sri Lanka is considered to be a convenient and also a respectable profession, given the respect that a teacher invites in these societies. To ice the cake, a graduate with an Arts degree is almost 'entitled' to a government teaching profession. Therefore, most of the learners in the lowest English proficiency levels end up having the 'ambition' of becoming a teacher.

However, in one particular year, when this question about learner ambition was asked, there was one student who said that she wanted to be a journalist while all the others 'wanted' to be teachers. When the year-end examination results were released, it turned out that this particular student has topped the batch! A friend informed me about the findings of a sociological study (which I am unable to find unfortunately) carried out in Belihuloya, a remote village in Sri Lanka where a large majority of the villagers are poverty-stricken: the findings show that the people remain poor because they do not plan for future, contrary to the general notion that when people are poor, no plans can be made beyond living for the day.

With regard to English language learners with low proficiency, the lesson that can be made use of is that, if different ambitions are formed, their performance can be enhanced. For altered ambitions, novel means to achieve them have to be created. They give a clear focus to student learning so that such ambitions can be achieved. If learners are taught to develop ambitions that are challenging and not given, the chances are that they will be more focused in their studies, including English language learning. It is commonly accepted that a good proficiency in English increases the employability of post-colonial South Asian graduates. If learners develop challenging employment ambitions that require English as a means to achieve and succeed, the need to learn English will become clear. This in turn will make learners approach English language learning with robust energy.

In our current study sample, some of the learners are from degrees offered in mother tongue instruction. While almost all of the universities in all four countries offer English medium instruction, opting for the mother tongue instruction at the degree level may be due to students having (a) a lack of proficiency and confidence to follow a degree course in English and (b) their future career purposes most likely seem to be divorced from using English. Therefore, it may be expected that their need to develop the skill they prefer the most being (speaking in English) secondary where their career 'ambitions' are concerned and more of a personal fancy that is expressed through the vague labels such as 'international language' that helps one 'communicate better' as opposed to most of the more focused reasons we found in our previous study, which were very specific: 'I want to be an accountant so I need English', 'I want to go abroad for my higher studies', etc., which were less frequently found in the current study.

Therefore, it is important that needs building is made a part of English language education. We see the possibility of achieving this goal through (a) the language attitudes discourse and (b) English language courses. When a specific need in terms of career prospects is built in the student to learn English, a clear focus is developed upon which even a new, more expansive ambition in life may be created. Therefore, apart from confidence building, needs building should also be part of language attitudes discourse and be further supported by English language teaching in universities and other higher education institutes. If and when, the core subjects fail to give a clear focus to students in terms of their future careers, the discussion of language attitudes can give them a clear focus, which can be strengthened through teaching English to reach out to students. Therefore, in the post-colonial-South Asian context, both confidence building and needs building can be considered pivotal to the language attitude discourse.

Significance

If language attitudes could be made into an academic discourse, the dissemination of such knowledge among professionals in the language field, especially among the teachers of English language, can help to change the existing language attitudes present in the field. As teachers are directly in contact with the student population, it is crucial that teachers are aware of their responsibility to help eliminate negativity in language attitudes among the student population.

It is noteworthy to mention that in the example analysis of language attitudes discussed above, none of the views contribute to a confluence of languages or languages complementing each other. The responses of the teachers, however, indicate that the co-existence of languages is not a friendly matter. As our current study reveals, in a context where language attitudes matter and their influence is detrimental to the language learner, it is important to reflect upon these findings in the two studies: it is the English language teachers who view the languages as co-existing in a non-friendly manner; the learners are affected by language attitude anxiety to the extent that they are unable to put what they learn into practice. We believe that resolving the major issues related to language attitudes needs to begin in the English language classroom. The attitudes that are reflected in the teachers' views inevitably seep into their teaching, error correction and in general discussion to affect their students and contribute to perpetuating the existing language attitude issues. A formal discussion on language attitudes can minimize the negative effects so that the new and better attitudes of teachers will have a trickle-down effect on the learners and the larger society.

Building bridges between the English language and local cultures/knowledge is important to create a harmony between the language learners' perceived attributes of the language and the practical use of it so that learners are not distanced from the language and learning it. This is another area that teachers and other professionals in the field should be made aware of, so that a conscious effort can be made in the teaching–learning process. Language attitudes discourse can help to create a group of personnel who can contribute significantly to achieving this.

To this end, it is crucial that teachers of English are well equipped with knowledge of language attitudes, acquire necessary skills and correct attitudes towards teaching English, the English language itself and all of its representations. A formal discourse will help them to obtain the necessary professional education in the area and to take the responsibility for guiding the student population to perceive languages in their proper perspective without being affected by language attitude anxiety.

Conclusion

The chapter discusses the timely need for developing an academic discourse on language attitudes in order to better understand the current language attitudes prevalent in societies and their influence on language learners. In postcolonial South Asia in particular, language attitudes play a very significant role vis-à-vis the relationship between the English language and native languages as our study reveals. Therefore, this discussion emphasizes the examination of the existing language attitudes in different societies, analysing them in diverse contexts and identifying the implications in the context of their effects on the language learner in particular and on society in general. The effects of language attitudes are further elaborated in terms of the consequences that are manifested in post-colonial societies and this is followed by a number of remedial measures to rectify these issues.

Note

1 The reasons for Sri Lankan Arts students' low proficiency in English have been discussed at length elsewhere.

References

Abu-Krooz, H. H., Al-Azzawi, Q. O., & Saadoon, M. M. (2018). Code switching and code mixing: A sociolinguistic study of Senegalese international students in Iraqi colleges. *Journal of University of Babylon for Humanities*, 26(3), 112–123.

Attanayake, A. U. (2017). *Undergraduate ELT in Sri Lanka: Policy, practice and perspectives for South Asia*. Newcastle upon Tyne: Cambridge Scholars Publication.

Attanayake, A. U. (forthcoming, 2019). The contribution of the Sri Lankan media to the construction, consumption and representation of white supremacy: Living white while being non-white. In H. Park and M. Dodd (Eds.), *Media culture in transnational Asia: Convergences and divergences*. NJ: Rutgers University Press.

Crystal, D. (1997). *English as a global language*. Cambridge: Cambridge University Press.

Esen, S. (2019). Code switching: Definition, types, and examples. Retrieved from: https://owlcation.com/humanities/Code-Switching-Definition-Types-and-Examples-of-Code-Switching.

Fernando, D., & Sivaji, K. (2014). Towards and inclusive standard Sri Lankan English for ELT in Sri Lanka: Identifying and validating phonological features of Sri Lankan English of Tamil speakers. In K. de Abrew, N. Abayasekera, and C. Jayasinghe (Eds.), *Changing paradigms in English language teaching* (pp. 17–26). Colombo: SLELTA.

Gramsci, A. (1971). *Selections from the prison notebooks*. Ed. and trans. Q. Hoare and G. Nowell Smith (p. 12). London, UK: Lawrence and Wishart.

Gunesekara, M. (2005). *The post-colonial identity of Sri Lankan English*. Colombo: Katha.

Lears, J. (1985). The concept of cultural hegemony: Problems and possibilities. Oxford University Press. *American Historical Review*, 9(3), 567–593.

Phillipson, R. (1992). *Linguistic imperialism*. New York: Oxford University Press.

Ramanathan, V. (2005). *The English-vernacular divide: Postcolonial language politics and practice*. Clevedon, England: Multilingual Matters Ltd.

Samarakkody, M. (2001). Motivation and acquisition of English in Sri Lanka: A linguistic and social psychological study. In D. Hayes (Ed.), *Teaching English: Possibilities and opportunities* (pp. 37–47). Colombo: British Council.

12 Conclusions

Introduction

The first half of this concluding chapter summarizes the outcomes of the previous chapters while examining the issues common to English language learners in the South Asian region, pointing to the relevance of the study and its findings. The second part of the chapter examines the study in terms of achieving the set objectives. The discussion takes the form of a reflection on the outcomes by locating them in the main objectives as outlined in the introduction.

The study and its findings

Post-colonial South Asian countries such as Sri Lanka, India, Pakistan and Bangladesh invest a considerable amount of money and resources into making enormous efforts to improve English language education. Despite all of that, the results are very unsatisfactory. Even though the influence of social, economic and political factors on these outcomes are unarguable, there is also an undeniable impact stemming from methods and approaches borrowed from the west that do not suit the English language learners in these countries. The needs of the post-colonial English language learner vis-à-vis English language are different from the needs perceived by the educators who profess to have uncovered second/foreign language teaching methods suitable for the whole world. The context within which these learners function is often very different from what may be generalized. This study attempted to uncover the language attitudes that are prevalent in the sub-continent towards the English language and its speakers in order to analyse their effects on the language learner and find corrective mechanisms.

The context of the study in this book is located in the four post-colonial South Asian countries of Pakistan, Bangladesh, India and Sri Lanka, with 4,630 respondents covering several regions within these countries. This data was collected over one year from October 2017 to October 2018. The preliminary research that led to this study was conducted in Sri Lanka over ten years from 2007 until 2017. The contrasting and similar nature of responses to those initial studies from the international academic community, both in the west and Asia, respectively, stimulated us to extend that research to Sri Lanka's neighbours. The outcomes of our study reveal an unmistakable influence from the attitudes that exist in the larger society outside of the English language domain in addition to the influence of the attitudes found in the 'inner society' of the English language classroom. Further, the study demonstrates the impact on learner performance in English as a foreign/second language, predominantly in regard to the primary mode of communication, i.e. speaking.

Our study identifies some interesting language attitudes that exist in South Asian societies in relation to the English language and its speakers, and they seem to be unique to the region. The discussion deliberates about the effects of language attitudes on the English language learners in post-colonial South Asia, which is manifested in a lack of confidence that inhibits the learners from speaking English, their most desired skill. We identify the cause for a lack of confidence to be due to a specific type of anxiety and introduce it as language attitude anxiety (LAA). LAA stems from the language attitudes that create norms and set standards, and the existence of prejudice against learners who do not meet these expectations. The vast majority of South Asian learners, especially rural and semi-rural learners, develop LAA. The influence of LAA is manifested in their speech performance and exhibits itself in a lack of confidence to speak English.

The study puts forth the argument that Foreign Language (Classroom) Anxiety (FLCA) and the associated scale that is extensively used throughout the world to discuss language anxiety related to foreign/second language learning is not able to capture the complexities attached to social attitudes and their influence on foreign/second language learning. It limits the anxiety in foreign/second language learners' experiences strictly to the classroom, and does not take into account the anxiety related to the use of a foreign/second language outside the classroom context. In addition, its Likert scale structure does not capture the complex nature of the anxiety that is caused by language attitudes. The Attitude Motivation Test Battery (AMTB) is also restricted in catching the context-specific attitudes in the foreign/second language learning settings that are prevalent in South Asia, thus establishing the existence of and the need for analyzing a different type of anxiety, which we call LAA. This anxiety is experienced by most foreign/second language learners in post-colonial South Asian societies. LAA stems from the language attitudes in the larger society that the foreign/second language learners come into contact with, both inside and outside the language classroom, and manifests itself in the learner's lack of confidence to speak in English. We have identified the fear of negative evaluation and communication apprehension as the two main constituents of LAA by analysing learner responses.

We further point out the fact that as a result of learners developing negative attitudes towards their own speaking of English there may be a gloomy projection of this negativity onto their own language learning in general. There is a need for a platform for intervention that needs to be created to help learners develop positive attitudes towards their own English-speaking ability. Building confidence to speak English is the best way to eliminate LAA.

In order to make use of the platform to build confidence to speak English, it is crucial to fully comprehend the learners in their current, failed states. We analyse the characteristics of English language learners in post-colonial South Asia vis-à-vis their social, mental and educational constructs of learner identity, possible selves, role conflict and in terms of the language acquisition stages. These are well recognized concepts that describe language learners' problems. In so doing, the problem of a lack of confidence to speak English and how that lack of confidence seems to project its effects onto English language learning in general are better situated. The learners are trapped within a complex power structure and this is evident from their responses to questions about their experiences of speaking and history of learning English.

The analysis of the problem of LAA permits us to find a strategic platform for an intervention to rectify the problem. As stated, learners' lack of confidence is an expression of the influence of LAA. Therefore, building confidence to speak English is the best rectifying measure to address this issue. The fear of speaking is addressed in the Building Confidence to Speak English course by using speech activities to build their confidence. This is accomplished by specially designed materials and specially trained teachers with a correct understanding of what is needed to teach these types of learners. The Building Confidence to Speak English course has a solid psychological approach in which habituation is used as the main mechanism to eliminate LAA.

The discussion about the specific course to build confidence is situated in the larger picture of an entire curriculum which is developed with thematic and theoretical links. The philosophy of BICS, CUP and CALPS is used as an overarching theory with our newly devised sub-divisions illustrated to develop a complete curriculum in three different, but connected courses, with the aim of developing the English language proficiency of weak learners. It establishes the relations between the three courses of this curriculum thematically along the lines of confidence: ***building*** confidence, ***developing*** confidence and ***maintaining*** confidence. The first course aims at building confidence and makes use of BICS, while the second, Narrative-based Course to Learn English, is designed to develop confidence and uses the principles of CUP. The third course, namely, the EAP/ESP course aims at maintaining the built and developed confidence with the use of CALPS principles.

We discuss the Building Confidence to Speak English course in great detail since it is the focus of this study. The course uses the principles of Speech Act Theory to design materials. It makes use of two different activity potentials, namely, Communicative and Cognitive Potential Development and their scales for the sequencing and gradation of activities. We highlight the significance of repetition of speech acts in an order of increasing difficulty for reinforcement. In addition, the context familiarity of the content is another significant feature when considering the rural and semi-rural backgrounds of the language learners. The module structure and format are important as detailed instructions, simple language and a simple format in the modules are a way, however insignificant they may seem, to bridge the existing gap between the learner and the learning.

To understand the psychology of language learners, an attempt is made to locate it in the LAA that most South Asian learners struggle with in learning English. There is a need to create an artificial society where learners feel safe from their fears of competition, over-correction and most importantly, the watchdog who is looking for mistakes. Therein, it is of paramount importance for a teaching methodology that is devoid of the teaching strategies that make the learners experience LAA. The principles of Cooperative Language Learning (CLL), qualify as the most compatible, hence CLL is at the heart of our teaching methodology. The deliberate transformation of the English language classroom into a safe zone has to be accomplished by way of special features such as no individual work, no individual performance, no error correction, no grammar teaching, no mandatory performance, no homework and no use of mother tongue. It is important to comprehend that these features are the complete opposite of the ordinary South Asian classroom. In addition, there are other important supporting strategies such as a phrase every day, having the teacher sit at the same level as the learners and summing up the errors/mistakes encountered during the day in general terms, etc., all of which are significant in fortifying the safe zone. It is necessary to train teachers to make them aware not only of the creation and maintenance of the safe zone, but also of the process-oriented nature of the approach to build confidence. In addition, teachers should be made to understand the significance of their role in the confidence building classroom, as they are the main agents who can build bridges between language attitudes and language needs.

The assessment of the Building Confidence to Speak English course is a simple stage play. However, what is mandatory is that all the members in the class take part in it. The responsibility for finding the theme/plot is given to the learners themselves. The teacher is supposed to help them with the script after the learners have developed it on their own. Grading student performances is not necessary and is therefore not encouraged. Nevertheless, if required, there is one criterion that is banned: using English language proficiency as a measurement variable. It must be remembered that the course objective is to build learner confidence to speak English. What has to be assessed and graded is the learner's confidence level to speak in English. At the same time, the collective performance of the group can be considered as a grading criterion since maximum collaboration among the group members facilitates the use of the English. Therein, fluency and accuracy are not evaluated but the use of English in a trial and error manner. The other criteria for evaluation are as usual: theme/plot, stage props, costumes, etc. In addition, a weekly formative assessment is encouraged to assess and monitor the changes in the exhibited confidence level (if any) of students to work and perform in English as team players.

Course evaluation mechanisms have been designed to be used after the course is taught. Pre- and in-course evaluations are not usually very practical in South Asia given the length of time it takes to process the data and make changes to the course. At the same time, evaluation at pre- and whilst stages may not contribute much in changing the course given the fact that the course objectives have already been identified against the need for confidence to speak English. Also the comparatively short duration of the course may not permit changes for an in-course evaluation. Therefore, these two types of evaluation are not discussed at length. The post-evaluation employs a questionnaire to collect data from students and teachers about the contexts where students show a lack of confidence to speak in English, i.e. inside and outside the classroom with teachers, their peers and outsiders consisting of 'others' in front of whom they are afraid of making mistakes. Interviews are recommended to obtain student and teacher feedback while teacher journals and records of teacher observations are also weighty contributions for extracting qualitative data. If a pre-evaluation is conducted, it is emphasized that the confidence to speak English prior to the course is to be assessed against their confidence level after the course. In such a case, a complete course evaluation in terms of course material, teaching methods and assessment practices cannot be expected and the evaluation will be a simple comparison of the confidence level to speak in English before and after the course. The outcomes of course evaluation need to be considered to improve future course content.

There is a clear need for developing language attitudes as an academic discourse to understand existing language attitudes in societies and their impact on language learners. This study brings out the major role of language attitudes in post-colonial South Asia in regard to the relationship between the English language and native languages. Therefore, it is important to examine the existing language attitudes in different societies, analyse them in diverse settings and identify the implications in the context of their effects on the language learner in particular and on society in general. The magnitude of the effects of language attitudes do not end with affecting the language learner in his speaking and in learning the language; in post-colonial South Asia, the impact of language attitudes is felt in all areas of society including where cultural artefacts, leisure activities and even where personal relationships are concerned. Therefore, it is important to situate the problems caused by language attitudes and their impact on society to find remedial measures. There is hope that via an open academic discourse, these issues can be brought to light and rectifying strategies can be found.

Upon reflection

There were a number of general and specific objectives our study aimed to achieve. We feel it is time for reflection to see to what extent they have been achieved.

Through this book, we set out to create awareness among the experts in the field on the necessity of considering context-specific features vis-à-vis English Language Teaching (ELT) in designing ELT curricula. We believe that this book has taken the reader on a journey through the feelings and emotions of post-colonial South Asian English language learners with their fears, shyness and uncertainties about speaking in English. Despite the benefits learners believe the ability to speak English can bestow upon them, their LAA overrides all of them leaving these learners with a lack of confidence to speak English, even though it is their most desired skill.

In addition, giving a comprehensive analysis of curriculum design for ELT with a strong theoretical framework was another aim which we attempted to achieve. Chapter 7 was dedicated to this purpose with layers of structures built not only on theoretical principles but on thematic aspects as well, on the theme of confidence: Building Confidence to Speak English is used to ***build*** confidence, the Narrative-based Course to ***develop*** confidence and English for Academic/Specific Purposes courses to ***maintain*** confidence. The theoretical perspectives provide an overarching theory for the three-course curriculum while each course has its own internal theoretical principles. The specific theory (Speech Act Theory) and the other principles that went into designing the materials of the confidence building course were discussed in detail and we believe that a reader who is interested in developing a course or a curriculum will benefit from that discussion. The significance of this dialogue is that the selection of the thematic and theoretical aspects have been identified as per the needs of the learners; in that learners' most sought-after skill is speaking and they lack confidence to speak English. Hence, confidence building is to be achieved via speech activities.

One of the most compelling aims was to understand the attitudes related to and prejudices attached with the languages that are in use in the post-colonial South Asia. The western societies may not experience the same type of prejudices and attitudes related to languages based on the hierarchical, competitive and unfriendly nature of linguistic co-existence, as most languages co-exist in the west harmoniously as tools of communication, knowledge and culture without conflict. In contrast, the co-existence of languages both during the pre-independence and post-independence eras in the South Asian region was not of a peaceful nature. Far from that, with or without the English language, some native languages have exerted their powers over others with the political powers of the dominant groups resulting in certain attitudes and prejudices being attached to languages. To add to this, English, as the colonial master's language, has a supremacy that creates power dynamics in every domain even into the 21st century in South Asia, now with the dominant power of the USA and no longer England. We found that societal language attitudes towards the English language and its speakers are creating prejudices that lead to LAA in post-colonial South Asian learners.

We introduced a new dimension, namely language attitudes, to academic discourse and discussed it as a crucial factor to consider in designing curricula for teaching English in the region. Therein, the co-existence of languages in a non-friendly manner with language competition, language hierarchies, language replacement, etc., came to the foreground with the analyses of students' and teachers' perspectives. The necessity of addressing the issues that affect the language learners and arising from language attitudes is discussed in the backdrop of the failure of teaching English in the region over 70 years.

Considering the lack of confidence to speak English, which is surprisingly common to post-colonial South Asian language learners, we attempted to demonstrate the importance of creating a 'safe zone' within the English language classroom, especially for low proficiency English language learners. The features of this 'safe zone' were discussed at length so that the way to create a special classroom, completely in contrast to the traditional English language classroom, was explained.

In so doing, we attempted to bring to attention the context-specific nature of problems related to English language teaching by contextualizing the material and the teaching methodology to address the problems faced when teaching English in the region. Thereby, we emphasized the importance of understanding the context-specific issues related to teaching languages in different localities.

In order to have a thorough understanding of the context and related problems encountered in teaching English, we made an effort to show the necessity of conducting a needs analysis prior to the design of ELT curricula. For instance, the need for speaking English has been ignored from the beginning in all four countries. Student needs are assumed as per teachers' perceptions, which are not always accurate. If needs analyses are made a compulsory part of ELT course design, we believe, most of the context-specific issues related to the teaching of English in South Asia can be better understood and remedial measures can be found.

Conclusion

A vast majority of the learners in the four post-colonial South Asian countries of Sri Lanka, India, Bangladesh and Pakistan, despite their desire to speak English, and a plethora of extremely positive attributes they perceive being able to speak English would endow them with, experience LAA manifested in lack of confidence to speak English. This may be projected onto learning English in general, which results in an unsatisfactory performance with a large majority of failures coming from rural and semi-rural locales. The course, Building Confidence to Speak English, is proposed as a rectifying measure to embark on teaching English in an innovative way, in contrast to the traditional, conventional and stereotypical methods that have failed our learners. Instead, we aim at taking these learners on a journey towards success. Learners' confidence to speak, in any English they are able to, is built, first within the four walls of the language classroom so that that their confidence is projected outwardly to ignore the watchdog waiting in society ever since the colonial master left these nations.

Appendix A
Module 4 (An example module)

Activity 1 – Getting to know more about others

Time: 40 minutes
Procedure:

Step I: Find information about the group members and report it to the class.

- i Get into groups of 4–5.
- ii Find answers to the questions given below.
- iii First ask the questions from the group members.
- iv Your teacher will put the question formats on the board.
- v Then report the findings to the class.

Questions:

- a Find someone who lives in Maharagama.
  - Do you live in Maharagama?
- b Find someone who likes to wear bright colours.
  - Do you like (would you like) bright colours?
- c Find someone who doesn't like music.
  - Don't you like to listen to music?
- d Find someone who likes soft drinks.
  - Do you like soft drinks?
- e Find someone who loves small children.
  - Do you like small children?
- f Find someone who is afraid of flying.
  - Are you afraid of flying?
- g Find someone who likes dogs.
  - Do you like dogs?
- h Find someone who is irritated by beggars, but gives them money.
  - Are you irritated by beggars, but still do you give them money?
- i Find someone who is interested in social service.
  - Are you interested in social service?
- j Find someone who would like to visit a country that has a cold climate.
  - Do you like to visit a country that has a cold climate?

Step II: Find information about your classmates and report to the class.
Time: 40 minutes

i Work in the same groups.
ii Take 2 questions from the above list and go round the class asking the questions from all the others.
iii Then come back to your group and put everyone's answers together and make a report.
iv Your teacher will help you with grammar and vocabulary.
v In groups, report the findings to the class, if you like.

Activity 2 – Where would you like to go?

Time: 15 minutes
Step I: Listen to your teacher and mark the route.
Procedure:

i Discuss with your teacher about the cities you like to visit.
ii Your teacher will put the names of the main cities on the board.
iii Mark the main cities on the map.
iv Now your teacher will read out a description of a trip.
v Listen and mark the route.

Mark the route on this map.

Step II: Discuss and present your findings to the class.
Time: 35 minutes

- i Get into groups of 4–5.
- ii Your teacher will give you five destinations (Anuradhapura, Polonnaruwa, Jaffna, Galle, Kandy).
- iii In groups, discuss the important places you can visit in those cities.
- iv Your teacher will help you with the language (grammar and vocabulary).
- v Now write a description of the important places you would like to visit in those cities.
- vi You may present the description to the class.

Activity 3 – Shall we tell a story in a different way?

Time: 45 minutes
Procedure:
Step I: Look at what you drew and tell a story.

- i Your teacher will draw a picture on the board (e.g. a tree, a man, a hut, a boat).
- ii Each one of you can come to the board and add another item to the picture on the board.
- iii Together with your teacher, write the words (vocabulary) that can describe the picture.
- iv You may use one side of the board to write them.
- v Now form different groups.
- vi A group can have 4–5 members in it.
- vii In your groups, create a story by looking at the picture on the board.
- viii One member of the group or all the members in the group can present the story to the class.
- ix After telling the story to the class, you can write the story.

Module 4 (Teacher's copy)

Activity 2 – The description of the route

Last weekend I went on a three-day trip with my friends. We started our trip from Colombo. First, we went to Kandy. We went to the *Dalada Maligawa*. Then we enjoyed a boat ride in the *Bogambara* Lake. In the Evening, we went to *Anuradhapura* via *Dambulla*. We stayed the night in *Anuradhapura* and visited the important places in the city. We were eagerly waiting for the next day: the day to go to *Jaffna*! Early in the morning, we started our first trip to *Jaffna*.

Appendix B

Ground rules to teach in the 'Building Confidence to Speak English' course

Course designer – Dr Asantha U. Attanayake

Part I

1 No use of mother tongue/s
2 No translation in to the mother tongue/s
3 No need to make students understand everything you say
4 No student can use mother tongue/s during English lectures
5 No grammar teaching
6 No home work
7 No individual work/performance is required
8 No error correction when students in groups/pairs get up to speak
9 No compulsion for students to perform in front of the class; only volunteers can perform

Part II

10 Use English and ENGLISH ONLY for classroom interaction with students.
11 Use a lot of body language to make students comprehend what you say.
12 Student MUST use English when they speak (even in wrong English).
13 Give them only group or pair work
14 Give a phrase that is required to work in groups every day. Put it on the board and get everyone to repeat it for practice.

> E.g.: Move your chair please.
> Is this correct?
> Can I see your answer please?
> We will note it down.

From time to time, go back to these phrases and make students repeat them. By the time all the modules are complete, count the number of phrases they have learned to use in speech.

15 Give simple language structures only when necessary.
16 Do not give more than three language structures at a time (for one Activity or a Step).

17 Put it/them on the board and leave it /them there until the Activity/Step is over.

18 Ask to volunteer and when they do, get the entire group to perform in front of the class. If they hesitate, then pass.

19 Appreciate each group performance by clapping/commenting, 'Wow!', 'Great!' 'Excellent', etc.

20 When students make errors while speaking, overlook them. Once the lesson is over, you may generally correct them without pointing at a particular group/student.

Very important

The objective of this course is to build student confidence to speak English and NOT to develop their English language proficiency/accuracy/fluency.

Appendix C
Questionnaire

Dear students,

We would be thankful to you, if you could kindly answer the questions given below. Your honest response will be very useful for us to develop new methodologies to teach English to our students in South Asia.

University: ....
Year of Study: 1st Year/2nd Year/3rd Year/4th Year ....
Degree programme you are following: BA/BSc/MA/Other ....
in (e.g.: History) ....
Medium of study: Mother tongue/English/Other ....

1 The skill you want to develop the most when you learn English

   a Listening
   b Speaking
   c Reading
   d Writing
   e Other ....

2 Why do you want to develop it the most? ....
   ....

3 Do you like to speak in English? Yes/No – Give a reason ....
   ....

4 Can you speak in English ***well***? Yes/No – Give a reason ....
   ....

5 If you want to speak English but you don't speak it (or you are reluctant to speak), what are the reasons for it? Underline the response/s that suit/s you the best.

   a Because I fear that others may laugh at my mistakes
   b Because I am shy
   c Both (a) and (b)

- d Because I don't like English
- e I am not shy or afraid to speak English
- f Any other reason: ....

6 If you are afraid/shy to speak English, that is,

- a in your classroom
- b outside the classroom
- c both inside and outside classroom
- d nowhere (not shy or afraid anywhere)

7 If you are afraid/shy to speak English, that is, in front of

- a your teachers
- b your friends
- c outsiders
- d all above
- e no one (not shy or afraid to speak with anyone)

Write anything that you have to say about your English language learning experience or your English language speaking experience, your suggestions to improve ELT in your country, etc.

Interview questions

1 Do you *like* to speak English?
2 How useful is speaking English to you? Give reasons.
3 Do you speak English? When? Where? With whom?
4 If you do not speak English, what are the reasons for that?
5 Tell me, how do you feel about people who speak English *well*?
6 Who do you think you are more comfortable in speaking English? With a native speaker of English (British or American) OR with your teachers, friends? Why?

Thank you
Asantha U. Attanayake Barborich
University of Colombo, Sri Lanka

Appendix D

Questionnaire for teachers' feedback on the 'Building Confidence to Speak English' course

Dear Teachers,

This course has been planned with the aim of building students' confidence to speak English. As you are a very important part of this course, your honest feedback would be very useful for its improvement.

1 According to your observation, what can you say about the improvement of <u>student–student</u> interaction in using English during the intensive course?

  i Highly improved
  ii Somewhat improved
  iii Slightly improved
  iv Not improved at all
  v Cannot say

2 According to your observation, what can you say about the improvement of <u>student–teacher</u> interaction in using English during the intensive course?

  i Highly improved
  ii Somewhat improved
  iii Slightly improved
  iv Not improved at all
  v Cannot say

3 How would you rate the present level of student confidence in speaking in English when you compare it with the same at the beginning?

  i Highly improved
  ii Somewhat improved
  iii Slightly improved
  iv Not improved at all
  v Cannot say

4 What is the most suitable duration you would suggest for a course like this designed for your students?

i One month
ii Three weeks
iii Two weeks
iv One week
v Other (Please write the duration) ....

5 Time given for the activities were (average)

i Sufficient
ii Somewhat sufficient
iii Not sufficient
iv Cannot say
v Any other comment ....

6 Variety of themes covered through activities were

i Adequate
ii Somewhat adequate
iii Slightly adequate
iv Not adequate
v Cannot say

7 How would you consider the teaching method used (Cooperative Language Learning associated) for a confidence building course like this?

i Highly appropriate
ii Somewhat appropriate
iii Nothing special
iv Not appropriate at all
v Cannot say

8 By looking at the stage performance of your students, do you think they have gained confidence to speak English <u>outside</u> the classroom?

i Yes
ii No
iii Highly doubtful
iv Maybe
v Cannot say

9 When you consider laying the foundation to teach/learn English in the university, as a language teacher how would you rate the course?

i Very effective
ii Somewhat effective
iii Nothing special
iv Not effective at all
v Cannot say

10 Any other comment you wish to make to improve the course:

i ....
ii ....
iii ....
iv ....
v ....

Thank you.

Index

Note: **Bold** page numbers refer to tables; *italic* page numbers refer to figures and page numbers followed by "n" denote endnotes.